This original and engaging book investigates American
television viewing habits as a distinct cultural form. Based
on an empirical study of the day-to-day use of television
by working people, it develops a unique theoretical
approach integrating cultural sociology, postmodernism,
and the literature of media effects to explore the ways in
which people give meaning to their viewing practices.
While recognising the power of television, it also empha-
sises the importance of the social and political factors
which affect the lives of individual viewers, showing how
the interaction between the two can result in a disengagement with corporately produced culture at the same time
as an appropriation of the images themselves into
people's lives. Accessibly written and at the cutting edge
of Cultural Studies and television research, this book is
essential reading for students and academics in Cultural
Studies, television research, and Media and Communication Studies.

RON LEMBO is Associate Professor of Sociology at
Amherst College, Massachusetts.

D0912816

Thinking through Television

Cambridge Cultural Social Studies

Series editors: JEFFREY C. ALEXANDER, *Department of Sociology, University of California, Los Angeles, and* STEVEN SEIDMAN, *Department of Sociology, University at Albany, State University of New York.*

(list continues at end of book)

Thinking through Television

Ron Lembo

CAMBRIDGE
UNIVERSITY PRESS

PUBLISHED BY THE PRESS SYNDICATE OF THE UNIVERSITY OF CAMBRIDGE
The Pitt Building, Trumpington Street, Cambridge, United Kingdom

CAMBRIDGE UNIVERSITY PRESS
The Edinburgh Building, Cambridge CB2 2CRU, UK   http://www.cup.cam.ac.uk
40 West 20th Street, New York, NY 10011–4211, USA   http://www.cup.org
10 Stamford Road, Oakleigh, Melbourne 3166, Australia
Ruiz de Alarcón 13, 28014 Madrid, Spain

First published 2000

Printed in the United Kingdom at the University Press, Cambridge

Typeface Monotype Times 10/12.5pt   *System* QuarkXPress™   [SE]

A catalogue record for this book is available from the British Library

Library of Congress cataloguing in publication data

Lembo, Ron.
  Thinking through television / Ron Lembo.
    p.   cm. – (Cambridge Cultural Social Studies)
  Includes bibliographical references and index.
  ISBN 0 521 58465 5 (hardback) – ISBN 0 521 58577 5 (paperback)
    1. Television broadcasting – Social aspects – United States.   2. Television
viewers – United States.   I. Title.   II. Series.

PN1992.6.L45   2000
302.23′45′0973–dc21   99–056422

ISBN 0 521 58465 5 hardback
ISBN 0 521 58577 5 paperback

For Phyllis,
her dad, Chris,
who would have been proud,
and for Addie,
who was behind me all the way

Contents

Acknowledgments

So many people deserve recognition for their support of my work. It was Stanley Aronowitz who introduced me to the work of the Frankfurt School, which included his own, as he used to say, "immanent" critique of it. When it came to television, Stanley demonstrated how and, more importantly, *why* the knowledge and insight of ordinary people was different from but certainly no less valid than the sophisticated theories of formally trained intellectuals. I owe a very significant intellectual debt to the late Ed Swanson, not only for validating my "brand" of sociology, as he used to put it, but, more importantly, for showing me how one can hold on to complex, theoretical ideas in the pursuit of an empirically grounded sociology. Ed Swanson posed the key questions and did a considerable amount of the dirty work that enabled my conception of a viewing culture to come into being. Similarly, David Wellman's intellectual presence can be found throughout the pages of this book. Having disabused me of false hopes for a quantitative study of television use, David led me to see how one can develop a nuanced understanding of the meaning–making process, one that accounts for the sometimes very subtle ways that people maintain integrity, dignity, and respect in confronting social conditions not of their own making. I am grateful, too, for his unending support and encouragement; it kept me focused on what was most important as I struggled to complete this book. His writing served as a model for mine by showing me that clarity and simplicity in the expression of ideas need not come at the expense of depth and elegance.

Being able rely on Margaret Cerullo as a friend and colleague during my time in Amherst has made the writing of this book that much easier. I am grateful for her editorial support (at a time when I simply tired of the manuscript), but, more than that, I feel fortunate in having been able to share her vision of what a critical sociology is and can be. Margaret opened me to new ways of thinking about poststructuralism and allowed me to explore interrelations between theoretical, political, and practical domains in ways that I had not anticipated.

Todd Gitlin continually posed tough, political-minded questions regarding the power of television, and mass media more generally, in people's lives. He was influential in leading me to a critical engagement with cultural studies in the early years of my dissertation research. I am grateful to Todd for taking me into his circle of graduate students at Berkeley and providing me with the opportunity to support myself teaching over a period of several years. Dick Flacks supported me in many ways while I was a graduate student at Santa Barbara, and, together, Dick and Todd helped me to acquire a political sensibility in my thinking about television. I also want to acknowledge the support of Jim Blackwell. It was Jim who helped me to discover sociology and, perhaps more importantly, he was the first person to instill in me a belief in my abilities to pursue graduate work in sociology.

I want to thank Bob Dunn for his many years of friendship. Bob's intellectual support and encouragement over the years has meant a great deal to me. It was in conversation with Bob that many of the ideas expressed here were first tried out, critiqued, and thought through to arrive at more adequate formulations. Ken Tucker has been similarly supportive, always posing smart questions regarding matters of both theoretical and practical import, questions that required me to rethink and rework my ideas. Thanks, too, to Craig Reinarman for his support and willingness to share his insights regarding the politics of television, particularly its representational world, and the cultural contradictions of the viewing experience. My sincere appreciation goes to Paul Lopes, Joellen Fisherkeller, and Rick Fantasia for providing encouragement and a sense of the sociological importance of my project. They were always generous with their time, their support, and their constructive criticisms of my work. Thanks to Danielle Bessett for her careful and thorough research into the more recent of cultural studies' accounts regarding television use. I also want to thank Megan Brown for her editorial assistance with an earlier draft of Part III of the manuscript.

Thanks to my graduate student colleagues, particularly those at Berkeley, who offered support, advice, and intellectual challenges as I developed ideas for this book. I am speaking here of Andrea Press, Jon Cruz, Paul Lichterman, Terry Strathman, and Tom Andrae. A deep sense of appreciation goes to my colleagues in the Anthropology and Sociology Department at Amherst College for being so supportive of me and my work over the last eight years. I am especially grateful for the time and effort put in by Jan Dizard, Deborah Gewertz, and Jerry Himmelstein in reading earlier drafts of this manuscript and offering insightful and constructive criticisms. Each of them helped to make this a better book. Thanks also to Fred Errington, Barry O'Connell, Frank Couvares, and Susan Douglas for their help with the manuscript.

Most of all I want to thank Phyllis Larimore, without whose help this book would not have been written. What she has done for my intellectual development over the past twenty years is almost impossible to put into words. She listened to all the half thought-out formulations that eventually, with her help, became successive drafts of the chapters for this book. She read and edited so many pieces of this book in its various stages of development that I long ago lost count. But most importantly, perhaps, she did something that none of my academic colleagues were able to do: she asked the questions of my research that television viewers themselves would ask. In doing so, Phyllis challenged me to think through academic formulations in order to reconstruct as faithfully as possible the worlds of everyday television use that were made available to me by my informants. In short, she was unfailing in her support of me, and for that, well, I am grateful beyond words. Thank you Phyllis.

Introduction: Situating my experience with television

In my studies of television, I have wanted nothing less than to, figuratively, get inside people's heads to determine the mindfulness that emerges from their use of the medium, and, further, to understand its ritual significance within the culture of television use. In doing so, I have wanted to gain a better understanding of the roles that the structural features of television and the broader, meaningful context of everyday play in giving shape, or form, to this mindfulness. I have wanted to know how it is that television viewing actually becomes a ritual practice for people, and what participation in this ritual as opposed to others means for people over the long run.

In research that I conducted with working people over several years, research that included indepth interviewing, watching television with people, the completion of viewer diaries, and more casual conversations with people at work, in the home, and elsewhere, I found that one third of the people included in my study used television in a continuous manner on a day-in and day-out basis. Watching television, they said, served as their primary form of relaxation and enjoyment during the time they spent away from work.

What I have come to call the "continuous" use of television is familiar territory to me. Like the people I watched with and talked to, I, too, grew up with television and, as it was for many of them, the television was on much of the time when I was at home. Watching television or just having it on needed no explanation or justification in my family. The same was true in my changing circle of adolescent friends. In fact, for countless working- and lower-middle-class people who inhabited the many towns and small cities in the New York metropolitan area during the 1960s, watching television was an indispensable part of living everyday life.

I, my family, my friends, and my friends' families – all of us enjoyed watching television. At times, we reveled in the pleasures it provided.

Television gave us Judy Garland and Bob Hope. It gave us the Cartwrights and The Barkleys. It gave us Matt Dillon, Kitty, and Chester. It gave us all the families we came to know so well: among them, the Cleavers, the Nelsons, the Ricardos, and the Reeds. Television gave us Ed Sullivan, who let us see The Beatles, the Rolling Stones, The Who, and The Animals, along with countless other British bands that soon faded into obscurity. It also gave us *American Bandstand* and *Soul Train*, where we first saw Smokey Robinson, The Four Tops, The Temptations, Otis Redding, Sam and Dave, among other singers and performers. Television gave us the *Laugh-In* of Rowan and Martin and *The Smothers Brothers Comedy Hour*. It gave us Steve Allen and Johnny Carson, and their countless late-night guests. Television gave us Walter Cronkite and Huntley and Brinkley, and other big name journalists who, on the way to becoming fixtures in our homes, told us what was going on in America and in the rest of the world, too. Television gave me and my brother and our friends a common currency of sports action and sports heroes: Mickey Mantle and Willie Mays, Joe Namath and Jim Brown, Bill Russell and Jerry West, Muhammad Ali and Howard Cosell, to name just some of the sports figures who made an enduring impression on all of us. And television gave us marches and demonstrations for civil rights, it gave us urban rioting, the Vietnam War, and student protests against the war. I could go on and on in this way, and still my recollection of the role that television played throughout my childhood and early adolescence would not be even close to being exhausted. Hardly. What we saw on television almost automatically became what we talked and argued and agreed with one another about. Television was that significant in my life, and in the lives of others like me who came of age in the 50s, 60s, and early 70s.

Looking back on my childhood, especially the grammar school and junior high years, I can see now that, aside from the shows and stories we followed or the characters we liked and disliked, television viewing was an activity of varied and sometimes ambiguous meaning for me and my family. My earliest memories of television involve the Saturdays and Sundays that I spent with my older sister watching cartoons and various movies that aired throughout the afternoon. I can recall, too, those Friday and Saturday nights when my mother, and, later, my mother and stepfather, would go out for the evening. With some hesitation I am sure, they entrusted my sister with the responsibility of "baby-sitting" me. When her time was not taken up talking on the phone with her friends, it was typical for us to make popcorn, ice-cream floats, a cake, or some other treat and tune into late-night movies such as *The Mummy*, *The Invisible Man*, or *Frankenstein*. Even now, I can still recall the frightening feeling that would come over me when we watched horror movies such as these. After my sister and brother left the house, it was my mother, my stepfather, and me that constituted our family.

In the simplest sense, watching television was a way for the three of us to be together – to be in the same room, at the same time, and share our experience with one another. The endless succession of programs, most of them formulaic, were just distracting enough to enable our watching together to become a kind of conflict-free, or conflict-neutral, environment. While the conflicts and tensions that perhaps prompted arguments at other times were still there, nevertheless, we looked forward to settling into the comfort zone provided by television. Even if we communicated little of what outsiders, particularly middle-class people, might have regarded as matters of substance, we were together, we did share ideas, and, perhaps most importantly, I think that at the back of our minds we all understood that television brought and kept us together.

Over time, watching television came to be an important way for us to share our lives together. To this day, I can still recall the warmth and comfort – the safety, even – that came with watching *Kojak*, or *Baretta*, *The Rockford Files*, or any one of so many other police, detective, or western shows with my stepfather. Because little else was shared between us, watching these kinds of shows together became a way for me to learn about his life. Oftentimes, Sal's commentary on the settings, the characters, and the situations that they found themselves in, or his comments on the stories and their moral implications, prompted him to recall instances from his own life that somehow resonated with what he saw or heard: his experiences growing up in Brooklyn in the 30s and 40s; the recollections he had of his mother and father and brothers and sisters; his still vivid memories of the war and army life; his post-war experiences; his gambling; or even his casual encounters with the wiseguys and politicians who frequented the New York restaurants and bowling alleys in which he worked. Our roles were reversed when he began to watch sports with me. Since this was my area of expertise, I could offer background information on particular teams or players to help him make better sense of the games or events we were watching. I taught him about some of the differences between college and professional basketball, about why one or another play might have been selected at a particular time by the coach or quarterback in a football game, about what a hitter might be looking for, or why a pitcher pitched a batter the way he did at different points in a baseball game – and, in all of this, I revealed something of myself, too, by recounting my own involvement in the school sports or playground games that were so central to my life at the time but which, for one reason or another, he never seemed to attend or ask about.

Through all of this, my mother had little to say, since she did not ordinarily watch these kinds of programs. When they were on, she chose instead to busy herself in the kitchen. Things changed for her, however, when we tuned in to *The Ed Sullivan Show* or any of the other variety shows regularly featuring the likes of Frank Sinatra, Judy Garland, Dean Martin, Bob Hope, and Sammy Davis Jr. During these times, the three of us sat and watched together, and my mother, too, would have stories to tell: about her parents coming from Italy and settling into life in America; about her early years in school; about the basketball and football games she went to with her friends; about the various jobs that she and her brothers and sister had when they were growing up; about her ballroom-dancing days, or about how she learned to cook or be a beautician. Along with mealtime routines and the extended family gatherings that took place on holidays and birthdays, it was our time watching television together that provided me with the sense of what everyday life was like in two of the many Italian–American communities in and around New York City in the years before I was born.

But our television viewing was not always so focused on programs, nor did it necessarily prompt the kinds of recollections that I just described. Not at all. In fact, in our house it was commonplace for me or my stepfather to turn the television on when we came into the house. Either way, it was just "on" much of the time when we were home. (Curiously, my mother did not care to watch television when she was home alone. She preferred instead to take care of her housework, which she did most of the time.) With the television on as a kind of background for us, my stepfather, I, and sometimes my mother, too, might sit and watch for a bit, depending upon what was on and what could hold our attention; but it was just as likely that any one of us would be up and about the house, talking or attending to any number of other things. I was perhaps the most attentive of all three of us, since some of my favorite shows – *Abbott and Costello*, *Soupy Sales*, and *Superman* – were on later in the afternoon. But, even with these shows, watching television for me did not necessarily preclude my doing other things, like homework for one, or categorizing my stamp or rock collection, doing household chores that were assigned to me, or even reading. In our house, television had acquired a kind of permanent presence.

We sometimes recognized, both individually and collectively, that having the television on as much as we did kept us from doing more constructive things with our time. But we also knew that television provided us with so much in terms of the persons, places, and events we could see, or the stories and the character's lives which we could enter so easily, and, because it did, whatever recognition we had of its power often faded rather quickly. None of us was ever at a loss, really, when it came to finding other things to do.

My mother and stepfather had work and bowling and family and friends. I had my hobbies, besides watching television, and I also had my cousins, my friends, and the sports we all played together. All of this was important in defining what was meaningful in our everyday lives. But so, too, was the ritual of watching television. In addition to bringing us together and fostering a sense of togetherness, our continued use of television sometimes diffused or deflected our energies for doing what we ourselves understood to be more worthwhile things. The regularity of my television watching often placed me one step removed from reading, or talking with my mother and stepfather without the television on, or really losing myself in the world of rocks or stamps or model cars and trains. I can see now that all of these things were more imaginatively engaging and, ultimately, more personally rewarding than watching television, but in an emotionally troubled family such as ours, where the initiative for undertaking more productive activities was in one way or another often stifled anyway, the turn to television was a path of least resistance. So, in addition to the worlds outside our own that television gave us access to and allowed us to enter so easily, television viewing also provided a distinctive kind of imaginative space, one that enabled me and my family to avoid asking more revealing questions about ourselves than we ordinarily did.

Outside my home and the world of my family and friends, watching television took on yet another meaning. When talk about television surfaced in my encounters with middle- and upper-middle-class people, be they junior-high or high-school classmates, their parents, or other adults in town, suddenly, my viewing habits became something suspect, something that I felt I needed to hide. Confronted by more educated people, people who had, in society's eyes, made something of themselves, I felt embarrassed by my close and continued contact with television. The fact that neither I nor my parents limited television use or that we did not watch shows that were deemed, again, in society's eyes, to be more informative or educational, and therefore more enlightening, was taken by me at the time to be indicative of a personal deficiency or some sort of character flaw. To speak about my familiarity with television would mark me, I thought, as not only less educated than they were, but, in a more insidious way, as a less capable and competent person than they were, too. Among my family and friends, television viewing was a source of pleasure. It also served as an important way of knowing the world; and, on occasion, it provided me with insights that were unobtainable elsewhere. But in the world of middle-class values and tastes, a world that we inevitably had to enter, television viewing often resonated with numerous hidden injuries of class and ethnicity.

I offer this brief account of my recollections regarding television because I think that how I used television when I was growing up, the role it played in my home, as well as the broader significance it carried in my life, all figured importantly not only in the questions I asked as I researched other people's experiences with television, but also in the answers I formulated and the conclusions I came to as I made sense of the accounts they provided to me. I shared with many of the people that I interviewed some common experiences of class in American culture, and, partly because of that, something of a common vocabulary of television use, too. This was especially true in terms of my formative years at home with my family and out on the streets and in the playgrounds with my friends. Like me, the people I talked to and watched with often lived through the stories that television provided for them. Some of them told stories, too, or had stories told to them around the television, in much the same way that I did. Like me, some of them simply kept the television "on" much of the time when they were home. And, like me, when they entered the world of middle-class values and tastes, they sometimes felt the embarrassment associated with watching too much television, and the defensiveness that came with having to justify it.

But, when these particular people met me, I was a sociologist as well as someone who watched television. Despite the similarities of class and television use, at the time of my research, our lives were, in fact, very different. None of them had undertaken graduate work, let alone at a place like Berkeley, which symbolizes prestige, privilege, and power. The jobs they had were similar to those that people in my family and in the families of friends had when I was growing up, but these jobs were certainly different from the research and teaching positions that I now held. Many aspects of their family situations resonated with what mine used to be, but, at the time of the research, their families were arranged very differently from mine. They had hobbies and spare-time activities that were different from mine, too. And many of these people had chosen or were burdened with very different responsibilities – regarding their families, their friends, their communities, indeed, their futures – than those that I faced at the time of my research. In short, despite affinities of class and, in many cases, race, and, despite the world of television viewing that we had in common, these people had different values and valued different things than I did.

Others that I interviewed lived lives that more closely resembled mine at the time of the research. Many of them had completed college, and some had gone on to do graduate work in various fields, as I was doing at the time. They were engaged in professional work, much as I was. The rigors and requirements of completing my graduate degree made me recognize, as they did, the value of making productive use of one's time. When these well-educated, professional people spoke of television, they often did so disparagingly. They made it clear that they knew the difference between, on the one hand, PBS programming and "higher quality" network fare, and, on the other hand, the more formulaic, run-of-the-mill programming that constituted the bulk of what commercial television had to offer them over the years. Distinctions such as these had become more familiar to me, too, as my colleagues, friends, and acquaintances were drawn in increasing numbers from the middle and upper middle class. The values and tastes held by my middle-class respondents were becoming my own. While I recognized and, in some cases, shared the hierarchy of tastes they cultivated, or the values and value distinctions they made, because I had grown up differently from them, what it was that led them to these values and tastes remained somewhat of a mystery to me.

I say all of this to make it clear, first of all, that I am a user of television. Television was and still is an integral part of my everyday life. Like other regular users of television, I am situated with the medium in particular ways, due to my class background, my class position, my gender, my ethnicity, my whiteness, and other factors, too. None of this is inconsequential when it comes to what I see (and hear) when I watch television, or how I see television working in other people's lives and in the culture more broadly. Second, my past experiences with television were very much like the present situation (at the time of the research) of some of my respondents, and the television viewer I had become resonated in important ways with the experiences, both past and present, of others. I am not, then, a disinterested investigator of television, of television viewing, or of the people that I interviewed and watched television with. Yet, as an analyst, I have reconstructed the experience that my respondents had with television as something other than my own. This proved to be one of the more objective and enlightening moments of the social research process. In the end, the validity of my account rests on the fact that achieving this kind of objectivity goes hand in hand with my continuing to recognize the inextricable links that exist between my own subjectivity and the subjectivity of the people whose patterns of television use I write about in the pages that follow.

Beyond mine or anyone else's personal account of television use lie the social facts of the viewing culture. Casual observations and prevailing opinions to the contrary, television use is actually a quite complicated cultural activity – both to participate in and to study. Considering the variety of patterns that can comprise television use as a cultural activity, it is the pattern of continuous use, a pattern in which different activities start, stop, and occur simultaneously with television viewing, that is perhaps the most complicated of all. Partly because of this, but due to other factors as well, the social facts of continuous use have been underrepresented if not neglected or altogether ignored in the scholarly literature pertaining to television. Among other things, this book is my attempt to correct such an oversight, to fill in some of the empirical and theoretical gaps in television studies, and, in the process, to provide an occasion for ordinary, working people to have a say, however indirectly, in expanding the parameters of what academics claim to know about the viewing culture. As I said, the social facts of the viewing culture encompass a wide range of viewing practices – wider, certainly, than this pattern of continuous use – and in this book I will discuss other patterns of use in some detail, and will also account for important similarities and differences among the patterns of use that emerged from my research. So, for example, in addition to meeting Dennis and Brenda, who are "continuous" users of television, you will meet "discrete" users, people like Jeanne, for whom television is merely one of numerous other focused activities that have become a part of her everyday life. You will also be introduced to "undirected' users, people like Steve, for whom the daily use of television involves an almost constant struggle to keep it under control so that it does not interrupt or overrun his desire to get other things done in his life. In the process, the cultural complexities of television use will be made that much clearer. But, again, it is continuous use, including what I will later call the "disengaged" forms of sociality that comprise it, which is at this point most in need of sociological explanation.

Situating television as an object of study

It was not until I encountered critical theory in graduate school that the power of television emerged as an intellectual issue for me. In the work of Adorno (1957; Adorno and Horkheimer, 1972), especially, I was directly confronted with a profound and carefully crafted argument that understood mass culture, including television, as an ideological form of capitalist domination, pure and simple. For a life-long viewer who admittedly enjoys watching commercial television, taking this perspective seriously invited a collision of worlds. I continued to read critical theory, and, even as some of its major weaknesses became clear, including a fetishism of high culture and an ignorance of the complexities of many traditions of American popular culture, including jazz, the analytical power of this perspective stayed with me. The interrogation of my own and others' viewing practices, both past and present, continued, as Adorno, Marcuse (1964), and other critical theorists became some of my most persistent and challenging critics. Time and again, I posed questions to myself. Among them: What did my television viewing really mean? Was I dominated by television in the ways that they said I was? Or, what did it mean to say that I was not dominated by the ideology, or the standardizing power of television? How was I to know if it was I or the television that was really in control of my viewing? On what basis could I even make such a judgment? Was there a way to understand what television viewing in general meant?

When I first began asking these questions, satisfactory answers were in short supply. Critical theory was *that* challenging to me. But, the more I read, I came to realize that television, and television viewing were much more complicated than either I or critical theorists, had imagined. Certain strands of thought in the work of Dwight Macdonald (1983), Edward Shils (1969), and Gilbert Seldes (1957) – noteworthy American critics of mass culture – resonated with the neo-Marxism of critical theory, but others validated the democratic tendencies at work in television, television viewing, and in the reception of the popular arts more generally. They recognized that there was more than ideological domination at work in mass culture, and this idea figured importantly in my continued reflections on the meaning of television viewing.

I saw, for example, that my own personal life became politicized in small but not insignificant ways in the 1960s and early 1970s, partly as a result of what I saw on television. The carnage and the political schisms of the Vietnam War, the protests that marked the civil rights and anti-war movements, the often-times violent police response to sit-ins, marches, and demonstrations, and the lyrical and rhythmic challenges to normative order found in rock and roll, soul, and rock music – all of this found its way onto television screens and into my life. It provided me, and television viewers like me, with ways of seeing and thinking that were not available to us at home or school, the two places where we spent most of our time. Even though these social conflicts and tensions were often depicted in ways that muted, to say the least, their political force, nevertheless, they were there, on television, something that authorities and media gatekeepers would have preferred to not have happen.

Furthermore, the writing, acting, and directing in a wide range of entertainment programs enabled critical insights to emerge regarding a variety of contemporary issues. The stories and characters presented on shows such as *Eastside/Westside*, *The Twilight Zone*, *The Outer Limits*, *All In The Family*, among others, often supplied fresh perspectives on familiar things, or provided depictions of worlds that were altogether different from our own. I mention all of this simply to say that, when it came to television viewing, to *my* television viewing, there was much more than ideological domination at work. Curiously, none of this figured importantly, if at all, in the work of critical theory.

Over the years I spent toiling away in graduate school, I became more deeply involved in studying what it means to watch television. I soon came to realize that nothing less was at issue in my studies than an intellectual understanding of the fate of people's ability to think for themselves and to act on their own terms in a culture that was dominated by large corporations which increasingly controlled the production and distribution of ideas and images not only on television, but on radio, in films, and in newspapers and magazines, too. As my studies progressed, discourses regarding television's power continued to be set off against many of the more practical claims to truth regarding the meaning of viewing that emerged from my own and others' everyday experience with television. A disjuncture took shape in my thinking with regard to power, one that was not going to be dissolved, displaced, or bridged all that easily.

Enter cultural studies, where elaborating on what was at stake in this disjuncture was in my mind one of the strategic purposes that propelled the work of Hall (1975, 1980; Hall et al. 1980), Hoggart (1966), McRobbie (1991), Morley (1986, 1980), Thompson (1966), Williams (1983, 1982, 1974), Willis (1978, 1977a), and others. Despite the newfound concreteness afforded me by notions such as encoding and decoding, discourse and text, the act of reading, dominant, oppositional, and negotiated interpretations, practice, and so on, I found that much of the cultural studies' work on television remained, in a peculiar sort of way, abstract. It worked one step removed from what constituted my practical realities of television use. This was especially true when it came to my encounters with poststructuralist accounts of power and resistance and theories of postmodernity. As my readings expanded to include the work of Deleuze (1983; Deleuze and Parnet, 1987), Foucault (1980, 1970), Lacan (1977, 1968), among others, I quickly became aware of subtleties regarding the workings of power and complexities in accounting for subjectivity that complicated my thinking about television use. In the place of ideological domination, I now saw multiple discourses working simultaneously or at cross-purposes, even, to constitute the power of television. Similarly, in place of naïve notions of consciousness and action, I saw multiple identities or subject positions that, like discourses, worked simultaneously and at cross-purposes to constitute resistance to power.

Nevertheless, even with all these sophisticated notions regarding the multiplicity of discourses and subject positions, the person who used television remained ambiguous to me. Not only that, but the very attempts by poststructuralists to clarify the socially constructed nature of subjectivity blurred my vision of the person even further. I found it odd that in conceptualizing the subject as socially positioned in various ways, as implicated in or resistant to discursive power, or as split by the disjunctures of discourse, there was no real mention made of the complexities of mind and emotion that, in some disciplines, were understood as indispensable to meaningful action. I found it particularly odd that constructs of symbolization and self – constructs found in perspectives as far apart as psychoanalysis and symbolic interactionism – were either reduced to politicized notions of social location, identity, and reading strategies (albeit against the grain), or ignored altogether in favor of even more abstract notions of practice or nomadic subjectivity. While I agree with much of the critique of essentialism found in cultural studies and poststructuralism, nevertheless, I do find these perspectives lacking when it comes to explaining many of the concrete conditions and practical actions that comprise the viewing culture.

I came away from my initial encounters with cultural studies and poststructuralism with a heightened awareness of the more subtle workings of television's discursive power. As a result, I proceeded more cautiously in my investigation of people's practical experience with television as something self-made, something constructed at least partially on their own terms, distinct from power. Even with my exposure to this work, the disjuncture that I spoke of earlier between, on the one hand, discourses of power, and, on the other hand, practical experience, was far from bridged. As time went on, I realized that I needed to take into account what cultural studies and poststructuralism were telling me. I decided to do so not by ignoring the mindful and emotional experiences of the people who watch television, but by moving further inside them. In as concrete a manner as possible, I needed to account for the complexities of sociality that were absent in their critical accounts. I knew, too, that I needed to come back out of this inner world of mindful and emotional experience and grasp the connections between it and the discourses of television programming. Furthermore, I needed to account for the relations that existed between these meaningful complexities of television viewing and the broader, social context of people's everyday lives, because I knew, both from my own experience and from the experience of those around me, that people's work lives, their family responsibilities (or lack thereof), and what they did besides watching television figured importantly in why they watched and the meaning that television held for them on a daily basis. And I understood that this entire line of inquiry must be understood without abandoning the idea of power.

This book takes shape in the disjuncture of discourses regarding television that I just described, because this disjuncture is still with us. Rather

than attempting to synthesize discourses of power and discourses of practice in yet another more abstract meta-level discourse, I have decided
instead to take on the more modest task of exploiting the space that this
disjuncture provides for thinking differently about television. In the chapters that follow, I use the documentation of television use provided through
depth interviews and participant observation to think through notions of
the medium's power. At the very same time, I continue to employ these
power constructs to reveal what is sociologically significant in the taken-
for-granted world of everyday television use. My critical inquiry into the
social world of the viewing culture is undoubtably partial and therefore
limited, shaped as it is by my own "situatedness," both as a scholar and as
a user of television. It is from both of these locations (at least) that I seek
to understand the workings of television's power and, at the same time, val-
orize the practical abilities of people in giving meaningful form to their own
experiences, on their own terms. My inquiry, then, is highly personal but
decidedly sociological. And it is deeply political, too, because people are
making meaning in image worlds that are always already inscribed with
social logics of power and the powerful.

In the chapters that follow, I move from a critique of prevailing conceptions
of television use, to a reconceptualization of use, and to the documentation
of the viewing culture. Part I of the book focuses on several paradigmatic
approaches to media study. In chapter 1, my criticisms are directed at sociologically based theories of television use, and media use more generally,
that fall outside the more contemporary framework of cultural studies. In
this regard, structural functionalism, critical theory, and Gramscian-
inspired Marxist perspectives are the focus of my critique. In chapter 2, I
critique the social-science model of media research by arguing that variable
analysis techniques are ill-suited for the study of socially emergent aspects
of television use. For that reason, among others, the scientistic study of
media use has yet to conceptualize or document adequately the sociality of
viewing cultures. In chapter 3, I look critically at cultural studies and argue
that, while it is certainly the most sophisticated of analytical approaches to
the study of television, it, too, fails to capture adequately the sociality of
use. In the case of cultural studies, however, this has more to do with the
emphasis that analysts have placed on a power-resistance model and,
within it, the role that identity is believed to play in the formation of cultural practice.

    In Part II, I develop an alternative conception of television use (and
media use more generally). In chapter 4, I make explicit the ideas of sociality that have guided my critique of social theory, social science, and cultural

studies in Part I, and I begin to elaborate on those social–psychological aspects that will advance further the study of television use. In chapter 5, I integrate elements of that social–psychology with a conceptualization of a "viewing culture" in order to broaden the sociological scope of the study of television use beyond the social–psychological *per se*.

In Part III, I report the results of empirical research regarding the viewing culture. Chapter 6 focuses on the sociological significance of the ritual of turning to television, and considers whether or not, or to what extent, people have become habituated to television, and what that means for them, given the other things that they do besides watch television. Chapter 7 focuses on the different kinds of viewing relations that emerge from the act of watching television, and it is here that issues regarding power and resistance are set in a new context, compared to the ways in which they are typically handled in cultural studies research. Chapter 8 presents a typology of television use based in large part on the documentation reported in the two previous chapters. In concluding the book, I re-examine issues of power and cultural politics in light of the documentation provided through my empirical research.

PART I

Conceptions of television use

1

Social Theory

Years ago, in *Social Theory and Social Structure*, Robert Merton (1968) distinguished between the "European" and "American" traditions in the study of mass media. The former theorized power in broad-based, social structural and historical terms and the latter focused on the systematic, empirical study of "the processes and effects of mass communication" (1968: 498). Writing in the 1960s, Merton believed that a substantial gap existed between the truth claims advanced by social theorists and those of social scientists.

Many years have passed since the time of Merton's assessment of the literature. In the intervening years, much has changed in the analysis of the mass media, including, of course, the emergence of cultural studies and, along with it, a newfound prominence given to interdisciplinary work. Those developments will be the topic of my third chapter. In this chapter and the next, I want to focus attention on the paradigmatic work of social theorists and social scientists in media studies, work that, for a variety of reasons, has fallen outside the purview of cultural studies, but which has nevertheless remained influential in shaping what more mainstream analysts conceptualize as important and document as "real."

The gap in truth claims that Merton spoke about still exists and continues to divide what is understood as "scientific" and what is not. But, beyond scientific concerns *per se*, what this gap really signified for Merton was the failure of media analysts to translate ideas about broad-based and deeply rooted forms of social power that were believed to be operative in the media into the terms of systematic empirical research, whether quantitative or qualitative. Writing in the 1990s (post cultural studies), when corporate control of media institutions and imagery has reached unprecedented proportions, when the circulation of such imagery can, via television, reach into the minds of virtually all Americans, I see this failure that Merton spoke about as a failure, really, to account for *culture*: that is, to account for the sociality that emerges from media use, for the meaning sometimes made there, and for the forms of power that continually shape this cultural terrain.

This may seem to be an odd position to take, since it is clear that theorists (both past and present) have identified the economic, technological, political, social, and cultural transformations integral to the emergence of mass society, mass media, and hence, television. They have focused attention on the issue of power – be it social structural, institutional, ideological, or, more recently, discursive power. They have often conceptualized how the various structural and institutional requirements of corporate production and distribution take shape as patterns of media imagery. They have identified what they believe to be myriad ways that television works to order and organize the everyday lives of the people who watch it. They have done so, however, by positioning themselves outside the day-to-day world of television use. Absent in their accounts is any clear conceptualization or empirical documentation of how television imagery, or media imagery more generally, actually enters into the meaning–making activities of the people who use it on a daily basis. Absent, too, is any systematic understanding of how television or other media contribute to the formation of a distinctive sociality of use, or how media-based practices are situated over time in people's everyday lives. The *culture* of viewing is unrecognized in these accounts; or, alternatively, if it is recognized, it is understood only as a derivative of power. As a result, valuable insights regarding television's power come at the expense of more fully understanding the complex social dynamics that comprise the everyday worlds in which it is used.

Typically, theorists analyze the social, or societal – as opposed to only the persuasive – power of television. This power emerges, they say, from the political, economic, technological, and discursive transformations that have characterized the rise of advanced capitalism in the West. Television is understood by them to carry something of these changes forward, touching and transforming the social, cultural, and social–psychological domains of people's everyday life experience. So, for example, while Lazarsfeld and Merton wrote in the pre-television age, their analysis of the mass media was – and still is – applicable to television. In fact, many of the key ideas found in their classic essay, "Mass Communication, Popular Taste, and Organized Social Action" (1977), have become staples of functional analysis regarding the mass media (Wright, 1975, DeFleur and Ball-Rokeach, 1982).

For Lazarsfeld and Merton, the mass media works first and foremost as a "structure of social control," serving to integrate individuals into the culture of industrial capitalism. How? By extending the corporate market economy, and, along with it, the interests of political and economic elites, directly into the social psychological experience of ordinary people (Lazarsfeld and Merton, 1977). The mass media, they say, has taken on the job of rendering the mass public "conformative to the social and economic status quo" (1977: 558).

Lazarsfeld and Merton have much to say about the broader, normalizing powers of the media. They talk of the patterning of values and norms in the media as representative of elite interests. They talk as well about how these values and norms work as a kind of symbolic fabric in supplying people with what, today, would be called the "discourses" for making their social experience meaningful, including the all-important ways that people find their place in the larger culture. The media does this, they say, by conferring status on people, places, groups, and events; by enforcing mainstream social norms and marginalizing challenging, or "deviant" behavior; and by substituting the taking in of information for political action – its "narcotizing dysfunction" (1977: 565–566). While their functional perspective leads them to see all of these forms of social regulation as, ultimately, something consensual (save for the narcotizing dysfunction, which has a peculiar status in their analysis), it does not, however, prevent them from seeing how elites maintain hierarchical control over personnel recruitment and the organization of the work process within bureaucratic institutions, or how media discourses become standardized in satisfying the requirements of capitalist production and distribution.

Lazarsfeld and Merton identify important, unintended cultural consequences of the consolidation of elite power in the mass media, and it is not difficult to envision how these functional processes work in the case of television. Certainly, television sanctions and enforces social norms; it confers status on people, places, policies, and events, simply by giving them coverage; and it sometimes removes people from more active forms of involvement in their own lives.

In a second example of this kind of theorizing, Todd Gitlin (1978) focuses attention on something called the institutional power of the mass media. This includes, he says, the preference given by the media to particular ideologies, the shaping of public agendas, the mobilization of support networks for the policies of political parties and the state, and, in a more general sense, the conditioning of public support for these kinds of institutional arrangements.

According to Gitlin, the repetition of certain "ideational structures" is indicative of the media's preference for ideas and values that harmonize with elite interests. Most importantly perhaps, Gitlin sees these structures working to solidify ordinary people's opinions and attitudes into more enduring configurations of consciousness – what he calls ideology. Once in place, ideologies shape how people will respond to and interpret media messages in new situations. Dominant ideologies are the most fundamental of symbolic structures in the mass media because they represent most directly the interests and world view of elites.

But Gitlin does not see the media as some sort of static, or monolithic, ideological structure. Rather, he understands it as something processual, as so many sites of "ideological work." What this means is that, while challenging ideas can and often do find their way into the media, they are usually framed in a way that blunts their critical, or oppositional qualities. They are tamed, co-opted, normalized, and ultimately they become, for Gitlin, compatible with elite interests. This is why he sees the institutional power of the mass media not so much as a social fact, but, on the contrary, as something continuously negotiated. This is understood, following Gramsci, as a hegemonic process. It is this perspective regarding the media's power that informs Gitlin's later analyses of the framing process in news and the mainstream coverage of SDS (Students for a Democratic Society), the decision-making process in network television, and the ideological structuring of entertainment programming (1983, 1980, 1979).

The Frankfurt School can account for all of what is important in Gitlin's and Lazarsfeld and Merton's analyses, and much more, too. In the work of Adorno, Marcuse, Horkheimer, Lowenthal, and others, we find a thoroughgoing critique of the commodity form of the mass media. Sometimes using different constructs, and sometimes developing different emphases, over the years the Frankfurt School has demonstrated quite consistently and convincingly how the marketing logics that guide programming production and distribution decisions standardize the story-telling conventions of mass media and, as a consequence, extend corporate capital's influence that much further into the everyday life experience of people.

Of all the Frankfurt theorists, I find Adorno's work to be particularly interesting, since he carried out systematic empirical studies of the media, even working for a time with Lazarsfeld at the Bureau of Applied Social Research in New York. In such studies – for example, "The Stars Down to Earth" (1974), "A Social Critique of Radio Music" (1945), and, most notably for my purposes, "How to Look at Television" (1957) – Adorno identifies how the objective forms of the mass media work in structuring the meaningful experience of people who encounter them. Radio broadcasts of classical music, films, television shows, astrology columns, etc. – all of them exhibit, in one way or another, the standardizing influences of commodity production. When people listen to the radio, go to the movies, watch television, or read newspapers and magazines, they encounter a world of standardized media imagery, are inevitably drawn into it, and, as a result, Adorno says, their mindful and emotional experiences become standardized, too. Under such conditions, real life becomes indistinguishable from commodified representations.

For Adorno, and others at the Frankfurt School, the historical emergence of mass culture carries consequences both numerous and profound. Not only does the ideology of elites become a social fact of everyday living for the vast majority of ordinary people, but so, too, they say, do the standardization of ideas and, imagery and, eventually, the commercialization of public discourse. Personal involvement in the image worlds of mass media inadvertently circumscribes whatever awareness people might otherwise have of more diverse and challenging ideas. Over time, Adorno says, that capability that people have for reflexive engagement with the social world – a cornerstone of modernity – is no doubt diminished and, furthermore, their ability to envision a world different from the one in which they presently live becomes increasingly problematic. In the end, the idea of a public sphere, of something separate and separable from commodity culture, is rendered obsolete.

When it comes to television, Adorno sees its power working at multiple levels simultaneously. At one level, what he terms "the multi-layered story structure," television serves as a "technological means" for the culture industry to "handle" the audience, because, Adorno says, the way in which the story depicts people and their social actions becomes the way in which the viewer understands people and their social actions (1957: 222). At a second level of analysis, Adorno sees the formulaic structure of the television narrative as pre-establishing "the attitudinal pattern of the spectator before he is presented with any specific content" (1957: 226). Because of the repetitions of formula, the viewer, according to Adorno, can "feel on safe ground all the time," and, as a result, he or she can always anticipate how the story will unfold (1957: 224). At both levels, Adorno conceives of television's power as working through standardized and repetitive depictions of social life to constitute fully what he refers to as the psychodynamic responses of the people who watch. This is the power of ideology in action.

Adorno's work is indispensable for the study of television because he demonstrates how its objective structure (namely, programming) is tied to the logic of producing and distributing commodities. The result is a series of transformations in story-telling conventions, and their repetition, as crucial determinants of television's power. Whether one uses the term industrial, postindustrial, late, post-Fordist, or some other one to designate the workings of capitalism, the fact remains that Adorno has theorized the relationship between television's institutional workings and its discursive power. By synthesizing Freud's idea of the unconscious with Marx's notion of the commodity form of social relations, Adorno moves beyond the abstractness of say, Lazarsfeld and Merton's, or Gitlin's conception of the media's institutional power, and articulates specific dimensions of internalization that characterize media use. Armed with psychodynamic constructs, he is able to theorize a complex interplay of conscious and unconscious processes that could conceivably make up people's social experience with television or other media. Interestingly enough, because Adorno's work remains theoretical in *the way* that it does, he is able, in comparison to others who analyze power, to deal more concretely with the sociality of television viewing. Adorno attempts to think through the social psychology of power relations. Yes, it is power that Adorno sees, and sees practically everywhere in mass culture. But his is a multi-layered conception of power, one that enables us to see the relationships that form between the outside world of media imagery and the internal world of thinking and feeling as something that is socially and culturally significant.

The language of these kinds of theoretical accounts is taken up with articulating the broader structure and functioning as well as the deeper workings of the media. The analysts mentioned have theorized quite nicely the *social*, or *societal*, power of television. The medium is linked with profoundly important, and, in some cases, irreversible economic, technological, and political changes. Television, in turn, is understood to carry something of these changes forward, touching and transforming social, cultural, and even social–psychological domains of people's everyday life experiences.

Many things are explainable using such an approach: the imperatives of industrial capitalism, the institutional structure of the mass media, marketing logics, ratings; the various facts of elite control, the commercial concerns that shape decision-making and, hence, programming; moving product; ideology; class; power; control; the idea of there being "preferred" ideologies, the idea, too, that these preferred ideologies reflect elite interests even, or especially, in their widespread popularity; the regularities and the changes in social life that become reflective of, and, at times, actually become the world outside of the media; the public sphere; the disappearance of the public sphere in the age of the image; and consumption patterns documented as on the rise.

But "top-down" approaches such as these must eventually touch bottom. So, much of the language of these accounts is also taken up with assumptions and assertions about how these broader structures and functions have become interwoven with one or another aspect of the social experience of those who use the media. Woven into this language, then, are ways of seeing the people who watch television. These ways of seeing, imbedded in language, make sense of what it means to watch television; or, less directly, but no less importantly, what it means simply to live amidst its presence on a day-to-day basis. The theories of Lazarsfeld and Merton, Gitlin, the Frankfurt School, as well as many other analysts – Postman, Kellner, Meyerowitz, and Miller, among them – offer, then, a whole series of judgments and understandings of proscriptions and prescriptions regarding the meaning of television in people's lives. In and of itself, this is not a problem. Theorists theorize by abstracting social logics from the particularities of more concrete conditions. This is a good thing. As I see it, the problem lies not in theorizing or making statements about institutional or ideological processes, or even in their influence upon or incorporation within the everyday life experiences of people. The problem arises when such theorizing occurs in the absence of any attempt to account for the experiences of those who are understood to be effected.

Certainly, Lazarsfeld and Merton saw the merit of grounding their theoretical ideas in the empirical world. As social scientists, they recognized the need for data in advancing truth claims. But, as Merton (1968) himself pointed out, the logic of variable analysis (their chosen methodology) limits what can count as evidence. The research techniques that they relied on were of little help, it seems, when it came to conceptualizing and operationalizing such things as the consolidation of elite power or other aspects of the media's societal power which they theorized as important. Methodological and technical issues aside, their theory itself – a theory of structure, of function, and of power – fails to conceptualize the emergence of power in the very social experiences that people routinely have with the media. Lazarsfeld and Merton do not inquire as to what normative functions or societal power or elite influence or unintended consequences look like from the vantage-points of the people who read, listen, watch, or otherwise encounter the media on a daily basis. In fact, a depth understanding of reading, listening, or watching never really materializes in their otherwise insightful and intellectually compelling theoretical account. Despite their brilliance as sociologists, they fail to elaborate a construct of culture that would enable them to reconstruct the very practical ways that media power is made meaningful by people.

Similarly, Gitlin's theorizing – of such things as the media's institutional power, of ideology and ideological conflicts, or the workings of the hegemonic process – is no doubt illuminating. So, too, is his critique of early social science research. I find no fault, really, with these formulations of power. The problem, however, lies with Gitlin's failure to explicitly account for how people who watch, listen, and read actually confront this power in the context of their own lives. For him, the meaning of media use unfolds out of institutional regularities or the ideological structuring of media imagery, among other things. Like many other theorists who position themselves outside the world of day-to-day media use, Gitlin understands the people who use media only as an audience, and, I might add, a somewhat passive one at that. This is not to say that ideological struggle and social change are unaccounted for. They are. But it is journalists, academics, and political activists who struggle and change things, and who therefore "count" as social actors, not people whose daily lives are lived in and through the media. Gitlin fails to adequately distinguish between the analysis of power as something institutional and ideological, and the ways that this power may actually work, concretely speaking, in people's everyday lives. "Ordinary" people who use the media are incapable of any kind of reflexive engagement with the ideas and imagery that they encounter. Gitlin is too quick to dismiss what they do with media imagery, and, as a result, he, like Lazarsfeld and Merton, is unable to properly theorize the sociality of use as an integral aspect of power. The idea that there is a culture of *use* never arises as a significant factor in his analysis.

In treating mass media as objects of social experience, Adorno, unlike Gitlin, fails to give any serious consideration to the ways in which challenging ideas may surface as representations of broader social conflicts and struggles. Furthermore, his conception of mass culture, dependent as it is on notions of repression and commodity fetishism, leaves little room, really, for the consideration of sociological realities that emerge in day-to-day media use. When it comes to actually investigating the lives of the ordinary people who occupy the role of audience members in his theory, Adorno appears to have had little patience for the subtleties of systematic, ethnographic research. Adorno never even attempts to accord the same status to reconstructions of people's actual experience with media as he does to ideas of commodity production, instrumental reason, reification, or the unconscious structuring of thought and action. In the case of television, Adorno was unable or unwilling to consider how the text and esthetics of programming might enable viewers to disengage themselves from dominant ideology, to question the supposed normalcy of story-telling conventions, and, in these ways, open up new possibilities for seeing the world. As brilliant and as far-reaching as Adorno's theory of mass culture is, his failure to develop a construct of sociality makes it impossible to theorize the meaningful complexities that come with actually watching television as something intrinsic to the workings of power.

Lazarsfeld and Merton, Gitlin, Adorno and the Frankfurt School, are three examples of sociological theorizing about the media, about power, about the culture that takes shape amidst the media, and, consequently, three theories about the meaning of media in people's lives. If my aim were comprehensiveness, then I would certainly want to account for the theorizing of other scholars, both past and present, who have made significant contributions in their own right when it comes to understanding the role television, mass media, and mass culture play in people's lives. For example, there is the work of Kellner (1990), Miller (1988), Postman (1985), and Meyerowitz (1985), to name some of the more noteworthy of contemporary media theorists who have yet to be identified with cultural studies. Further discussion of, say, Kellner's analysis of the political economy and regulatory environment of contemporary commercial television, or Miller's ideas regarding the (inherently) limited horizons of television programming, or even Meyerowitz's notion of the loss of a sense of place resulting from the more subtle and pervasive effects of media imagery in people's lives – all of this would add much to our understanding of the objective structural features of television as well as the sociological influence they may carry in day-to-day living. And, going back in time, the contributions of Seldes, Shils, Lippmann, and Macdonald, among others loom large in defining American media criticism. Ideas about the construction of distinctive "taste cultures" in the age of television, or about gaps between the world outside and the pictures in our heads, or even about the democratizing tendencies that accompany the introduction of media – all of this, too, would figure importantly in an expanded view of the object, television, and the ways it may work in structuring social experience.

My aim, however, was not comprehensiveness but clarity: clarity, that is, regarding where and how the people who use television fit within analytical frameworks that, while outside of cultural studies, have defined and continue to define the sociological significance attributed to television by successive generations of scholars. While many scholars have made significant contributions to what we know about the media, the theorizing of Lazarsfeld and Merton, Gitlin, and Adorno is, I believe, paradigmatic. Why? Because ideas about a capitalist political economy, norms and what becomes normatively appropriate, status conferral and legitimation functions, structures of elite control, institutional requirements, ideology, ideological power, the hegemonic process of fashioning consensus, commodification, story-telling conventions and their standardization, the growth of consumption, the passivity of the audience, and the disappearance of a viable public sphere, are all elemental in critical analyses of the mass media, and they receive elaborate and original treatment in the work of these theorists. Other scholars certainly articulate the significance of, say, legitimation, or the hegemonic process, in distinctive ways, accounting for particular conditions or specific circumstances that are not addressed by Gitlin, Lazarsfeld and Merton, or Adorno. And yet, their frameworks of analysis, their ways of seeing the media and the people who use it, the logics they deploy, are derivative, really, of the elemental ideas that form the backbone of sociological theorizing for Gitlin, Lazarsfeld and Merton, as well as Adorno and the Frankfurt School. In aiming for clarity in my critique of theorizing (again, outside of cultural studies) about media, then, I have focused attention on seminal aspects of their work. I leave it up to the reader to decide the extent to which the theorizing of other media analysts is subject to the same critique.

While there are real differences between structural functionalism, critical theory, and Gramscian-inspired forms of ideology critique, nevertheless, as perspectives for media theory, they all share what I call a "top-down" mode of analysis. Lazarsfeld and Merton, Gitlin, Adorno: each of them *read out* of the media as objects in order to explain things social and cultural associated with their day-to-day use.

In their work and in the work of other "top-down" theorists, too, a rather complex and sophisticated *reading out* of the object occurs. In today's parlance, theirs are *situated* readings; situated, that is, by an understanding of history, politics, and social logics, including the logics of capitalism, corporate institutions, dominant ideologies and political struggle, among other things. All of this is constituted in explanations, elaborations, and critiques of the objective structures, the functioning (or dysfunctioning), the power of mass media in social life. The phrase "in social life" is key here because, in using it, I want to underscore the fact that in such top-down theoretical accounts, what is read out of media as its objective forms, as its objectivity, is, at the very same time, unavoidably subjective. The media, after all, is believed to order and organize what things mean to people. That is, what people who use media on a routine basis take to be the meaning of their experience with it is understood by these theorists as something already structured, behind the backs of people, as it were. Their meaning–making activities take persistent social and cultural forms as a result of the objective workings of media – where it comes from, historically speaking, how it is structured economically and politically, the ways in which it functions, socially and culturally, and its power, ideologically, to shape thinking and acting.

The top-down mode of analysis enables theorists to deal with the meaning of the media in daily life. They account, sometimes very effectively and with great insight, for how the broader and deeper workings of the media can become inscribed within the everyday, common-sense, and taken-for-granted experiences that people have with it. This is precisely how they theorize the social, or societal power of the media. It is, as I said, a power to direct actions, shape thinking, and channel desires. It is, really, a power of cultural formation that they describe.

I am certainly supportive of this kind of theorizing. After all, it is clear that television, for example, takes shape amidst broad-based political, economic, technological, and discursive transformations characteristic of the rise of mass society. It makes sense to speak about the day-to-day workings of television as an elite controlled institution, or to use terms such as legitimation, normative consensus, standardization, mainstreaming, ideological domination, and so on to account for television's sociological significance in people's lives. Television's power can be understood to cut across virtually all domains of social life – work, home life, public culture, and private thoughts – and to touch virtually every social location that analysts deem important, including class, race, gender, sexuality, ethnicity, religion, and age, among others.

In the objectivist perspectives like those of Lazarsfeld and Merton, Gitlin, or Adorno, theorists are outsiders to the world of day-to-day media use. Analysis proceeds from what Bourdieu has called "an intellectualist standpoint of deciphering" (1977). Those who theorize in this way (and intellectuals in general) no doubt use the media, whether it is reading newspapers, attending movies, listening to the radio, or watching television. It is probably the case that their own media use, including their critical reflection upon it, becomes incorporated into the formation of their theories, especially when it comes to concerns about the meaning of day-to-day use.

But their pattern of use could hardly be considered typical of most Americans. When it comes to television, for example, few if any of those who do this kind of theorizing currently watch or have watched commercial programming for even several hours a day, let alone the seven hours that is average for American households. When they do watch, they probably focus attention on what they are watching and, as a result, are less likely to just have the television on for hours at a time while they do other things, a way of watching that has, in fact, become quite routine for many people. And, unlike many people who live and work outside intellectual circles, media analysts and scholars of culture are often hesitant to acknowledge the pleasure and purposelessness that comes with watching television. They are also less likely than others who watch to recognize that such pleasure and purposelessness is often integral to the meaning of viewing, quite apart from the information gained, the knowledge derived, or the understandings made while watching.

While media theorists do indeed watch television, their world of use differs in frequency and in kind from the worlds of day-to-day use that others who watch television typically inhabit. There are ways of thinking, feeling, and acting that occur when people watch television that remain unfamiliar to these theorists. Among people living outside more purely intellectual domains, there is often a sociality that emerges in the presence of television and becomes a persistent feature of their day-to-day use. I am speaking here of varieties of mindful and emotional relations between and among people, but also, and perhaps more importantly, between people and the television set, that can occur in routine use. Over time, the repetition and ritualization of these social relations may even come to constitute distinctive cultures of use. Yet, those who theorize in a top-down mode lack the practical experience that comes with continual involvement in such social relations. Consequently, they lack a certain knowledge and understanding – call it an "insider's" knowledge – of the cultures that take shape in and through uses of television other than their own. As a result, there are worlds of television use that remain invisible in their theorizing, theorizing that purports, as Merton has said, to "capture the broad movement of ideas in relation to social structure" when it comes to media. These theorists see themselves primarily as thinking through various intellectual traditions pertaining to the study of media and culture, recasting the findings of previous empirical research into new theoretical abstractions, unmasking class power or ideological domination and mapping the formation of political interests in media, or, more simply, recognizing and critiquing the kinds of media use that go on in society at large. It is this kind of intellectual work that typifies the critical stance of top-down theorizing.

This is not a problem, really. Over the years, valuable ideas and keen insights regarding media have emerged from intellectuals positioned outside worlds of day-to-day use that are much more familiar to most Americans. Rather, the problem lies with the *unacknowledged nature* of their outsider status. For, as long as the position of the analyst as outsider remains unacknowledged, the gaps, the distance, indeed the differences that exist between their positioning and the positionings of those who use the media more regularly, and admit to enjoying it, can remain camouflaged, they can be abstracted away, or naturalized under the rubric of an intellectualist standpoint of deciphering.

Conclusion

In theorizing about television and media more generally, analysts must deal directly with issues of power. Functionalists, critical theorists, and

Gramscian-inspired Marxists are quite correct to emphasize the importance of social structures and processes that give rise to mass media in the
first place and shape the meaning it can have in people's lives. In the case of
television, theorists should continue to focus attention on the medium's
influences, since it is clear that broader social and historical forces are at
work – through discourses and ideologies as well as the set itself – in constituting much of what people take for granted in using television.

But assertions about the power of television cannot only be *read out* of
what theorists see as the structure of the object, no matter how complicated
and nuanced their conception of that object, television, might be. This is
true for the study of any other form of mass media as well. If the power of
television, for example, is understood to work socially, then theorists must
make the sociality of television use an explicit part of their conception of
power. In addition to focusing analytical attention on the meaningful consequences of more broad-based social structures and processes, theorists
who share something of the top-down perspectives that I have criticized
must examine the actual experience that people have when they watch television regularly. This includes, of course, consideration of the ways in
which those more broad-based structures and processes work via the television set and the symbolism of its programming in the meaning–making
activities of people. This is not simply a matter of grasping the normative
or ideological outcomes of viewing. When watching television, people participate in an oftentimes complex social world, one in which they routinely
exhibit varying levels of mindful and emotional involvement with television
and other people as well. These kinds of involvement stand on their own as
cultural forms, quite apart from what many theorists take to be their normative or ideological consequences. Furthermore, their involvement with
television and other people while watching is itself situated amidst a variety
of ongoing social and personal relations that constitutes the wider, meaningful world that they inhabit. This cannot be read out of the object, television, either. For far too long, sociological theorists have failed to
formulate clear conceptions of "viewing," choosing instead to link constructs of "television" and "culture" in fashioning their critiques of the
medium. What is needed in the approaches I have described is a commitment on the part of the theorist to reconstruct the standpoints of participants in a *viewing* culture. To speak about television viewing is to speak
about power as something socially and culturally emergent. To speak about
television viewing, then, is to speak about more than power in the very
attempt to designate what power is and does in the rituals of daily use.
Theorizing can, in Marx's terms, rise from abstract designations of television's power to concrete formulations of its sociological significance in

people's lives. In order for that to happen, media theorists must own up to their own outsider status regarding the worlds of day-to-day media use. In falling back on their own ideas about what it is that ordinary people actually do with the media – and consequently, what the media does to them – theorists must work harder, and differently, to enable the voices of the people who use the media, the people who they believe to be affected by it, to be heard.

2

Social science

In contrast to the work of media theorists, social-science researchers have proceeded inductively, replacing questions about broad-based historical changes or notions of societal power with a research-based scientific language of "problems." This analytical agenda has called for the specification of hypothesized relations between a given medium, usually a particular aspect of it, and one or another dimension of the subjective experience or behavior of the people who use it. The primary goal of social-science research has been to develop ever more precise techniques of *measurement*, and this, in turn, has led to a search for conceptual precision. In this tradition, researchers have sought an empirical test for hypothesized problems in the *variations* in data along specified dimensions of media effects or use among discrete users or whole audiences. By these means, social science has attempted to scientifically "validate" ideas about media power or the subjective dimensions of use, seeing this as forming a basis for generalizations and, ultimately, theories of television or the mass media generally.

Variable analysis techniques have provided an exactness to social science research that is unmatched by any other approaches to media studies. And yet, it is this very "scientificness" that has limited the vision of analysts in understanding and documenting power, meaning, and, most importantly, the sociality that comprises the distinctive cultures that emerge from television use. First, with few exceptions, the vast majority of social scientists (past and present) have failed to conceptualize power as something social, preferring instead to study it as a phenomenon of persuasion at the level of media effects. As a result, they, like social theorists, have been unable to identify how the various structural and institutional requirements of corporate production and distribution take shape as patterns of media imagery and to explain the constitution of power through this process. Secondly, social scientists do not offer any clear conceptualizations or empirical documentations of how television imagery, or media imagery more generally, *actually* enters into the meaning–making activities of the people who use it on a daily basis. Absent from their accounts, thirdly, is any systematic understanding of how television or other media contributes to the formation of a distinctive sociality of use, or how media-based practices are situated, *meaningfully*, in people's everyday lives. As was the case in the work of social theorists, the *culture* of viewing is unrecognized in social scientific accounts. Here, clarity and precision in the conceptualization and measurement of the effects process as well as the specification of different levels or kinds of effects come at the expense of understanding more fully the complex social dynamics that comprise the culture of everyday media use.

The social-science model of media research that Merton described some forty or so years ago has indeed operated with a language of specificity and precision in which broader notions of institutional or ideological power were inadequately represented and ideas of culture ignored altogether. The kinds of problems formulated and the data obtained are testimony to this fact, as is the critical commentary regarding the limits of scientism that has appeared over the years. At the same time, it is obvious that many of the guiding ideas of early media research, if not now treated as a given, have been superseded in the new directions of study that have come to characterize the field. It is obvious, too, that the methods of studying media have grown more sophisticated. Together, substantive and methodological developments since Merton's day now make it possible for analysts to treat even very complicated aspects of the media's workings, including power, with a sense of subtlety and nuance, all the while maintaining their commitment to precise and systematic measurement techniques. So, for example, Gerbner et al. (1982, 1980, 1977), Iyengar (1991), and Iyengar and Kinder (1987) provide evidence of the media's institutional power in shaping ideology and discourse, and, if perhaps less clearly or convincingly, they present data regarding the media's shaping of consciousness as well. But, as I will argue in the pages that follow, their work is exceptional. On balance, however, social-science media research is still very heavily committed to a communicative model in which the data of intentions, content patterns, or responses – in all their varied formulations – are preferred to that of ideology, elite control, institutional power, or the hegemonic process.

Questions of power aside, the social-science model is even less adequate when it comes to understanding the social and social psychological complexities of day-to-day media use. Even when analysts move beyond conceptions of audience and response, definitions of what is social (or cultural) typically are still too far removed from the processual nature of thinking, feeling, and acting. Consequently, social science research is unable to offer plausible reconstructions of how these aspects of sociality, including their interrelated and contradictory qualities, emerge in actual situations of use. And because it has, at best, an underdeveloped conception of social power, the scientistic perspective is unable as well to provide data regarding how that power itself shapes the sociality and cultures of use.

So, while substantive concerns have changed, and while the methods and strategies of research have grown more sophisticated, the discourses of social science do not ordinarily aid analysts in representing broader structures and deeper processes of power, or the varied forms of sociality that comprise a viewing culture as something empirical.

Limited effects research

At the time of Merton's writing, the limited effects paradigm set the parameters for American media research. For reasons both substantive and methodological, this paradigm was ill-equipped for studying social power or the sociality of media use. Social scientists instead studied the process of "communication," or, to be more precise, "persuasive communication." From the very start, sociological realities that gave shape and structure to this communicative process were taken for granted, pushed aside, ignored, or otherwise assumed away as analysts sought to obtain data regarding *who* said *what*, to *whom*, in *which channel*, and with *what effect*.

So, for example, the workings of industrial capitalism were treated as a kind of second nature by limited effects researchers. Private property, market mechanisms, and the profit motive, among other things, were simply accepted as they were given in the culture; rarely, if ever, were they seen as problematic or treated critically by these analysts. Similarly, technological innovations influential in the formation of mass media and mass society were seen as something progressive, a continuation of enlightenment traditions. Regarding the structure and functioning of the mass media, the normative frameworks that guide decision-making in media institutions were taken for granted, by practitioners and analysts alike. So, too, were the hierarchical divisions in the communication process between elites and masses. The fact that communicators were interested participants in the communication process, that they, like the masses to be persuaded, had predispositions, were engaged in ongoing networks of interpersonal communication, that they typically worked in group contexts and institutional structures of the corporate world, all of this was all too often assumed away in the early research. In fact, Joseph Klapper (1960), in his comprehensive review of the pre-television, limited effects research, went so far as to discuss the commercial nature of mass media as a mediating factor in the communication process; as if corporate capitalism could somehow be set apart from what it is that communicators do with mass media. The fact that ideological power accrues to social groups, and that elites should be afforded the legitimacy to direct public opinion and shape mass behavior went unquestioned by limited effects researchers. And, of course, it was quite natural for them to take the prevailing social logics of patriarchy, heteronormativity, race relations, and the nation state, indeed, of the West, for granted, too. As a result, the reproduction of dominant ideologies in the day-to-day workings of media institutions and the proliferation abroad of democratic ideals and an American way of life were never recognized as such; or, alternatively, they simply went unchallenged in limited effects research. What was assumed away was what was most in need of explanation: the power of elites, the ideological forms it took in the communicative process, and the role marketing forces played in shaping what and how communicators "communicate" in the first place.

In fact, Gitlin (1978) has argued convincingly that this research and the researchers were so ensconced within the ideologies of elite controlled institutions and so reliant on the funding and financial reward structures of those same institutions, that the study of such social conditions and processes, let alone any significant criticism of them, were rendered moot. Instead, substantive interest focused on something more immediate and identifiable: persuasive communication. In the scientistic scheme of things, the workings of persuasive power had to be operationally defined to obtain data that would confirm or disconfirm hypothesized effects.

This resulted in the now familiar strategy of measuring messages, responses to messages, immediate effects, and, shortly thereafter, the mediating variables. As a message or, more generally, as content patterns, the mass media was defined as a specific variable, distinct from other variables comprising the institutional matrix in which it operates, such as corporations, schools, families, and so on. The same was true of user responses. The social experience of media use was selectively broken down into its specific and variable component parts; notably, opinions, attitudes, and behaviors. The logic of variable analysis was quickly extended to the definition and measurement of a host of social psychological, psychological, and sociological variables that mediated, shaped, and contextualized responses and, hence, effects. It was these constructs and their indicators that became the preferred terrain of empirical research. The abstracting of persuasion went hand in hand with the abstracting of its variable effects, and these methodological operations together generated a suitable object of study out of the broader, deeper, and more complex workings of the mass media.

No doubt, these were separate moments of analysis; but, practically speaking, they became virtually indistinguishable from one another in conceptualization and measurement.

Nevertheless, limited effects research generated an extraordinarily impressive array of facts regarding the workings of persuasive power and audience responses to it. In study after study, analyses detailing variations in structures, patterns, and sequences of media imagery were set against the empirical evidence of opinions, attitudes, and actions, providing a series of snapshot accounts of the communicative process. The many variable analysis findings that emerged from this steady stream of studies established limited effects research as the preeminent scientistic paradigm of its day. Surrounded as it was by similar discoveries in other fields, limited effects research was shaped by and contributed to significant advances in the knowledge of human behavior. Among them were the facts of variation in motivations and attitudes; differences in the susceptibility of individuals to behavioral modification; data indicating the existence of selective attention, perception, and retention as key factors in the learning process; the knowledge that variability in social location – age, class, gender, race, ethnicity, religious affiliation, education, and so on – were correlated with patterns of exposure, selection, and response regarding media messages; and the finding that interpersonal interactions, group affiliations, and informal social relationships all routinely mediate the effects of communication. By the 1940s, all of this – individual differences, variability in social location, interpersonal interaction, and group dynamics – had become an integral part of scientistic thinking about mass media.

As a result, the audience, often seen as passive in earlier formulations of persuasion theory, was understood as an active component of the communication process. Persuasive power was no longer assumed to work uniformly or unilaterally, and message content was no longer equated in any simple and straightforward way with effect. It was in this way that the power effects of mass media were understood as limited. Furthermore, influential social scientists such as Lasswell (1938), Berelson (1971), and Lazarsfeld et al. (1948) used the evidence of limited effects research to question the idea that mass society was simply an aggregation of atomized individuals lacking any sense of connectedness with others or to normative frameworks that guided participation in local communities and public life. So, for example, Merton (1946), in his classic study of a 1943 Kate Smith war-bond drive, documented the structure and content of persuasive radio messages, but, more importantly, he obtained measures of behavior and opinions as indicators of an active audience. Merton's work in *Mass Persuasion* opened a door of mass-communication research to the systematic study of receivers and reception situations. Out of this line of research came, among other works, *Personal Influence,* in which Katz and Lazarsfeld (1955) discovered the "two-step flow" of mass communication. Contrary to prevailing scholarly opinion, they found that the diffusion of ideas through newspapers was oftentimes indirect, passing first to already established "opinion leaders" in a community and then to others who were less involved or interested in following the news. Like Merton some years before, Katz and Lazarsfeld validated the idea of an active audience. They provided evidence of the specific ways individuals mediated potential persuasive power effects.

Yet, what critical analysts call the social power of mass media was never named in these accounts. Institutional power, ideology, normative consensus, standardization, commodification, hegemony – all of this was outside the theory and operational logic of limited effects research. This comes as no surprise, really. Among limited effects researchers, some were professional communicators who worked with political elites to shape public opinion. They designed election campaigns or managed the dissemination of ideas regarding political and social issues of the day. The professed purpose of their audience research was to assess the responses to specific campaigns in order to better direct and control the thoughts and actions of individuals in managing social consensus. Others were situated squarely within media corporations themselves, where selling goods as well as images and ideas about goods was the primary capitalistic concern. Obtaining data regarding predispositions, needs, patterns of attentiveness, or other factors deemed likely to influence buying behavior was the focal point of scientific research. And still others were researchers in universities and laboratories, a step or two removed from the more instrumental interests of politics and the profit motive. Comparatively speaking, theirs was a disinterested scientism, one concerned with making presumably "universalistic" truth claims regarding the facts of motivation, perception, attitude formation, and behavior, something beyond the purview of persuasion studies *per se.* Whether it was in conjunction with political elites, in the corporate market-place, or in the universities, little, if any, of this work formulated empirically testable constructs of social power. For this to have occurred, analysts would have had to think through the ideological, institutional, and social structural arrangements that lent legitimacy to the study of persuasion and audience responses in the first place, something they were unprepared to do. In subsequent work on agenda setting, and in the more recent research of George Gerbner and Shanto Iyengar, among others, we do find measures of social power and data of its effects. But in the limited effects paradigm, such studies never came to pass.

With regard to media use, ideas that were (and still are) elemental in sociological and anthropological conceptions of social life were notably absent from the discourse of limited effects research. Meaning, meaning–making, self (or identity) formation, the construction of cultural forms – none of this ever reached the threshold of conceptualization in this paradigm. The sociality of use, then, remained hidden from view. Consequently, it could never be named, explicitly, as a constituent part of the empirical world of limited effects research.

Descendants of limited effects research

The American tradition of empiricism has certainly undergone many significant changes since the days of the limited effects model. Numerous schools of thought have taken shape, and, while each may have a distinctive approach to media study, they share a concern for clear operational definitions of constructs and precise techniques of measurement. So, for example, political learning and voting behavior studies, the most direct descendants of the limited effects paradigm, have used the survey method to measure cognitive as well as attitudinal and behavioral responses to media imagery. Data on how people process information have served as evidence of political learning, with particular attention paid to the role personality factors play in the learning process. Stages in political learning and different audiences have been identified, based on the kinds of information supplied and the attentiveness of people toward it. In a similar manner, agenda-setting research has made use of content analysis techniques, survey methods, and, to a lesser extent, field experiments to expand the study of media power beyond the evidence of persuasive effects. Measures of the preference given in the media to certain issues and not others, to the framing of issues and events in newspapers, radio, and television have been used to indicate a media agenda, while the measurement of responses from people regarding what they believe to be salient issues of the day have been taken to indicate a personal agenda. Correlations between them have allowed analysts to ascertain whether or not, how, or to what degree the media have the power to set personal agendas in everyday life.

From the classic radio research of Cantril (1935), to Bandura's (1965) influential studies of violence, to the recent work of, among others, Malamuth and Billings (1986), Zillman and Bryant (1982), Iyengar (1991, and Iyengar and Kinder (1987), the experimental method has been used extensively to test hypotheses of media effects. Both in the laboratory and in the field, examining causal relations between one or another aspect of media content and cognitive, attitudinal, or behavioral responses on the part of people has been the staple of experimental research. Data run the gamut of measurable effects, from studies indicating aggressive actions following the viewing of violence, to those linking desensitization toward rape and portrayal of sexual violence with increased viewing of pornography, to experiments revealing different cognitive routes to persuasion. In all cases, it is establishing facts, objective facts, through systematic sampling, clear conceptualizations, precise measurements, and explicit time sequencing that allows social scientists to claim validity and generalizability for their findings.

From the early days of radio and on through the television age, survey research has been used to chart and profile audience preferences and predispositions of all kinds. By emphasizing the audience and not power, this research served as a kind of precursor of uses and gratifications research. When it comes to the television audience, survey research has yielded an impressive array of facts, including data pertaining to the amount of time spent watching, whether viewing is a primary or a secondary activity, the activities that television replaces, the entertainment versus information functions of the medium in comparison to other media, the relationship of various demographic factors, such as age, race, gender, income, education, and so on, with the amount and kind of television viewing, correlations between these demographic factors and other activities, correlations between the viewing of violence and instances of aggressive behavior, as well as other facts too numerous to mention.

And then there is uses and gratifications research. Practitioners of this perspective abandoned the study of power effects – persuasive or otherwise – to systematically explore media use on its own terms. Of all the social–scientific approaches to media study, uses and gratifications research, with its emphasis on use *per se*, attempts to approximate most closely the actual social experience that people have with media. From the start, this research tradition understood the initiative for media use to originate with individual audience members, not communicators. Analysts presupposed that individuals strive for consistency and stability both in orienting themselves to activities and participating in them. Analysts also assumed that people can act with an awareness of their own motives, needs, or intentions and are capable of reporting them in response to survey questions. Typically, fixed-choice questions have been used to obtain self-reports from people of perceived needs, motives, and intentions, preferences for different media, frequency of media use, and patterns of participation in non-media activities, among other things. Using existing theories regarding human needs and prior categorizations of the structural features of mass media, analysts have employed survey data to compare empirically the uses of different media, the fit between perceived needs and the characteristics of different media, the degree of interchangeability between different media in satisfying the same or similar needs, the alternatives to media use that individuals employ in satisfying their needs, and the gratifications derived from both media and non-media activities. Ranging across media – from newspapers, magazines, and books to radio, television, and the movies – and considering a variety of needs – for information, entertainment, escape, companionship, or social interaction – uses and gratifications research has provided evidence of the functional role different media play in ordering and organizing everyday life. Like the data of limited effects, the cumulative evidence of uses and gratifications studies indicates that, far from being isolated, atomized, or otherwise powerless in a mass society, individuals remain connected with others in various ways both through media use and continued participation in other activities. What is different here, however, is that the compilation of data regarding variations in needs, motives, or gratifications is never set against or qualified by the measurement of power effects.

This is hardly an exhaustive account of recent or contemporary social-science media research. A more comprehensive review would capture the historical trajectory of particular perspectives in more detail, providing elaboration of issues that have mattered most to social scientists. Perhaps it would identify developments in concept-formation or innovations in techniques of measurement and data analysis, or discuss substantive "breakthroughs" in specific areas of study. Such an account might also assess what analysts themselves take to be the current state of knowledge in their area of specialization or provide a clearer idea of what they see as pressing problems or promising paths for further research.

Yet it is clear from this brief overview of this literature that the schemata for making sense of media power and media use have changed considerably and shown significant variation since the days of limited effects research. The most noteworthy of such departures has been uses and gratifications research, in which the privileged position of communicators, with all that it has entailed, was abandoned. Less dramatic departures are evident in the time-budget studies of radio and television use and in public-opinion polling as well; in research on "media agendas" as powerful but not (necessarily) intentionally so; in a wide range of experimental work that, like agenda-setting research, has used the data of correlations and causation as evidence of a power that is not, strictly speaking, something persuasive; and even in research on political learning and voting behavior, where studies of personality and persuasability have taken analysts further inside the subjective experience of media users and examined the very formation of predispositions.

At the very same time, and in some of these very same perspectives and approaches, affinities with limited effects research live on. While research is no longer carried out in that name, component parts of its scheme of messages, mediating factors, responses, and immediate effects continue to order and organize inquiry with regard to political learning and voting behavior, agenda setting, public-opinion polling, marketing strategies and consumer behavior, as well as in experimental work regarding violence, sex, gender, and racial stereotyping, among other things.

The logic of variable analysis

Amidst the affinities, the changes, the departures, the variations, and the overall diversity of substantive interests and concerns that constitute this brand of media research is a shared belief in and commitment to a scientific methodology. Variable analysis techniques, as Herbert Blumer (1969) referred to them, have been indispensable to the compilation of social facts and the cumulation of knowledge regarding the workings of the mass media. Above and beyond even so many substantive considerations, then, this "scientism" of social-science research is profoundly consequential in its own right. Simply put, the strictures it places on what and how things can count as empirical limits too narrowly the evidence of social power in media studies and actually prevents documentation of a sociality of media use from emerging at all.

The terms "scientism" and "variable analysis" thus can be regarded as shorthand designations for a logic of empirical inquiry, of scientific practice, including ways of thinking about it, that have become routine, something second nature for social scientists. Elemental to this logic is the requirement that empirical realities be "measurable." Practically speaking, measurement becomes synonymous with the identification of things that vary. Whether in survey research, experiments, or one or another form of content analysis, the operative assumption is that the media and the social experience of the people who use it can and should be treated as variable occurences. Through measurement, then, patterns of possible variation can be documented as actually occurring ones.

This logic of variable analysis, including its measurement requirements, originates, among other places, in the pioneering work of Durkheim. Writing a century ago, Durkheim (1967, 1938) spoke not of variable analysis techniques *per se*, but of "the social," "social facts," and "social fact analysis." The social was the name Durkheim gave to the terrain of collective life that emerged between metaphysical domains and psychological realities. The distinctiveness of the social required a distinctive mode of analysis as well, since neither philosophical constructs nor psychological theories were adequate as a language of explanation. A social fact represented the more objective aspect of the social. It had a life of its own, Durkheim said, independent of the people in whose lives it constituted something real, and independent of the sociologist, too. Suicide rates were social facts, as were laws and the myriad norms and rules that emerged from social life to orchestrate and shape collective thought and action. Social facts, then, were "things," they took on a thing-like appearance, and were capable, Durkheim said, of analysis on their own terms.

Social scientists who study mass media proceed with this idea of social facts in mind. For example, in the study of television, programming is routinely treated as something objective, since it very clearly exists independently of the analyst and independently of the people who watch it, too. As a social fact, it can be operationally defined and then measured as so many things that vary: as a discrete persuasive message, a series of such messages, a more general index of content patterns (as in agenda setting research), or as genre, plot, narrative structure, patterns of character's actions, or other formal features of programming. When it comes to television use, the same logic of variable analysis is applicable even if use proves to be a more complicated social phenomenon to study. There are aspects of television use (and media use more generally) that take a more objective form than others, and for that reason can be treated more easily as social facts than other aspects of use. The predispositions and background characteristics of people – age, class, gender, race, education, family size, and so on – along with the specific actions, and feelings that occur in relation to television, all of this can be measured as discrete variables, too. In this way, not only do the object and subject sides of the empirical equation vary, but, more importantly, the objective features of television – whatever they may be – are treated as something separate and separable from the subjective dimensions of use. Both the medium and its use are capable of measurement on their own terms.

Studying social power scientifically

This emphasis on the factual does not preclude social scientists from studying social power, although it does restrict what can count as evidence. After all, theoretical ideas, broad conceptions, or more specific ideas about media or media use must first be translated into conceptual constructs and then operationalized to permit measurement to proceed. When the legacy of limited effects research, with its lack of substantive vision regarding issues of social power, is added to these methodological restrictions, it is no wonder that topics like ideology, elite interests, the institutional workings of mass media, or the hegemonic process have failed to receive adequate treatment in social-science research. None the less, when analysts have thought through these substantive limits, variable analysis techniques have indeed proven effective in providing data regarding the workings of social power *in the mass media itself*.

For example, in the cultivation analysis carried out by George Gerbner and his associates (1986, 1982, 1980, 1977) social power is dealt with explicitly in study after study of television programming. Like Gitlin, Lazarsfeld and Merton, and Adorno, Gerbner's primary analytical concern is the institutional power of television to generate ideology. After first analyzing television as an elite controlled corporate institution with distinctive mass-marketing requirements, he operationally defines its ideological workings as the "message system" of programming: a widening circle of standardized images that cut across the widest variety of programs (1986). For Gerbner, it is the overall flow of imagery with its repetitions, rather than the messages of specific shows that provides the most compelling data of social power. By counting instances of, say, violence, across random samples of programming, and charting variations in such depictions over years of study, Gerbner uncovers facts that provide evidence of television's power: a power to limit the range of representations that people have access to and which they can use in making sense of their own social worlds. This power is, in a way, pre-established by the workings of television as an elite controlled, corporate institution.

The more recent agenda setting research of Iyengar (1991, 1987) is another example of how variable analysis techniques can provide evidence of social power. Based on Gitlin's idea of ideological framing, Iyengar manipulates the ordering of news stories in an experimental set-up designed to test whether or not and how the media agenda is incorporated into the personal agendas of people who watch television news. I will have more to say about the audience response component of this research in a moment. Here, however, I want to focus on Iyengar's analysis of the object, television news. In contrast to so much agenda-setting research, Iyengar is explicit in recognizing that news is a product of an elite-controlled, mass-market driven institution. At the outset, news stories are understood as shaped by the hierarchy of decision-making in the television industry, by professional norms that guide judgments about what is and is not news, by editorial control and supervision, and by marketing needs, among other things. Iyengar represents these institutional factors as categorizations of the content and form of news stories. So, for example, he identifies variations in the "episodic" and "thematic" as well as the "vivid" and "pallid" depiction of events in news stories. The predominance of episodic and vivid depictions is data that provide evidence of this institutional power working as ideology in the object itself. For Iyengar, this is an important first step in measuring how this ideology constitutes the personal agendas of people.

Armed with an understanding of what social power is and where it comes from, Gerbner and Iyengar were able to use variable analysis techniques to identify and measure its patterning in television programming. This is not so surprising, since the more objective or factual aspects of social phenomena fit the requirements of variable analysis quite nicely.

Difficulties arise, however, when social scientists must situate the media object in the culture of everyday use and employ variable analysis techniques to measure power as it emerges from the meaning–making activities of people. Gerbner was certainly interested in how the ideology of television's message system could shape the thoughts, feelings, and actions of viewers, and he used the logic of variable analysis to measure it. With his analysis of the object already in place, Gerbner turned to use. He operationalized exposure to television as a measure of light versus heavy viewing and the understanding people have of their own real-world conditions as a series of questions that presented a choice between a "television" (real-world conditions as seen there) and a "real-world" answer (corresponding to actual social conditions). Gerbner then correlated the data regarding a television or real-world answer with that of exposure and found that, in many if not most cases heavy viewers were more likely than light viewers to give the "television answer" (1977). This was evidence, he reasoned, of television's social power to cultivate a mainstream outlook in people. Technical issues regarding measurement and statistical analysis aside, these facts are hardly adequate as empirical indicators of the meaning television viewing has for people. Gerbner certainly understood that television viewing *had* meaning for people; how else could he hypothesize that their thinking changed as a result of watching? But he did not define or measure how people made programming meaningful or, for that matter, how their interpretive activity with television was linked with thoughts and actions that emerged elsewhere in their lives. Assumed but never made explicit was the sociality of use and the existence of a viewing culture. Measures of exposure and choosing a television versus a real-world answer serve as the more abstract indicators of this culture and the sociality emergent there. As a result, it was difficult if not impossible for anyone reading Gerbner to understand how this message system, with its ideology, was grounded concretely in everyday life.

Iyengar has fared much better in this regard. In *News That Matters* and *Is Anyone Responsible?* he links the social power of television – in his case, various ways that events and issues were framed in news stories – with the meanings people attribute to news shortly after watching it. Through a series of sophisticated experiments he demonstrated how exposure to television-news coverage influences the importance that people attach to particular issues of national concern. While the specific issues varied from experiment to experiment and the magnitude of the effects varied across different experiments, generally speaking, Iyengar provided evidence of modest but consistent effects that were statistically significant. For example, in *Is Anyone Responsible?*, he examined people's exposure to episodic and thematic news coverage and found that with greater exposure to episodic coverage, people were less likely to hold public officials accountable for social problems and less likely to see them as responsible for alleviating these same problems. This is indicative, Iyengar said, of television's power to discourage participation in the political process and to decrease the sense of control people think they have over elected officials. Furthermore, he argued that, by portraying issues primarily in terms of discrete events (episodic framing), television news impedes the recognition people have of the interconnections between issues which in the long run may generate inconsistencies in the formation of public opinion.

Not only is Iyengar's work scientifically rigorous, experimentally precise, and substantively convincing, but it also represents a significant step forward in measuring the workings of social power inside the meaningful experience of people. Unlike most social scientists, Iyengar understands quite well that data on responses and immediate effects are inextricably linked with institutional processes and broader societal structures of power. Gone are ideas of persuasive power, the privileging of communicator intentions, and messages that reflect those intentions; in their place, ideas of framing, ideology, the institutions of news production, and the situatedness of mass-communication amidst an elite-controlled political process. Now, the production of ideology and the interpretation of ideology are the key constructs of the mass-communication process, and Iyengar recognizes that they must be studied in conjunction with one another to provide data adequate at the level of meaning. So, responses become data, the facts of interpretation, which, in turn, serve as the basis for generalizations revealing the broader significance of those responses. In the end, Iyengar has generated a set of interconnected ideas extrapolated from evidence. These are ideas about what responses *mean*, not only in the laboratory, but in actual television use; and, further, they are ideas about what actual television use means for people in their everyday lives. Scientific disclaimers aside, acknowledged or not, mere responses made by people in a laboratory to news stories shortly after watching them are understood to stand for, to resonate with what it really means to watch television and live amidst its presence. The ideas that Iyengar has generated, then, are ideas about a sociality of television use and about ongoing participation in a viewing culture. And yet systematic documentation of this viewing culture or its sociality of use is never provided. In fact, such documentation is occluded by the very measurement of responses and the social power they indicate. This is not Iyengar's choice or his fault. It is, however, a consequence of using variable analysis techniques to position interpretation as a communicative effect.

Like other social scientists, Iyengar generates data through a series of abstractions. He generates social facts, a set of discrete things that vary. First, in terms of the object, television, variations in the content, placement, and, in some instances, the form of news stories are abstracted from a more complex and multi-layered symbolism of programming. This makes sense, given Iyengar's substantive interest in the effects of news framing. It also provides a communicative focus for measurement at the very outset of inquiry. If Iyengar were interested in other aspects of communication that occur through the news, or if he wanted to explore the workings of less explicitly communicative dimensions of programming, he would have focused the measurement process on different aspects of its symbolism to begin with: on different contents, on genre, plot, narrative, or characterization in the story-telling conventions in news itself, on the repetition and standardization of the commodity forms in programming, or on various aspects of programming esthetics. But, in this research, variations on the content, placement, and, on occasion, the form of news stories *are* the object, television. They stand for all of the symbolic complexities of programming, and, as such, they serve as the source for any and all subsequent measurements of response and, hence, effect. The variations abstracted as data are what matter empirically while other aspects of symbolism in the object become invisible to the measurement process.

Second, on the subject-side of things, variation in responses that people make to news stories shortly after watching them are abstracted out of a much more complex and multi-layered sociality that comprises day-to-day television use. To the extent that people actually respond to news stories when they watch, the measured responses of the experiment are themselves a reconstruction of an already indirect indicator of the meaning that news stories have for people. Nevertheless, as data, this variation in responses is, for Iyengar, indicative of an attentiveness that people bring to their watching of news; an attentiveness that is itself motivated by a desire to stay informed about events and, as he says, "attribute responsibility to news actors" for what goes on in their world.

But with the abstracting of this data comes the disappearance of various dynamics of news watching, dynamics that contribute importantly to the

actual meaning that news has for people. Gone from view are the less attentive ways of watching news stories, and, with them, any consideration of
the significance they carry, including their interrelation with attentiveness,
in determining the meaning of news. Gone, too, are the small and seemingly insignificant occurrences that often punctuate actual news watching
in the home: moving in and out of the room, listening to as opposed to
watching the news, doing other things while watching, especially talking
with others about things unrelated to what is on, flipping between channels,
watching one or two other programs along with the news, and so on. Gone
as well is any recognition of the exigencies of work, the routines of family
or household life, or the ordinary responsibilities that situate everyday news
watching in the home. While all of this is empirical, none of it is conceptualized or measured, therefore none of it can count as evidence of how news
is made meaningful by people. People who watch television news, who routinely exhibit a variegated sociality in their use of television, who participate in an ongoing culture of television use, these people simply become
receivers of mass communication.

Iyengar has abstracted significant variations in a communicative process
from a complex, multi-layered and indeterminate sociality of use (which
includes the symbolic complexity of programming). He has made this
sociality into something precise and determinate, into data, which enable his
analysis to be understood as scientific. At the same time, however, the
dynamics of meaning–making and cultural formation that comprise this
sociality of use are broken up, flattened, and compartmentalized, in order
to appear as facts for variable analysis. In privileging the more factual
aspects of news watching – responses about it, actually – Iyengar obscures
equally empirical if less easily definable social and cultural dimensions of
television use that give meaningful form to news watching. His extrapola-
tions from the evidence notwithstanding, it becomes difficult, if not impossible, to adequately determine the sociological significance of his findings
outside the context of their construction: i.e., the laboratory. In moving from
the laboratory and its controls to real life, the emergent aspects of actual
news watching become more visible, their grounding in a culture of television use harder to ignore. The logic and language of variable analysis leave
Iyengar and social scientists like him ill-equipped to explore the emergent
social and cultural dimensions of news watching, indeed of television use.

From social power to a sociality of use

Many years ago in *Movies and Conduct*, Herbert Blumer (1933) said that
eliciting the attitudes or opinions of individuals by using surveys and

experiments is crucial for generating data of media use. But this data, he said, was too far removed from what it is that people actually do with the movies and what the movies actually do to people to provide an accurate picture of what media use means to people. For Blumer, measuring attitudes or opinions about media use shortly afterwards is not the same as documenting what he termed their "actual experience": how people think and feel and imagine while they are using media. Furthermore, he argued that such data failed to capture how this thinking and acting, this feeling and imagining, actually fit into everyday life. As a result, Blumer said, social science deals with the emergent quality of social experience only in a second-hand way, reducing the "integrity of the person" to a mere set of responses to pre-given messages. In the end, Blumer's position mirrors that of Merton, who argued that a preoccupation with measurement reduced the documentation of social reality to a "technical problem" (Merton, 1946).

The power of Blumer's argument was evident in my own research. I used the survey method to profile viewers with regard to particular meaningful dimensions of their television use. The first step in this process was a quantitative one. I used the documentation of viewer diaries along with the recording of my observations and participation in various viewing cultures to formulate a construct of "viewing relations." I defined this construct as different patterns of mindful and emotional involvement that emerge as a result of viewers' situating themselves with television and becoming involved with the symbolism of programming over the course of their day-to-day use. I then operationalized it as a series of eight statements that people I interviewed would respond to in order to indicate which patterns occurred in their viewing and how typical they were. While my sample was too small for the use of multiple controls, the data were informative none the less. In addition to finding out how often people watched television in each of these ways, I found out, too, that this continuum of viewing relations accurately represented the parameters of their own day-to-day viewing habits. Contrary to expectations, I found that mindful attention to the text was not positively correlated with education, as more educated respondents ignored textual features of programming as much as or more frequently than, less educated respondents. On the other hand, I found that, generally speaking, age was positively correlated with mindfulness toward the text, as younger viewers were more likely to use television in distracted, image-based ways, where attention need not focus on a single story for viewing to be meaningful. Furthermore, when this data of viewing relations were combined with a series of qualitative responses to generate an overall profile of mindfulness, I was able to place and compare individuals across particular mindful and emotional dimensions of television use.

The survey method was of little help, however, when it came to documenting and explaining the dynamics of television use. The data of aggregate responses were abstracted from the actual culture of use by means of a prior, qualitative reconstruction of this culture that occurred through depth interviewing and participant observation, processes of abstraction in their own right. The initial choice of the survey method was driven by a need to generate objective measures rather than qualitative accounts of viewing, so that data free from traces of the researcher's subjectivity could solidify the validity of my findings. Yet, this compilation of social facts provided few if any clues regarding the interrelation of viewing relations that typically occurred in the *real* time of the viewing culture. Lost in the static data of responses were the various patterns of movement in and out of different viewing relations as well as the preferences of people for one or another viewing relation, or combination of viewing relations at different times or in different, recurring situations of use. While these dynamics of viewing may seem small, insignificant, or simply not worthy of analytical attention, in actuality, they constitute the most elemental aspects of a sociality of use, including the formation of a sense of self in use.

I found that documenting the sociality of television use requires more than reconstructing what people do with television as responses to fixed-choice questions. It even requires more than using brief, open-ended questions in a limited interview format to elicit more elaborated responses from people. Documenting this sociality requires the use of methods that enable, rather than close off, reconstruction of the mindful and emotional involvement people have with television, especially their sense of its duration. There are many practical aspects of watching television that are repeated over and over again, such as mindful movements in and out of different viewing relations, movements between different stories and characters, watching more than one show, switching between channels, being led along by fast-paced imagery, becoming absorbed inside the image worlds, and so on. Despite, or perhaps because of, this repetition, people take much of their involvement with television for granted. At first glance, they are not always aware of the conditions that shape this involvement or of the significance it carries in their lives. Such is the power of the unconscious. Furthermore, much of this involvement on the part of people cannot be observed in behavior because it takes place in their heads and often remains there. Documenting this sociality poses a serious problem for social scientists, since a good deal of it is not objectively given and cannot easily be translated into the terms of variable analysis. Yet, it can be documented.

Doing so, however, requires significant departures from a scientistic methodology.

First, the analyst must begin with the idea that some kind of unconscious processes are at work when people use television; without it, no amount of methodological sophistication will enable the reconstruction of these processes to occur. People may indeed be unaware, initially, of different dimensions of their television use, but that does not mean that they are always unaware of them, that they will remain unaware of them, or that they cannot, under certain circumstances, call them to mind and discuss them in conversation. This applies to their behavior as well as to what is in their heads.

Second, documenting this sociality of use calls for explicit displays of subjectivity on the part of the researcher that social scientists are not prepared to acknowledge. Such study calls for open-ended follow-up questions and a conscious directing of the path of inquiry to explicate dynamics of meaning–making that are not readily apparent and could not easily be formulated as responses to fixed- or limited-choice questions. Depth interviewing and participant observation, as opposed to survey methods, are appropriate for this task of documentation. Depth interviewing can be used to direct and redirect inquiry, in a flexible way, to the borders or limits of people's practical knowledge and self-understandings, enabling them to reconstruct thoughts, feelings, and actions that typify their television use. The analyst must enable people to reconstruct, both for themselves, since they may not ordinarily have occasion to do so, and for the analysis itself, the routines of their participation in the viewing culture. This requires a lengthy, open-ended interview format. Similarly, participant observation can be used to account for emergent patterns of television use that viewers themselves may be too immediately involved in to take notice of or to comment on. In this way, the sociality of use is treated concretely and need not be forced to fit the more abstract requirements of variable analysis. In addition, a variety of other strategies of documentation, ranging from viewer diaries, to focus groups, to television autobiographies, could be employed to draw out more of the ritual significance of continued participation in a viewing culture.

Variable analysis and the problem of subjectivity

Some social scientists would defend the use of variable analysis techniques by pointing out that a more sophisticated research design, along with more precise survey questions, would remedy whatever problems may arise in the study of sociality by enabling the analyst to measure dynamics of use as they occur in the viewing culture. I am not convinced of this. To my mind, already formed fixed-choice questions, no matter how sophisticated in design, do not allow for the more open displays of the researcher's own subjectivity that are essential in documenting the emergent qualities of television use, especially in bringing its hidden dimensions to the surface. As it is presently practiced, variable analysis is inadequate in this regard.

Practically speaking, the requirement that empirical realities be "measurable" means that the social, social–psychological, or even psychological aspects of media use must appear to analysts as facts, as "data" that exist objectively, free from subjectivity, whatever its origin or kind. Data, then, are the result of a scientistic process of abstraction that conflates the empirical with what is measurable, in so far as what is measurable is understood to be objective. Data can never include empirical aspects of media use that emerge out of an open acknowledgment of the subjectivity inherent in the research process. This conflation, understood by social scientists as an elemental act in establishing truth, is itself ideological, and actually constitutive of one of the more profound limitations of scientistic media research. Any sociality of media use that cannot present itself objectively, as a fact, will not fit the requirements of variable analysis techniques, and, hence, will not count as empirical. Consequently, it is difficult, if not impossible, for the cultural dimensions of media use to gain visibility and attain a position of importance in social-science research. The complex and multi-layered social processes that comprise media use never merit serious attention in their own right. The dynamics of reading, listening, or viewing as distinctive activities are then taken for granted or, worse still, ignored altogether. This is the case even if, or when, analysts are intent upon measuring dynamics of meaning–making to begin with. In this particular research perspective, ideas regarding a viewing culture are hard to come by, let alone to translate into empirical terms. As a result, the sociality of a viewing culture or cultures never acquires significance within scientistic models of media use.

I think it is possible, however, for social scientists to use variable analysis techniques reflexively. Among other things, this would mean that the significance analysts attach to social facts should be linked with an awareness that these facts are a reconstruction of what they, the analysts, believe people's actual experiences to be. Social facts, then, are understood as *not* the same as the social processes that actually emerge in the viewing culture, and *not* the same as the reconstruction of these processes either. To be reflexive is to recognize that the gap between the measurement of social facts and the social dynamics of actual media use is *as* important as whatever substantive significance analysts attribute to facts themselves.

Interestingly, within the social-science model, there are breaks with the conventional logic of factual measurement. These breaks provide insight into the social world of television use above and beyond what we usually see when the logic of variable analysis techniques are employed. One such break occurs in the empirical work that Merton himself undertook many years ago. In *Mass Persuasion*, Merton identified "the nature of the affective relationship" as a "third factor" in the study of persuasive effects, emerging between the structure and content of the message and the predispositions that listeners brought to their radio use. While much of this affective relationship was to be found in responses to messages, Merton argued that the measurement of responses did not exhaust what could be meant by an affective relationship to media. While he set out to measure immediate responses, in doing so, he was led to infer how psychodynamic (unconscious) processes and taken-for-granted societal ideologies influence conscious responses to messages as well as radio listening habits in general. These factors, while not measured by Merton, were nevertheless crucial components of the listening culture of radio. Merton knew this and thought that they must be accounted for if the analyst is to understand the meaningful significance of radio use in people's everyday lives.

But, beyond that, Merton's idea of an affective relation *emergent* from the act of radio listening really does point to media use as a distinctive social form in its own right; one that, while shaped by the objective structural features of the medium and by the predisposing factors and previous experiences that contribute to interpretation, is also independent of these factors as well. This idea is very close indeed to what I have referred to, somewhat interchangeably, as the sociality of media use and the viewing culture. In talking about this affective relationship, Merton recognized that an important direction for media research lay in conceptualizing and documenting this sociality and along with it, listening or viewing cultures.

Another break with conventional social-science logic is evident in Herbert Blumer's media research. In *Movies and Conduct*, Blumer wanted to document the "actual experience" people have with movies. This meant reconstructing the social situations that typify movie watching in order to account for what people think and feel *while* they are watching; but, just as important, it also meant understanding how these thoughts and feelings become a part of what people subsequently think, feel, and do while away from the movies. Like Merton, Blumer thought that media use was sufficiently complex to warrant close study as a distinctive, social world in its own right. This is a world emergent from media use, but one that extends back into people's previous experiences, since it is these experiences that prepare people to see and interpret movies in the ways that they do. In

Blumer's eyes, the survey method, with its emphasis upon eliciting responses, is "too far removed from understanding what motion pictures are actually doing," because the opinions or attitudes that people have shortly after attending the movies is simply not the same as how they think and feel and imagine while engaged with movie imagery (1933: 18). Alternatively, he employed multiple qualitative methods to study the social world of moviegoing: personal accounts of moviegoing activities, depth interviews, the recording of informal conversations, direct observation. As a symbolic interactionist, Blumer did not explicitly account for the social power of movies. Despite this limitation, however, Blumer was well aware that there is a distinctive sociality to media use that must be understood on its own terms. With the idea of an actual experience of moviegoing that is meaningful, one that emerges from previous interactions and social settings and extends into the formation of new ones, he undertook important steps toward the conceptualization and documentation of this sociality.

Conclusion

Notwithstanding these notable exceptions to the prevailing logic of research and analysis, the methods and language of social science in the field of media studies have gone wanting. Besides being too abstract and empirically ungrounded, conventional social science has been too preoccupied with measurement, conceptual precision, and the satisfaction of its own truth claims to understand what I have called the sociality and culture of media use, including the ways that the social power of media work within these. In social science, past and present, ideas of sociality or of a viewing culture simply do not exist. In their place, various constructs of communication have served as ordering and organizing principles for measurement. While social scientists are to be commended for the specificity and precision with which they generate data and discuss their findings, the lack of emphasis placed on the documentation of social and cultural dynamics or on broader notions of institutional or discursive power renders their contribution to media studies problematic at best.

3

___

Cultural studies

Cultural studies looms large in current thinking about television. Seen initially as a growing body of scholarly work inspired by the Centre for the Study of Contemporary Culture at Birmingham, England, nowadays, cultural studies is arguably the most sophisticated of critical approaches to the study of culture. It has focused on the study of cultural practice and power across a wide variety of social settings, both contemporary and historical. Analysts have paid attention to the ways that power orders and organizes even the most mundane aspects of everyday life; and, just as importantly, they have sought to demonstrate how people take issue with power and resist its normalizing influences. Over the years, cultural studies has encompassed wide-ranging work from different disciplines and in this way has become a repository of various terms and constructs that have been used to identify and discuss the workings of social power as something institutional, ideological, discursive, and cultural. Throughout its brief history, the substantive interests and political concerns guiding the work of analysts have changed, reflecting the simultaneous and successive influence of neo-Marxism, structuralism and semiotics, feminism, and, more recently, postcolonial and poststructuralist perspectives. As a result, initial concerns in cultural studies with capitalism and class-based identities and cultural practices have been expanded to include the study of patriarchal power relations, racial and ethnic divisions characteristic of advanced industrial societies, and the investigation of, as well as studies of, postcolonial politics and culture, among other things. At the very least, the diversity of substantive interests and strategic approaches to the study of power, culture, and social life attests to the interdisciplinary nature of cultural studies research. All of this has made cultural studies the important and innovative perspective that it is.

It is difficult to think of cultural studies as a singular paradigm, due to its interdisciplinary origins and the wide range of cultural phenomena that analysts have chosen to study. Yet, there are common themes to be found in the work that comprises cultural studies. Foremost among them is the idea that cultural objects and meanings are *situated* (Hall, 1980). A most important aspect of this situatedness is the recognition of a division in societies between dominant and subordinate groups that differ in terms of their access to social power and, following from this their ability to assert it: economically, politically, socially, ideologically, and, of course, culturally. Beyond the idea of groups, of group-based practices, of group interests and ideologies, many proponents of cultural studies see meaning as situated discursively as well. Discursive power, then, is another of the more important themes of cultural studies research. Discourses are understood to work normatively, ordering, organizing, and regulating everyday life in ways that reach beyond the power of values or even ideologies. Furthermore, in doing so, discourses are believed to possess relative autonomy: that is, while tied to social structures, state institutions and policies, and the workings of the economy, discourses also and at the very same time constitute distinctive linguistic domains in social life, powerful in their very naturalness and apparent invisibility.

Common, too, in the work of cultural studies, is a belief that mass media is crucial to the reproduction of elite power and privilege – institutionally, ideologically, and discursively. Central to media research is an understanding that representational forms of media are powerful in their own right. Cultural studies has identified dominant ideologies commonplace in media imagery, in some cases, documenting significant transformations in the ways they work over time. With an increasing reliance on tools of discourse analysis, cultural studies has opened up media study to account for a multiplicity of normative influences that work beneath the coherence typically attributed to ideologies. But, in cultural studies, distinguishing between this objective power and the ways it works in actual encounters that people have with media is just as, if not more, important to a critical understanding of contemporary culture. While analysts believe that the encoding process bestows certain preferred meanings on the text, they also believe that these are not the *only* meanings to be found there. Interpretation is understood as an indeterminate moment in communicative and cultural processes. In fact, textual interpretations are understood to vary considerably, since people who use media occupy differing locations in the social structure, which give rise to distinct, material interests and social identities, which, in turn, result in differing but persistent strategies of interpretation. Because this positioning is believed to be hierarchical with respect to power, under certain circumstances, textual interpretations can take issue with or provide an alternative to the preferred encodings representative of official culture.

Cultural studies has identified the way that media work to privilege some ideologies and discourses over others and, equally important, how social locations work to privilege some textual interpretations over others, all of which has illuminated just what constitutes dominant, negotiated, and oppositional meanings of cultural practice. In doing so, it has demonstrated that mass media does not work unilaterally nor achieve any complete or lasting power in everyday life. Resistant, oppositional, or transgressive meanings emergent from media use are believed to be an important basis for political empowerment (Lembo and Tucker, 1990). Analyses of power notwithstanding, the overriding concern of cultural studies has been to document the interconnectedness between the social locations of people, their identities and interpretive strategies, and modes of cultural resistance and political empowerment. As a perspective, then, cultural studies has insisted that interrogations of media power be grounded in everyday life. As a result, not only is culture itself understood to be political, but its "politics" must be thought about, discussed, and documented in new ways.

Familiarity with the work of cultural studies – whether it is the early of Richard Hoggart (1966), the encoding/decoding model of Stuart Hall (1975), the ethnographic studies of Willis (1978, 1977) or McRobbie (1991), Morley's television research (1994, 1986, 1980), or Fiske's (1987) revisions of the hegemonic model – is indispensable for anyone who thinks seriously about television. In contrast to both the theorists and social scientists whose work I have discussed, cultural studies' analysts pose much more concrete – and difficult – questions regarding television: how does its social power actually work in people's everyday lives? What does hegemony mean in practical terms? How do we know when people accept dominant discourses and when they do not? What does being implicated in power or resisting its influences actually look like? At the outset, then, cultural studies analysts propose to interrogate directly how the power of television actually meets the social experience of people who watch it. As such, it is possible for ideas about a sociality of use or of a culture emergent from viewing to be more fully recognized in the documentation process and in the theorizing that stems from it.

I am supportive of the critical project of cultural studies. I, too, want to understand the workings of television's power, especially how it operates as a commercial medium to structure and shape what people think and do, and, also, how it provides imaginative possibilities for them as they make their experience with it meaningful. Like cultural studies' analysts, I want to know how the worlds that television represents become inscribed in the ways that people live their own lives. I want to understand how television seeps into the most mundane things that people think and feel and do. And, like many proponents of cultural studies, I want to understand the limits of television's power to do any or all of these things, which means accounting for various modes of resistance or opposition that emerge from daily use.

Despite the strengths of cultural studies and the clear advantages it offers for media study, it remains limited when it comes to documenting the complex social dynamics that comprise the culture of television use. The construct of social power used by cultural studies' analysts who investigate viewing is focused predominantly on the discursive symbolism of programming, whether it is referred to as ideology, the text, or discourses themselves. The esthetics of visual imagery and the explicitly commercial forms of programming, distinct symbolisms in their own right, fail to receive adequate treatment. Lost to analysis is the interplay of each of these symbolisms with one another and with the discourses of programming. Lost as well is an understanding of how this symbolic complexity of the object, television, can shape the sociality of use in distinctive ways. On the audience side of things, a variety of constructs are used to identify meaningful activity: textual interpretation, reading strategy, social location, the workings of identity, discursive practices, and so on. Despite the different designations, most analysts end up at the interpretive process, deconstructing the power of the text by distinguishing between the dominant, negotiated, and oppositional meaning that people attach to it. The idea of sociality is intrinsic to all these constructs, especially interpretation, but is never itself made an explicit part of the analysis of power or use. The fact of the matter is, all that is social about television use cannot be conveyed by these constructs, alone or in combination. Lost to analysis is the inner mindfulness of different viewing relations, the sociality of self that continually traverses the various symbolisms of programming, the patterns of self-formation that occur between interpretations and identity positions, and ritualistic aspects of use that incorporate and move beyond readings of the text. Lost to analysis, then, is a wide-ranging and diverse sociality that comprises dynamics of power and resistance as cultural studies' analysts typically conceive of them, but much more as well.

In the remainder of this chapter, I will use a variety of constructs to elaborate my critique of cultural studies. Mindfulness, mindful and emotional involvement, symbolism, self, self-formation, viewing relations, viewing practices, ritual, meaning–making, and of course sociality and the viewing culture: all of these constructs will serve as key terms of an emerging discourse that accounts for what people do with television in ways that cultural studies has not. I will proceed by discussing, in turn, the constructs of "discourse," "text," and "discursive practice," identifying both their importance and their limitations in cultural studies' accounts of media power and use.

Discourse

There are many ways to think about the power of television, depending upon the particular aspect or aspects of its workings analysts wish to discuss. This fact alone is testimony to television's complexity as a cultural object. Much of the earlier work in cultural studies focused attention on the hegemonic role of television in obscuring or naturalizing the material interests of the powerful in the very reproduction of ideologies representative of those interests. Television was understood to provide people with partial and highly selective access to social realities. In this scheme of things, the limiting power of television became the focal point of analysis: television was understood to limit the range of ideas and imagery available to people; but, more that that, it was understood to limit the representation of social realities to reflect and reproduce the norms and conventions of official culture.

In more recent scholarship, the construct of discourse has taken center stage. In this version of cultural studies, power is seen not so much as a limiting of meaning or a hiding of underlying social realities, but more as a normalizing process that is productive: one that proliferates meaning and, in doing so, generates new fields and forms of cultural practice. It is by ordering and organizing the meaning of everyday life that regularities of discourse constitute a television culture.

For example, in *Make Room for Television*, Lynn Spigel (1992) discusses the discursive formation of television in the post-war United States by examining depictions of social life in popular magazines such as *Good Housekeeping*, *Life*, *Look*, and *Harper's Bazaar* (as well as various newspapers and the business press). The documents she analyzes, if not designed and produced by corporate personnel, were shaped by other professionals such as journalists, writers, and cultural critics who were, like corporate employees, positioned outside the world of day-to-day (radio or) television use. In the simple frequency with which products appeared, in the advertising pitches and the imagery that accompanied them, and in the narratives of magazine stories, among other places, she finds a repetition of themes that promoted consumption: ordinary aspects of domestic labor and leisure were represented in product-oriented terms; consumer behavior was promoted as an answer to a variety of life's little problems and concerns;

greater comfort and convenience were shown as the likely outcomes of consumer activity; consumption was held out as a desired way of life, an end in itself for human activity.

For Spigel, such themes were discourses: what Rabinow and Dreyfus (1983) would call the "significant speech acts" of official culture. They were regularities in the formation of television that in their objective form of images and text, extended the power of corporate capital into the private world of the American home. These discourses served simultaneously as normative ordering principles for people. They provided them with frameworks for finding personal meaning and securing a sense of social place in a society undergoing profound transformations. In this way, Spigel says, the social logics of corporate capital were normalized; they became integral to the everyday meaning–making activities of people in the domestic sphere. This was particularly true for women because they were principally responsible for the care, maintenance, and reproduction of domestic life.

Spigel accounts for resistance to this normalizing power, too. In the same magazines, newspapers, and journals, she found that the voices of cultural critics, public intellectuals, homemakers, and viewers were sometimes at odds with what was said in dominant domestic discourses about television. In these oppositional discourses, the benefits and comforts, the easy living, the miraculous and wonderfully transformative effects that the powerful envisioned as being ushered in with the advent of television, were called into question. In their place were various ways of recognizing the hollowness and falsity, even, of the claims made about television by advertisers and industry insiders, including their supporters and sympathizers. Compared to dominant discourses, oppositional ones generate a different, more concrete kind of knowledge.

A similar argument is made by Cecilia Tichi (1991) in *Electronic Hearth.* Seeking to understand the meaning of television in American society, Tichi analyzed a wide variety of texts, including those comprising the popular press, trade publications in the fields of marketing and advertising, intellectual journals of opinion, the scholarly publications that circulate in the academic world, as well as the artifacts of popular culture more generally. Like Spigel, she found regularities and repetitions in the ways television was spoken about. These were the discourses of television: multiple, overlapping, and sometimes conflicting with one another. Among the most prominent of them were discourses celebrating television as an instrument of technological advancement, those extolling its comforts and conveniences as a consumer good, and, somewhat paradoxically, those expressing myriad fears associated with television as it encroached upon and, in some cases, usurped the value and place of traditional cultural institutions and practices.

In Tichi's eyes, the dominant discourses of television were extensions, elaborations, of the social logic of science, technology, and the corporate market-place, especially consumerism, but they took distinctive and unprecedented forms. At the very same time, these discourses were understood to carry normative implications for people. They worked, like language did, in small and seemingly insignificant ways to order, organize, and give meaning to a wide variety of thoughts, feelings, and actions that emerged from everyday life, doing so in ways that coincided with other discourses of power. And yet, Tichi is well aware that this discursive formation of television did not work unilaterally or unequivocally in the service of power. Like Spigel, she saw in the writings of cultural critics and academics insights and understandings that challenged, opposed, and resisted any simple acceptance of the meaning television carried in dominant discourses. In this way, fears and anxieties regarding television became an integral aspect of its discursive formation and placed a critique of economic, political, technological, social, and cultural developments on a par with their presumed normalcy.

The accounts of Spigel and Tichi illustrate a prevailing way of thinking about television in the field of cultural studies. For these analysts and others like them, the construct "discourse" (and its related terms) designates workings of power that are distinctive and merit analysis on their own terms. Discourse refers to a kind of societal speech about television; it is a way of naming the significant speech acts that endure in the culture, even as they undergo modification and change. Discourse cannot easily or accurately be identified with the institution, television, with its structures, or with the beliefs and practices of the people in it. Discourse is not ideology either: it does not originate solely in group-based practices and it cannot be identified merely or exclusively as a representation of group or class interests. Discourse is more or something other than all of that, too.

Discourse, then, designates a distinctive, complex, and multi-faceted terrain of power relations. To talk about television's power is to talk about the existence of discourses, discursive regularities, that work to order and organize social life and, of equal importance, to resist and challenge this imposition of power. Beyond the most elemental notion, discursive analysis in cultural studies proceeds with the idea in mind that the complexity and multi-facetedness of television is best understood as different discourses working simultaneously in different domains of social life to produce their power effects.

This is evident in the work of Spigel and Tichi. The core of their analyses of television-as-discourse centers on the identification of normative regularities across depictions of social life found in advertisements, magazine and newspaper stories, trade reports, journal articles, and in popular culture more generally. They demonstrate clearly and convincingly that these regularities stand on their own as societal speech about television: the comfort and convenience associated with its use; its representations of social life as part of a product-oriented world; its functioning as a technology of freedom; the ways in which it serves as an instrument of cultural democracy; awareness of the emptiness of promotional claims made about it; recognition of the limits or outright falsity of its purported transformative effects; the fears and anxieties associated with its proliferation in social life, and so on. Apart from what people did in the institutions of the industry or in the actual use of the medium, television took on meaning in social life as the very production and circulation of these discourses. For Spigel and Tichi, this was the most important way that the power of television was constituted discursively.

Beyond magazines and advertisements and the like, Spigel and Tichi see these discursive regularities of television as constituents of even more elemental discourses that circulate in American culture. Among them: the scientific and technological ordering principles intrinsic to the workings of the economy, the academy, and other media, and that also find expression in one form or another in virtually all modes of social and cultural representation and practice; likewise, the patriarchal norms and assumptions that naturalize male power and privilege throughout the culture, especially when it comes to the control of science and the uses of technology; the social logics of the market that have become pervasive in the culture, providing the rationales and justifications for the ordering and organizing of an ever-widening range of social relations and practices. Normatively speaking, these different discourses – the televisual and the more elemental – overlap and resonate with one another. In the process of producing their power effects, the discursive regularities of television amplify, magnify, and extend the power effects of these more elemental discourses, too. They take on new meaning and influence in the discursive formation that is television. In sentences and phrases throughout their accounts, Spigel and Tichi move off the language of documentation and speak in terms that situate television amidst these more elemental discourses. The technology of television, the images of patriarchal power and personal freedom that comprise its discourses, the pleasures of consumption it generates and circulates, all of this becomes aligned almost automatically with the referencing of similar workings of power in other domains of social life. In this way, a more abstract discursive signification is attached to television, one that is more free-floating compared with the regularities of programming and the press, but which is also, at the same time, capable of conveying a deeper and even more profound sense of television's implied power effects. This patriarchal conception of television-as-discourse resembles very closely the analysis of television's social power put forth by the theorists I discussed earlier. In both perspectives, the workings of television – as functional, ideological, or discursive – derive their analytical significance from the fact that they are understood to be linked, inextricably so, with more broad-based forms of power, be they historical, social structural, institutional, or discursive.

Spigel and Tichi analyze television-as-discourse at still another level: that of everyday life. The normative regularities found in programming, the press, and popular culture, as well as the fusion of televisual discourses with more elemental ones that I just described, all of this is understood by them to operate closer in to the social world of day-to-day television use. There, discourses become inscribed in the meaningful experience of people, ordering and organizing the understandings they forge of themselves, others, and the world around them, and giving form as well to the play of imagination and the intensity of feelings that emerge from television viewing.

This mode of analysis is actually quite prevalent in cultural studies. In the accounts of Spigel and Tichi, but in countless others as well, phrases such as "television constitutes the viewer as a subject," or "television implicates the viewer in its discourses," or "television generates resistance to such and such transformations of the domestic sphere," etc., are commonplace and often represent the authors' most profound and totalizing statements regarding what they see as the sociological significance of television-as-discourse. These are provocative statements to make. They speak not only about the existence of certain discursive regularities – the patterning of advertising imagery, narrative themes in magazine stories, repetitions of programming content – but also about how these regularities have become a practical part of what people think and feel and do in the viewing culture itself. It is this jump from an analysis of television-as-discourse to television-as-culture that I find problematic. Why? Because descriptive analytical accounts of discourse and their workings are blurred into prescriptive judgments about the reach and meaning of discourse in people's lives without any attempt to reconstruct the sociality comprising the viewing culture in which such discourses are presumed to circulate and produce their power effects. Description, however, is not prescription. Establishing discursive facts of "television culture" is *not* the same as establishing the discursive facts of a "viewing culture." These are different domains that require different strategies and methods of empirical reconstruction.

In the case of Spigel and Tichi, their analysis of day-to-day television use remains abstract. Compared with the documentation and discussion of discursive regularities, the world of use is hardly represented at all, especially when it comes to accounts that reconstruct the practical knowledge and self-understandings of people as they emerge from the viewing culture. To speak of the patterning of advertisements and stories, what marketers and executives say about television, or even to document the criticisms of academics and public intellectuals regarding television, to identify the voices of viewers and homemakers as they appear in the press is one thing. It is, in fact, a necessary component of critical analysis. But to use these kinds of accounts to represent the social world of the viewing culture and assert that meaning–making activity is always, already constructed in discourse, to do this without relying on a systematic set of accounts that document the sociality of use and the routines, rituals, and contexts that constitute a culture of viewing, is quite another thing. At best, such a move obscures the meaning of using and watching television; at worst, it treats television viewers, and the social worlds that they make and inhabit, as beneath the threshold of analytical importance required for making truth claims about power, culture, television, and selfhood.

This blurring of boundaries between domains, this abstract treatment of the social world of use is not part of some deliberate attempt on the part of Spigel or Tichi or others to misrepresent the lives of people who watch television. Nor is it an effort to avoid an examination of viewing practices. Rather, it is, more simply, a conceptual problem. In this particular mode of cultural studies' analysis, ideas of sociality and social process, of mindfulness and meaning–making, or of culture and cultural formation are either not thought of at all, which means that what these ideas designate about everyday life remains invisible to analysts; or, what is more likely, such ideas are never treated with a sufficient degree of conceptual autonomy relative to discursive constructs, and, because of this, the distinctive aspects of everyday life that they illuminate are simply folded back into various notions of television-as-discourse. All too often in the study of media, cultural studies' analysts begin and end with ideas – sometimes very sophisticated ideas – about discursive power. They fail to see any need for grounding these ideas any more concretely by thinking through them and linking them with other ideas that identify specifically social aspects of day-to-day media use. Likewise, more often than not, analysts shy away from the difficulties involved in doing field research, which means that they fail to provide any documentation, drawn from the viewing culture, of what discourse actually does to people and, just as important, what people actually do with discourse. Critical analysis proceeds, but only by conflating the sociality of television use and the dynamics of a viewing culture with the abstract workings of television-as-discourse.

These days in cultural studies, conflating a sociality of use with television-as-discourse, of the viewing culture with television culture, is an accomplished fact. Discursive constructs now occupy a preeminent position in critical analyses of culture. "Discourse," "subject position," "constitution," "location," "resistance," "opposition," "transgression," the interchangeability of "television culture" and the "viewing culture" – terms such as these are commonplace in cultural studies. No longer do they invite interrogation or require explanation. In fact, we have become so accustomed to their use that when we see or hear such terms we nod our heads in recognition and move on to catch the import of what has been written or said. Analyst to analyst, we just *know* that to speak about television-as-discourse is to speak about the meaning of power, the place, the space, where discourse meets the social – all of this in an unproblematic way.

But when we turn our attention from theorizing and analyzing television-as-discourse to the empirical question, "how does discursive power actually work in the *viewing* culture?", the abstractness, the ambiguity, the uncertainty, the inadequacy, really, of using such terms to designate and explain things social becomes clear. Because of this, I think the distinction between television-as-discourse, a *television* culture, and the *viewing* culture, must be maintained. By doing so, critical attention is directed to the gaps and disjunctures that currently exist in explanations of the social uses of television that rely on these particular discursively based constructs.

Text

Those who study television and other media from a cultural studies' perspective may find my critique of television-as-discourse off the mark, a bit overdrawn, naïve, even. In their eyes, perhaps I have oversimplified what discourse is and how it works. Countering my critique, they might say that discursive constructs refer not only to things or thing-like structures but to processes as well, and that it is my thinking about discourse, rather than the workings of discourse itself, that is reified. Continuing, they might point out that this is precisely what prevents me from recognizing more fully the significance of discursive constructs in my own work. They might even pose the question: is not the sociality of use and the viewing culture you describe, as outside or beyond discourse, is not all of this able to be understood, discursively, as a *text*? – as a *social* text?

To a certain extent, this is true. Of all the discursively based constructs, "text" is well suited for explaining the social complexities of television use that I have been speaking about. Currently, it enjoys a near universal appeal in cultural studies, informing over the years the work of scholars such as

Hall (1989, 1975), Brundson (1991), Morley (1994, 1986, 1980), Silverstone (1995), Ang (1985), Radway (1984), Allen (1987), and Press (1992), among others. By conceptualizing television as a text, cultural studies analysts identify the specific and multiple forms that power takes in programming as well as a wide range of interpretive responses in which power is constituted as something meaningful by people.

The sophistication of this analytical approach to television (and other media as well) is perhaps best exemplified in the work of John Fiske (1987). His critical analyses of media imagery and audiences are important in cultural studies precisely because they build on developments in the field to draw out the sociological significance of discourse by discussing its workings as a text. For Fiske and others who utilize the construct, text enables multiple lines of analysis to proceed simultaneously. In terms of the object, television, analytical attention can be focused on different forms of hegemonic power that constitute the text. Fiske's account of television is quite comprehensive in this regard. In the first place, there is the realism of the medium; a realism that personalizes the social and historical circumstances of human action, and, in doing so, obscures the origins of those circumstances and the significance they carry in shaping everyday life. There is also genre, which establishes the parameters for story-telling as well as the conventions that enable it to proceed in culturally familiar ways. Then there are the conventions of story-telling themselves: patterns of plot, characterization, and narration, among other things, that lend predictability to the unfolding of action in socially acceptable ways. Fiske notes as well the esthetic dimension of programming, such as editing, lighting, camera work, set design, and so forth, things integral to the craft work of television production that become infused with story-telling or, alternatively, contribute to the distinct appeal of visual imagery itself. And also important for Fiske is what Raymond Williams (1974) referred to as the flow of programming, the continual movement of imagery that enables representations of social life to circulate on a seemingly unending basis.

For Fiske, and other cultural studies' analysts, too, it is in and through the combined workings of these formal features of programming that dominant discourses of all kinds – of gender, race, class, sexuality, ethnicity, and consumption – are produced. For cultural studies' analysts, the repetition of these discourses across different programs and channels is what constitutes the normative ordering of social life in programming; an ordering that is powerful precisely because it coincides with the canons and conventions of official culture and extends them across a new domain. Of course, in cultural studies, hegemonic power is, by definition, never lasting or complete. Oppositional or counter-hegemonic representations of social life can and do emerge in programming. When they do, they upset the balance of cultural power and challenge, if only momentarily, the normative order preferred by elites. All of this – realist portrayals of social life, multiple plots and story-lines, close-ups of characters, juxtapositions of scenes, resolutions of narrative action, the immediacy and tangibility of visual imagery, promises and pleasures of consumption, the organization of these elements of programming into dominant and oppositional discourses – all of it and more constitutes the object, television, as a text. In its objective form, the television text is generally understood to represent the social world in meaningfully coherent ways, even if, or when, the normative frameworks that provide such coherence are in tension or conflict with one another. Meaningful coherence is there. It simply needs to be found by people.

But this formation of the object, its situatedness in power, is only one aspect of a cultural studies' analysis of television-as-text. Equally if not more important for such analyses is a conception of the act of reading the text: the interpretive moments in which this complex and multi-layered object, television, is made meaningful by people. Fiske and others who study television understand people who watch television as always in the process of situating themselves, meaningfully, with respect to discourse, and, hence, with respect to power, too. As was the case with the object, television, the idea of meaningful coherence underlies cultural studies' conceptions of this situating process and the textual readings that result from it. The fact that people are located socially – by age, class, gender, race, ethnicity, sexuality, religious affiliations, and so on – is understood to lend coherence to their situatedness with television by aiding in the formation of identities which, in turn, establish the parameters for meaning–making activity with television. Since social locations are numerous and identities multiple in the cultural studies scheme of things, reading the text is understood to be a quite complicated activity. People can accept, reject, or negotiate in different ways the meaning that discourses will have for them. Compared to the structuring of the object, television, the act of reading or interpreting it is a more indeterminate process.

At certain times, people allow the coherence provided by dominant discourses to become their own meaningfully coherent ways of seeing things. Part of the power of attraction of these discourses lies in the resonance they establish with more mainstream social locations and identities, a resonance that leads people to situate themselves inside the social worlds that they represent. As they do, the meaning found in those social worlds becomes their own. For example, in Fiske's analysis of television-as-text, patriarchal discourse is constituted in the consistent and repetitive associations established across representations of masculinity, femininity, activities in the domestic and public sphere, the power dynamics between men and women, and other aspects of gender relations, too. Through the various formal features of programming I described, television provides people with coherent depictions of white male power and privilege in social life. Already ensconced in mainstream social locations and exhibiting the marks of conventional gender identities, people embrace such depictions and make the meaning found there their very own. In cultural studies, this kind of situatedness with television is understood as a dominant reading, or interpretation, of the text.

At other times, people refuse to allow the coherence provided by dominant discourses to become their own meaningfully coherent ways of seeing things. According to Fiske and other cultural studies' analysts, on these occasions, less conventional social locations and identity positions have come into play as the backdrop for interpretive activity. When this occurs, dominant discourses lose their power of attraction. Rather than situating themselves inside the social worlds they represent, people position themselves outside them, and use normative frameworks of their own, which are oftentimes critical of official culture, to read the text. They supply a meaningful coherence to things, but in ways not anticipated by the dominant scheme of things. Returning to the example of patriarchal discourse, Fiske and other cultural studies' analysts understand this kind of textual interpretation to occur more frequently among viewers who position themselves outside patriarchal and/or heteronormative frameworks of meaning–making and adopt feminist, gay, lesbian, or bisexual identities. In cultural studies, this kind of situatedness with television is understood as an oppositional or counter-hegemonic reading or interpretation of the text.

And at still other times, people are understood by cultural studies' analysts to situate themselves both inside and outside the social worlds represented in televisual discourses, accepting some of their normative ordering principles and rejecting others. Because people typically occupy more than one social location, they form and maintain different identities, which makes it possible for them to interpret any given text in different and sometimes contradictory ways. On the one hand, cultural studies tells us, certain meaningful aspects of dominant discourses can resonate with the more mainstream identities of people and become incorporated into their own meaningfully coherent ways of seeing things; ways, that is, that accord with the conventions of official culture. On the other hand, analysts understand that other aspects of those same discourses never achieve a meaningful hold on people, at least not in the terms presented, because less conventional identities come into play and generate a more distanced critical stance toward the depictions at hand. When this occurs, people may draw upon counter-hegemonic discourses to formulate an alternative reading of the text, or they may recognize what they see and hear as hegemonic and simply maintain their critical stance. Either way, cultural studies' analysts say, they know that the norms and practices of the worlds depicted are *not* their own, and it is this knowledge, not the power of discourse, that sustains their critical but still meaningfully coherent way of seeing things.

Returning once again to the example of patriarchal discourse, Fiske and others who study television as a text may find that depictions, say, of emotional intimacy between men and women, that, in different ways, accord men a subtle power over the interaction, are embraced as meaningfully coherent by people. Analysts explain this as a result of a mainstream gender identity coming into play, enabling the hegemonic power of such depictions to be felt, imagined, and understood as natural and normal. As scenes within a show change, depictions, too, may change, to those, say, of sexual objectification involving women. In the cultural studies view of things, when this occurs, viewers, especially women viewers, may alter their situation by drawing from a less conventional (from the standpoint of official culture) feminist identity to distance themselves from such depictions. In cultural studies, this kind of situatedness with television, where people are both inside and outside the frames of dominant discourse, is understood as a negotiated reading or interpretation of the text.

The world of negotiated readings is actually a quite murky domain of study. Despite the simplicity of the term "negotiated," the meaningful dynamics that comprise these readings are far more complicated than cultural studies makes them out to be. The ideas of differing social locations, multiple identities, and conflicted, contradictory, or ambivalent interpretations of the text can take cultural studies only so far in explaining adequately the complex sociality intrinsic to television use. I will elaborate on this point in my critique, which will follow directly. Prior to that, however, I want to reiterate the importance that the idea of reading, or interpretation, carries in the analysis of television-as-text. That is, it introduces the standpoint, the identity *standpoints*, really, of the viewer as an indispensable moment of the production of textual meaning. Almost by definition, the act of interpretation involves the recreation of one or another discursive formation of the object, television, as an ideational structure in the mind. This is true, even when interpretation occurs in group-based contexts. At the very least, two things follow from this. First, the workings of discursive power are now very clearly grounded in social–psychological processes of meaning–making. Subsequently, failure to specify these processes results in an understanding of power that is abstract with respect to the viewing culture. Second, by identifying this act of interpretation and elevating it to a position of importance in television research, cultural studies analysts, knowingly or not, placed the idea of coherence in meaning–making activity at the center of their analytical approach.

The analysis of television-as-text is important because it provides a conceptualization and, in some cases, an empirical documentation of social power that has yet to materialize in the work of either social theorists or social scientists. Power is now grounded as, among other things, an interpretive process. Through a language of dominant, oppositional, and negotiated readings, cultural studies analysts have identified a distinctive politics to viewing; and, along the way, they have also illuminated social aspects of viewing – significant in their own right – that figure importantly in the construction of this politics. What people find plausible in programming, the meaning made of characters, scenes, and stories, the role of social locations and identities in stabilizing interpretive activity, the strategies people employ to distance themselves form television's normalizing power, how television is or is not constitutive of more broad-based discursive regularities of leisure and consumption – these processes and others like them are now understood politically, thanks to cultural studies.

Yet, something is missing from the analysis of television-as-text; something social and cultural, and something "political" as well. As insightful as cultural studies' accounts of television viewing are, they, too, remain limited when it comes to conceptualizing and documenting the sociality that comprises a viewing culture. The textual metaphor is, after all, only one way of characterizing television use. Despite its near hegemonic status among analysts and its presumed prevalence in viewing, the activity of reading or interpreting texts is just one form of sociality emergent from day-to-day use. To see people who watch television as always locating themselves, normatively, with respect to power, to see them as using their identities to interpret the text and produce coherent meaning of one sort or another, is to circumscribe, unnecessarily, the sociological significance attributable to other forms of sociality that recur in everyday television use. By emphasizing the production of textual meaning, cultural studies has displaced the study, say, of mindfulness, self-formation, or of sociality itself to the margins of critical media analysis. Furthermore, to the extent that cultural studies' analysts focus their attention on resistant or oppositional interpretive strategies, they fail to consider the political implications that these other less explicitly textual forms of sociality can carry as they take shape in the viewing culture. Even with the use of textual constructs, constructs that emphasize the processual and productive aspects of television use, ideas about culture, and especially its sociality, continue to be conflated with notions of discourse. Consequently, the complexities of sociality and power, as well as the distinctive cultures emergent from television use, remain unexplored. From a vantage-point of everyday use, the textual analysis of television remains unnecessarily abstract. This is true of the way that both the object, television, and its use are understood.

First, reconsider how the object, television, is conceptualized in cultural studies, including what it is purported to "do" in the viewing culture. What happens to those symbolic features of television programming that do not conform to ideas about normativity implicit in the idea of "text"? For example, is visual imagery to be understood as merely textual? Must it be seen as conveying one or another kind of normative ordering principle in its representation of social life, as is the case with story-telling conventions? In contrast to most cultural studies accounts, Suzanne Langer (1957) argues that esthetic qualities of visual imagery operate more by their form, including colors and contrasts, and the feeling they provoke than by depicting what is normative in social life. If visual imagery can work as much by form and feeling as it does by supplying people with coherent and conventional meaning, then is the text as much about form and feeling and mood as it is about normativity? While most cultural studies' analysts readily acknowledge these other-than-normative workings of visual imagery, they have yet to treat them as a distinctive kind of symbolism by granting them the same kind of conceptual autonomy they bestow upon story-telling conventions or discourse or ideology.

Similarly, what do analysts make of what I call the "commodity forms" of symbolism: flow, segmentation, and repetition. For example, does the continual flow of programming always work in the service of normativity by lending coherence to social action, either on the screen or in the act of viewing? Is the sheer movement of imagery on the screen coincident with what cultural studies' analysts take to be the normative significance of imagery? Is flow, or movement, textual too? Is this true of the segmented programming structure as well? Are the breaks between shows, or those between commercials in shows, or the different worlds shown simultaneously across channels, objective features of programming to be understood as always contributing to normativity, too? Certainly, many cultural studies' analysts understand that television programming sometimes exhibits disjunctures in meaning, as do other discourses. But, other than referring to the fact that disjunctures exist in programming, cultural studies' analysts do not ordinarily think through the abstractness of such assertions to see these breaks with normativity as a distinctive symbolic feature of programming, as they do with normative regularities of various kinds.

And what of the repetitions of discourse found in programming? Is the presentation of stereotyped characters, conventional scenes, and the usual

stories over and over and over again *itself* something normative, and, therefore, something to be understood in textual terms? If this were the case, then
what, specifically, is the normative content that is referred to? Even if attention were directed to the norms repeated, this would say nothing, really,
about the fact of repetition itself, nor would it aid analysts in theorizing the
logic of commodity exchange that generates repetition as a symbolic feature
of programming in the first place. Alternatively, the repetition of story-
telling conventions, like the segmented programming structure, could be
understood as a non-normative feature of programming. If this were the
case, then cultural studies' analysts would have to provide a more elaborate
account of exactly what it is that distinguishes normative from non-normative workings of the text, something they have not yet done. Here, too, the
logic of commodity exchange awaits more adequate theorizing.

These commodity forms of symbolism do much to provoke an unsettling
of meaning in programming, and, consequently, in the viewing culture. As
products, or outcomes, of market relations, they do not conform to the
same communicative logic that underlies the workings of story-telling conventions – the usual focal point of textual analysis. Flow and segmentation,
and, to a lesser extent, repetition, generate a symbolic field consisting of
movements, combinations, juxtapositions, and disjunctures in programming that are indifferent, relatively speaking, to any particular normative
content that is or could be depicted. What Fiske and others typically refer
to as the text is actually contained within a broader symbolic field, one not
based, solely, in a communicative logic of normativity. As a result, the
reading or interpreting of texts need not be the sole focus for television use,
and, because of this, the sociality of use need not revolve only around the
production of coherent meaning. Importantly, all of this is made possible
by the symbolism of the object, television.

Cultural studies' analysts are certainly aware that the logic of commodity relations shapes programming in important ways. For example, in
Television Culture, Fiske discusses flow and standardization as representational forms of commercial interests, interests that place a premium on the
production and continuous circulation of "familiar" programming. Hence,
the stereotyped characters and the formulaic scenes and stories that comprise so much of what people see on television. His discussion is insightful
in this regard. It is true, too, that other scholars whose work falls within the
frame of cultural studies – among them, John Ellis (1982), Andrew
Goodwin (1992), Lawrence Grossberg (1988, 1987), Fred Jameson (1991,
1983), and Raymond Williams (1974) – have discussed in some detail the
commodification of meaning in television and in mass culture more generally. Like Fiske, they, too, have often demonstrated keen insight into the

logic of commodity relations, especially as it takes social and cultural form. It is my contention, however, that, when it comes to television, none of these analysts have identified commodification as different forms of symbolism that work simultaneously and in conjunction with one another as a part of programming; none of them have conceptualized how this symbolism of commodity forms works in conjunction with other forms of symbolism, notably the esthetics of imagery and story-telling conventions, to constitute a broader representational structure of programming; and, lastly, none have grounded a theory of these symbolic forms empirically, in the viewing culture, in order to document the various roles they play in shaping the sociality that emerges there.

To reiterate: cultural studies' analysts do often conceptualize specific differences in what is understood as textual. Distinctions are made between, say, the esthetics of programming, its flow, standardization, the workings of various story-telling conventions, or discourses of consumption. Such differences are recognized. The problem is, the insights opened up by this recognition are thought through a language of discursive constructs, a language that cannot name these differences as differences in symbolism or elaborate on their origins, the forms they take, or their workings without employing a textual metaphor. As a result, the insights opened up in the analysis of the object, television, are closed down prematurely.

As I said earlier, the analysis of television-as-text provides much insight regarding how power works at a social psychological level. By focusing attention on the reading or interpreting of texts, cultural studies' analysts are able to ascertain the degree to which discourse has a meaningful hold on people versus their ability to maintain a critical distance from its normalizing power. And yet, even with the emphasis placed on interpretive activity, the textual metaphor is still too abstract to understand adequately the social world of day-to-day use. As was the case with the object, television, important questions remain to be answered on the subject- or audience-side of things, too.

In fact, a series of questions can be posed to cultural studies' analysts who see television use in textual terms, all of which derive, really, from a prior, more important, and more broad-based question: what happens to our understanding of television use when the reading or interpreting of texts is no longer accorded its privileged status as the centerpiece of critical analysis? For example, in a more concrete sense, how do cultural studies' analysts make sense of more playful uses of imagery – those in which mindful and emotional involvement need not exhibit the consistency in positioning and coherence in meaning–making that prior social locations and identities are understood to provide for interpretive activity? Besides interpreting the text, people who watch television often just play with visual imagery. Colors, contrasts, and movements in imagery can simply be felt or become part of diffuse imaginative experiences that are mindful, without being *thought of* by people as communicating something or having a "meaning." Visual imagery can provoke layered, simultaneous, and non-linear forms of mindful and emotional involvement on the part of people, again unsettling meaning that is tied to communication. None of this is interpretive, yet it is something social, and, hence, something significant. Similarly, it is often the case that people watch television by becoming mindfully engaged with a scene, a characters' actions, parts of a story-line, or even the movements of images in a particular program, move on to repeat something of this process in another program, move back to the first program and repeat something of it again, and so on, continuing this kind of back-and-forth movement for the duration of their television use. In such situations, interpretations are made, but they hardly constitute all that is social in this kind of use. Furthermore, it is unlikely that ideas about prior social locations or identity, with the fixity and stability they imply, are adequate in understanding the more fluid and textually detached aspects of this sociality. Along this line of thinking, are textual constructs adequate for making sense of the movements people make between watching television and doing other things, something that occurs routinely in the viewing culture? Viewing like this proceeds with numerous starts and stops, the specific movements in and out of programming or other activities can be quite arbitrary, and people do not necessarily identify themselves, consistently, with a point of view and follow the normative regularities depicted in social action through to their conclusion. The same could be said about the brief, imaginative excursions that people take off on while they are focusing their attention, ostensibly at least, on the text of programming. During these excursions, they routinely move between the image-worlds of television and the real-life and fantasy worlds that make up their everyday lives. In doing so, they range across any number of different settings and contexts of social action, sometimes with no discernible order to their movements. They might focus attention on one or another aspect of story-telling conventions, interpret them, and make them meaningful, but these interpretive moments can hardly be said to constitute *all* of what engages them, mindfully speaking, during the time that they consider themselves to be watching television. Certainly, the normative regularities of programming play a role here, as do social locations and identity positions. But, if analysts focus only on the role that these factors play, can they understand adequately the complex and multi-leveled sociality that comprises this particular use of television?

And then there is the simple fact of inattention to programming, a common characteristic of any viewing culture. How do cultural studies' analysts incorporate the wide range of activities that occur regularly when people watch television – eating, reading, talking, ironing, writing letters, and so on – as something textual? Is the idea of text simply extended to these activities so that analysts can compare the patterning of normative regularities, power effects, or the potential for resistance across all of these activities, including television use? Certainly, analysts may proceed in this way. But can they do so and still preserve a sense of the differences in mindfulness that constitute this kind of television use?

Reading or interpreting the text, then, is only one form of sociality emergent from the viewing culture, and day-to-day television use does not necessarily revolve around the formulation of coherent meaning, at least as cultural studies' analysts see it. Television programming routinely presents people with more than coherent meaning to begin with, and, just as routinely, people draw upon capabilities for mindful action that do not require the stability and coherence of an identity position. Because of this, ideas of discourse, text, prior social locations, identities, interpretive strategies, and the act of interpretation itself can take analysts only so far when it comes to understanding the complex sociality that comprises television use in a viewing culture. Making sense of this sociality, of power, of how they emerge in all their varied forms to constitute cultures of television use, making sense, too, of how such cultures are situated amidst more broad-based and deeply rooted rituals of everyday life, making sense of all this requires much more than textual constructs. If cultural studies' analysts believe that the analysis of television-as-text can account for social and cultural complexities I have referred to, fine; let them demonstrate it conceptually and empirically. The point is, to account adequately for such complexities. But, if what I say is true, if textual constructs fall short in this regard, then it is incumbent upon cultural studies' analysts to think through the limitations of these constructs to arrive at a more adequate understanding of what day-to-day television use means to people as well as what it means for us, as analysts.

Discursive practice

Nowadays in cultural studies, the idea of practice, especially discursive practice, has become a preferred way to talk about power and resistance, both in media research and in analyses of culture more generally. By linking the construct *discourse* with another one, *practice*, cultural studies' analysts have at their disposal one of the most sophisticated means of critical interrogation. As perhaps the most concretely oriented of discursively based and, hence, power-based, constructs, "discursive practice" has come to stand for what might otherwise be referred to as social or cultural processes. What I have spoken about as the sociality of television use, including the other-than-interpretive aspects of viewing, can be understood in cultural studies as so many practical workings of discourse.

In talking about discursive practice, cultural studies' analysts are talking about power and everyday life in a way that is actually quite complicated. Discourse can certainly issue forth from various social institutions, but it is not reducible to the workings of those institutions, including their ideologies, nor, for that matter, is discourse reducible to the ideological perspectives of the people who work in them. Its power is more diffuse than that.

For cultural studies' analysts, the term "practice" is used to designate both a particular way of acting or doing things as well as the actual doing, the carrying out, of activities. In either or both cases, the construct practice draws attention to the unfolding of activities, to their temporality, whatever the content or focus of the activities themselves.

To speak about discursive practice, then, is to speak about a number of things simultaneously. From one vantage-point, it is to speak about discourse, like text, in a way that makes the temporality of its workings more explicit: its ordering and organizing, its normalizing functions – its power as well as the resistance it generates, is understood to unfold in even the most mundane thoughts and actions that comprise daily life. From another vantage-point, it is to speak about practice in a way that, unlike the reading or interpreting of texts, makes the decentering of meaning–making on the part of people more explicit. That is, the meaning that people make is never understood to be all, or only, of their own making; likewise, the very sense people have of themselves, others, and the social world does not originate with or in them as makers of meaning. Rather, their knowledge, their powers of reasoning, and the ways of knowing and understanding that they possess are understood as inseparable from discourse because discourse is always already there, itself giving shape and form not only to the act of meaning–making, but to the very capabilities for meaning–making that people think of as underlying such activities. So, in this particular cultural studies' scheme of things, discourse is understood to constitute meaning–making activity just as meaning–making activity is understood to always already be constituted in discourse. Discourse exists outside of people, but it dwells inside them, too.

In the construct of discursive practice, then, there is the idea of power; there is the idea of meaning; there is the idea of temporality; there is the idea of possibilities for movement and change, too. Because practice is constituted in discourse, because discourse is constitutive of power, and because power is understood dynamically, as a play of forces, the specific forms that practice takes cannot necessarily be fixed, analytically, or otherwise known in advance. As a result, there is also the idea of an agency to discursive practice.

With the use of this construct, agency moves to the forefront of critical analysis in cultural studies. Furthermore, it does so in ways not bounded by the use of a textual metaphor.

In some cultural studies' accounts, this agency of discursive practice is understood as synonymous with the workings of identity. As I said earlier, identities can be constructed in the terms of dominant discourses, and be understood to work to produce "power effects" of those discourses, enabling the practices of people to fall well within the mainstream of social life. But it is generally understood that identities can also be constructed outside of dominant discourses, in more marginalized social locations, enabling practice to resist, oppose, subvert, transgress, or overturn the normalizing power of dominant discourses. This way of thinking about discursive practice is in fact widespread in cultural studies and typifies the important work carried out by Morley (1986, 1980), Fiske (1987), Ang (1985), and Press (1992), among others.

More recently, there are cultural studies' analysts who have been influenced to a greater degree than others by what is called poststructuralism. They use the construct of discursive practice in a way that dispenses altogether with the idea of identity either because it is believed to bear the mark of essentialist thinking or its qualities of stability, coherence, and continuity are believed to be too fixed, too static, to deal adequately with the fluidity and instability that these analysts understand as characteristic of the postmodern condition of cultural practice. In these accounts, reference is made to the workings, not of identity or identities but subjectivity – a more abstract and indeterminate construct, but one which none the less designates an agency of discursive practice. For example, Lawrence Grossberg (1987) refers to a "nomadic subjectivity" which is understood to traverse fixed determinations of ideology, discourse, and identity, and, in doing so, to elude the marks of essentialism. Variations on this idea are indeed plentiful in recent critical scholarship. Gloria Anzaldua (1987), Renato Rosaldo (1989), Gilles Deleuze (1983; Deleuze and Parnet, 1987), and Judith Butler (1995, 1990), among others, offer sometimes very sophisticated accounts of the indeterminateness of discursive practice. These authors share a concern with finding the borders and breaks, the cracks, the disjunctures that emerge from the day-to-day workings of discourse. It is these places and spaces rather than identities that are understood to serve as sites for the resistance and transgression of power. From this viewpoint, then, subversive practices can be valorized without having to attribute their workings to the stability or centering presence of consciousness, mind, identity, or any other form of subjectivity believed to exist prior to or independent of discourse. Analysts who speak of agency in this way are attempting to think through dualisms of subjectivity and objectivity in order to open up lines of critical inquiry into dynamics of power, meaning–making, and social life that have been closed off in more traditional cultural studies' accounts. This "problematizing of subjectivity," as it is often called, is what results when the deployment of discursive constructs is taken to its limit.

The work of Judith Butler stands as a fitting example of this position. While she does not concern herself directly with television, viewing activity, or even media use more generally, Butler is arguably one of the most prominent and sophisticated of contemporary theorists of agency and power. Many cultural studies' analysts who interrogate television and other media are familiar with Butler's work and they often use it, as they do Foucault's work, as a framework for situating their own inquiries regarding power and cultural practice.

Because Butler understands social life to be thoroughly discursive, the idea that qualities or capabilities constituting identity are intrinsic to the individual smacks of essentialist thinking. Even when identity is thought of in constructivist terms, Butler understands the stability and coherence attributed to its workings to be just as fictional as the belief in a hidden essence; they are qualities invented by analysts to confirm the centeredness of subjectivity, something they assume is simply "there" to begin with. So, for example, in the case of feminism, the construct of identity enables some feminists to speak of a community of interests and concerns, a "We" that provides a stable and coherent grounding for different women's practices *as women*. It also serves, Butler says, as a reference point for strategies and tactics that characterize specifically feminist claims upon the public sphere. In this way, identity has defined "the political" for the vast majority of feminists. Butler does not dispute the necessity for or even the efficacy of identity-based politics. But the idea of identity is problematic in so far as it precludes activists and analysts alike from considering as "political" a range of critical cultural practices that do not originate in the presumed commonality of a feminist "We" or exhibit the stability or coherence typically associated with group-based political action.

In contrast to this (conventional) view of identity-based practices, Butler sees agency emerging from the very *repetitions* and *disjunctures* of discourse itself.

[T]o understand identity as a practice, and as a signifying practice, is to understand culturally intelligible subjects as the resulting effects of a rule-bound discourse that inserts itself in the pervasive and mundane signifying acts of linguistic life . . . As a process, signification harbors within itself what the epistemological discourse refers to as "agency" . . . [W]hen the subject is said to be constituted, that means simply that the subject is a consequence of certain rule-governed discourses that govern the intelligible invocation of identity. The subject is not determined by the rules through which it is generated because signification is not a founding act, but rather a regulated process of repetition. [A]ll signification takes place within the orbit of the compulsion to repeat; "agency," then, is to be located within the possibility of a variation of that repetition . . . [I]t is only within the practices of repetitive signifying that a subversion of identity becomes possible. (1990: 145)

Agency is not located in the person, but rather in the repetitions of discourse. For Butler, there is no "doer" behind the deed, and the analyst need not posit one, especially one with an identity, in order to talk about contestation, transgressions, or other ways in which power is destabilized. It is no longer necessary for analysts to set "identity" against discursive power in order to speak about agency. As such, the stability and coherence believed to comprise identity, the interiority understood as integral to it – these foundations are abandoned. In their place are aspects of practice – latitude, indeterminacy, maneuverability – that issue forth from the very logic of the signifying system itself.

Butler moves the talk about practice from the interior of persons to the surface of discourses – to their repetitions and disjunctures. Practice no longer corresponds to the inner qualities of persons, but instead becomes synonymous with its enactment. Practice is performance. It is performativity.

Butler's account of discursive practice is intriguing, provocative, and quite illuminating when it comes to the study of television use or of the activities that recur in an image-based culture more generally. In the case of television, the perspective Butler offers enables analysts to identify normative regularities that comprise the discourses of institutional decision-making and of programming itself. More importantly, it allows them to look beyond regularities of this kind and examine the repetitions and disjunctures of these discourses, highlighting, in ways that textual approaches ordinarily do not, the instability and lack of coherence that can characterize the workings of power. When it comes to the viewing culture, Butler's ideas enable analysts to account for the role identity plays in stabilizing and lending coherence to viewing practices; but again, and more importantly, perhaps, her ideas make it possible for analysts to see past such regularities and consistencies and document how repetitions and disjunctures of discourses and imagery enable more fluid and dissociated practices to emerge from television use. So, instead of looking to the stabilizing tendencies of discourses or identities to explain the coherence of viewing practices, analysts can turn to an examination of what lies beyond or between such tendencies to explain what lies beyond or between coherent practices, too. For cultural studies' analysts who adhere to more conventional notions of power and practice, Butler's ideas can be disconcerting, to say the least. But for analysts, like me, who find the conventional to be unduly limiting when it comes to talking about what people do with television, Butler's vision of agency and practice provides insight and clarification regarding the social world of watching television that is unavailable elsewhere.

Of all discursively based constructs, it is discursive practice that is most closely allied with ideas of agency, and, hence, with an understanding not only of the "productivity of power relations," but of the partial, fractured, and destabilized forms that this productivity can take as well. By itself, the construct "discourse" cannot reference the concrete in this way; it is too normative, too abstract for that. The construct "text," with its emphasis on reading or interpretive activity, fares better in this regard; but it, too, is overly normative and, therefore, unnecessarily abstract when it comes to capturing so many of the practical aspects of living in an image-based culture. With the construct of discursive practice, things are understood to be different. The particular limitations of the constructs "discourse" and "text" are left behind and attention focuses on what is believed to be a new-found concreteness of practice. Cultural studies' analysts who deploy the term can now reference an almost infinite range of "things social" – discursive conditions and contexts, actions and reactions, responses and refusals, interpretations, imaginative forms and feelings, and much more – as a productivity of power relations, a practical productivity of power relations, one that can matter sociologically and politically without taking on conventional markers of cultural order and coherence.

The construct of discursive practice, then, fills in significant conceptual gaps and solves important theoretical problems within cultural studies. This is not in dispute. What is in dispute, however, is the belief prevalent among cultural studies' analysts that the term discursive practice can adequately conceptualize and document, say, the complex sociality that comprises cultures of television use. First of all, the "master" terms in this kind of cultural studies' analysis – "practice," "agency," "subjectivity" – are themselves rather abstract designations for what it is that real people may actually do, say, think, or feel when they watch television or become involved with other objects or people in their world. The referencing of the concrete that occurs in the name of practice is peculiar, then, in so far as the person who practices is abstracted out of the analysis, an unfortunate casualty, it seems, of the critique and abandonment of essentialist or other, identity-based constructs. Curiously enough, so many of the practical and concrete aspects of television use – the decision-making involved in turning to television as opposed to other activities, the mindful and emotional form that people give to their viewing activity, the continuities that they create and sustain as part of their rituals of everyday use – simply do not count, analytically speaking, when viewed through the lens of discursive practice. Regardless of the terms used or their degree of sophistication, if conceptions of practice fail to include at least some idea of a person who practices, especially a person who's practice is not only or always and already constructed in discourse, then cultural studies' analysts who study television, for example, will never account adequately for the sociality of use or the distinctive viewing cultures that emerge amidst the very productivity of power that they purport to explain.

Grounding discourse as practice does not eliminate the need for explanation as to why distinctions between "the discursive" and "the social" or "the cultural" are no longer necessary; or, alternatively, if such distinctions are to be maintained, what it is, exactly, that distinguishes "the discursive" from these other analytical and practical domains. To the contrary: precisely because discourse is understood, explicitly, to work in very practical ways, there is a greater and more immediate need for explanations of this sort. But cultural studies' analysts do not ordinarily move in that direction. Instead, they continue to assume that social and cultural processes simply *are* discursive practices. Furthermore, they believe that ideas about the mindful and emotional capabilities of people who practice serving as sites, as locations – socially constructed, no doubt – for the generation of practices, that these ideas are no longer necessary to explain practice or theorize agency. The analytical and empirical gaps left by this disappearance of "the social" and "the cultural" are covered over by one or another of the myriad terms that have come to stand for it: resistant practices, oppositional practices, transgressive practices, interpretive practices, dominant practices; performance, the performance of practice, performativity, fluidity; nomadic practices or nomadic subjectivity; or, more simply, agency, subjectivity, or just practice. In every case, the dynamics of self-construction, sociality, and cultural formation, among other things, continue to be treated abstractly.

Sympathies aside, there are real ambiguities within cultural studies, not only regarding what it is that constitutes this agency of discursive practice, but, more importantly, regarding how practice, agency, and subjectivity will be understood in the postmodern condition. This is symptomatic of the fact that the study of television, mass media more generally, and culture itself is a contested terrain. Over the years, in scholarly accounts too numerous to mention, conceptual ambiguities and differences in terminology have become commonplace. They have appeared, for example, as the fault lines between Marxist, feminist, poststructuralist, and postcolonial perspectives within the broader framework of cultural studies; as conceptual differences that were translated into differences in emphasis which, in turn, defined what was problematic about television, film, or particular arenas of cultural study; as the gaps or absences that appear routinely in cultural studies accounts when analysts attempt to name the ostensibly less political aspects of television use or cultural practice more generally; and also as the divide between the critical approaches of cultural studies and those that characterize more conventional sociological or social–psychological schools of thought.

It is not my intent to overestimate the limitations of cultural studies' conceptions of practice, or to highlight differences or gaps in the ways that practice is designated, simply for the sake of identifying limitations or differences. I think that what is shared in cultural studies as well as what I share with cultural studies is, in the long run, more important than the marking of limitations and differences, especially when the scope and depth of cultural studies' analyses is compared to the much more limited vision of traditional social theory or positivist social science in exploring issues of power and practice. Nevertheless, significant conceptual differences remain between what I understand as cultural studies and my own developing perspective when it comes to interrogating and theorizing what people do with television. I think that these differences need to be talked about, questioned, and thought through in order to arrive at a more adequate empirical grounding for the critical sociological study of television use.

Conclusion

It is understood in cultural studies that power is always already there in social life, working to order, organize, and normalize thinking and acting while at the same time providing the very conditions for challenges to it. Everything and anything must be explained, it seems, in terms of power. This was evident in my discussion of the conceptual constructs that have figured most importantly in cultural studies' accounts: discourse, text, and discursive practice.

I do not wish to dispute this assertion because I really cannot say that power (or resistance) *is not* always already there in what people think and do. The more important issue, however, is whether or not we see power and resistance as *all* that is always already there in what people think and do; in my case, what they think and do with television. My own view is that, like power, sociality, too, is always already there in the practices that comprise daily life, and, if cultural studies' analysts were to acknowledge this, then their understanding of power would be that much more sophisticated and complicated. Many if not most cultural studies' analysts believe that, in talking about power, they have already accounted for this sociality and the ways it works in the viewing culture. Ideas of reading, practice, agency, or subjectivity serve adequately enough, they say, for capturing the social ground of power constructs. And yet, the question remains: Where *is* sociality in all this? How, exactly, is "the social" as opposed to "the discursive" understood to work as an integral part of what cultural studies' analysts wish to explain as the empirical world? What degree of autonomy, if any, are cultural studies' analysts willing to grant to something called sociality, the social, or the cultural, as opposed to discourse or power or resistance? It is not enough to say, as cultural studies' analysts sometimes do, "Well yes, of course what I am talking about here as power or resistant practices is social – that is understood, really"; or, alternatively, to simply *incorporate* what I or someone else might designate as sociality or as one or another of the cultural forms emergent from television use within languages of power and resistance *as they now stand*. This does not change anything, really.

What is needed in cultural studies at the present time is a more concerted effort in thinking through power as something social. Constructs of power must be taken to their limits, which means explaining how something called power comes up against or is confronted with something called sociality or culture.

PART II

Reconceptualizing television use

4

Sociality and the problem of the subject

In the course of my critique – of social theory, social science, and cultural studies – I pointed to limitations, absences, to significant gaps and ambiguities in the ways that the culture of television use, and media use more generally, was understood. I argued there that cultural studies is the most sophisticated of contemporary approaches to the study of television use. It allows analysts to conceptualize multiple dimensions of social power inscribed in the object, television, and to account for how this power actually works in the everyday lives of people, too. For these reasons alone, cultural studies constitutes the cutting edge of television research and media research more generally.

But, more than that, cultural studies has challenged conventional wisdom when it comes to thinking about things social and cultural. Time and again, cultural studies' analysts have refused to conceptualize subjectivity, social life, or cultural practice as distinct from power or from the workings of discourse more generally. Analytical accounts of television or other media that identify discursive regularities highlight the fact that cultures of viewing are always already implicated in power. Similarly, accounts that focus on textual reading strategies indicate very clearly that people are indeed agents in meaning–making processes, but in ways that legitimate, negotiate, and resist various power effects. And the very construct of discursive practice names the ways in which the workings of discourse and power have become coincident with the social experience of people, sometimes in very subtle ways. In short, cultural studies has introduced a new language of power into sociological analysis. As a result, time-honored assumptions that have guided inquiry into the social, assumptions about the coherence of the self, about the integrity of meaning–making, or about the autonomy of culture, these assumptions and more have been exposed *as* assumptions and, for that reason, are now deemed problematic. These days, in thinking about television use, or media use more generally, analysts must re-establish the social ground of empirical and theoretical inquiry rather than simply taking it for granted. This is what I, following many other critical analysts of media and culture, refer to as "the problem of the subject."

Certainly, much of what is social in television use is currently explainable by the use of power constructs. But the fact of the matter is, power constructs, as they are presently formulated in cultural studies, do not capture *adequately enough* the complexities of social life – including the practices of meaning–making and the inner mindful and imaginative dimensions of those practices – that emerge, with regularity, in the day-to-day world of the viewing culture. If they did, then there would really be no need to continue with attempts at distinguishing something specifically *social* from various constructs of power and resistance that have been deployed in cultural studies. In my mind, the question comes down to this: can we continue to say that there is an *interiority* to persons, an interiority that is integral to the thinking, feeling, and acting that emerges from their use of television, but that is not captured adequately, if at all, in the current repertoire of power constructs – discourse, text, textuality, practice, or, even, identity? Furthermore, can we continue to say that this interiority is integral to the formation and reproduction of a *self-made* ground, a *social* ground, of *cultural* practice, *even after* we acknowledge the persistence of both the thought and unthought workings of power? And, if we continue to rely upon ideas of interiority, as *a* social ground to practice, then what importance do we attribute to these ideas in conceptualizing and documenting television use and in theorizing about its sociological significance?

Despite (or perhaps because of) the multitude of references routinely made to practice and agency in cultural studies, especially its oppositional or transgressive forms, nowadays, there is *less* clarity or certainty regarding the role of the agent, the actor – *the person* – in what cultural studies' analysts refer to as "practice." To reassert the idea of something social, of something cultural, is, in the current climate of critical intellectual work, to challenge cultural studies' analysts to think through their use of ideas such as discourse, power, identity, practice, and so on, in order to reveal where and how they fail to capture certain social grounds of television use. A grounding for practice as something *self*-made has yet to be distinguished discursively.

In part, this uncertainty regarding the role of the actor in conceptions of practice stems from the fact that some cultural studies' analysts use the construct "identity" to explain the processes of thinking and action that constitute the everyday practices of people. Across these accounts, identity is sometimes used differently, with different reference points in mind, which adds yet additional grounds for uncertainty.

For those analysts who deploy the identity construct, the processes involved in reading, or interpreting, texts are certainly understood to reference something social in the workings of power. These particular cultural studies' analysts share with sociologists the idea that identity is constructed in relation to significant "others," and that it is a most important outcome of the socialization processes that typically occur in everyday life.

But, beyond that, what is distinctive about this particular body of cultural studies' work is that identities are understood to take shape as repositories for the material interests, the practical knowledge, and the ideologies, even, that are understood to attach to salient social locations: those of class, race, ethnicity, gender, and sexuality, among others. Interestingly enough, then, *even when* it is *processes* of reading or interpreting the text that are foremost in the analyst's mind, the construct of identity tends to be used in such a way that the *already* constructed aspects of the social – structural locations, present inequalities, objective interests, existing dispositions, current knowledges, recognizable ideologies – are emphasized.

So, when Fiske, Morley, Press, and others say that people who watch television accept, oppose, or negotiate power by deploying identities, they draw from the authoritativeness that ideas about the *already* constructed aspects of the social carry in cultural studies in order to explain the motive force of identities. Typically, it is by virtue of what *already exists, socially* speaking, that the reading, or interpreting, of texts is able to occur in the first place. In this scheme of things, there is usually no need, really, to explore further the dynamics of interpretation, the interior complexities of mind of the persons who do the interpreting, or the actual elaboration of meaning that occurs in time; these *emergent* aspects of the social are either taken-for-granted or subsumed within what is understood as *already* socially constructed. Identity does indeed designate a specifically social aspect of media use, and of cultural practice more generally. But the way it is used in so many cultural studies' accounts tends to reduce the significance that analysts attribute to *social processes* to that of a mechanism, a mechanism for illustrating, primarily, the resiliency of human agency in the face of power.

This is true, even when analysts refer specifically to *both* social *and* discursive aspects of agency in formulating their accounts, which is often the case in cultural studies these days. The intermingling of neo-Marxist, structuralist, and "poststructuralist" conceptions of subjectivity and practice leads some analysts to speak about identities both as situated in social life and as effects of discourse, or to talk of interpretive activity as at one moment grounded in social relations and at another moment constructed-in-discourse. Some accounts may privilege a terminology of the social while remaining mindful of the discursive underpinnings of the social, and others may favor a terminology of the discursive but continue to refer to material interests and conditions as shaping practice. In all cases, however, the outcome of the analysis is much the same: the motive force of identity, and of the processes of reading, or interpreting, that it makes possible, lies, in a curious kind of way, in what is understood to be *already constructed*.

In using the construct "identity," analysts are able to account for the myriad ways that people read, or interpret texts and, in doing so, they are able to theorize the role that *already-constructed* aspects of the social (and/or discursive) field play in this negotiation of power. Still, I am not convinced that this construct of identity, with its reliance on the "already constructed," is the most adequate means of explaining the social (and discursive) complexities of agency and practice, and, in particular, the role that the actor plays there.

In deploying identity constructs, analysts simply do not deal adequately enough with the full range of thinking, acting, and feeling that takes place, day-in and day-out, in the cultures that comprise media use. For, after all is said and done, after everything that can be explained by identity has been explained, I am still left wondering: what is it, exactly, that is *emergent* in television use, or in practice more generally? What role do *emergent* aspects of thinking and acting play in constituting the temporality, and the form, not only of interpretation, but of innumerable other practices as well? How are the emergent and already-constructed aspects of practice to be distinguished? And where, in these accounts, do we find a *person* capable of initiating thought and action?

What I find curiously absent in most of these particular cultural studies' accounts of media use, or of practice more generally, is any significant distinction between, say, identity and self, where the construct "self" designates, among other things, the *actuality of* as well as the *capability for* reflexive thinking. It is well documented in sociology that people act as a *self*: that is, they routinely make *internal* objects of what occurs in their social world as a part of what they do. This includes their making internal objects of their own and others' identities as well as of the actual objects, such as the television and its programming, that they typically encounter in their everyday lives. I think that cultural studies' analysts who use identity constructs actually assume that this kind of reflexive thinking is an integral part of the workings of identity, and that it "goes on" all the time, so to speak. The problem is, they do not ordinarily acknowledge it, explicitly, as a *distinct* aspect of agency and practice. If they did, then what can count, conceptually speaking, as practice, would certainly be enlarged, and this would complicate considerably (and in a good way) how they could speak about power. Perhaps more importantly, acknowledging the self as something distinct from identity would enable analysts to locate identity within a broader field of *sociality*, which, in turn, would allow them to accord the *emergent* and *already-constructed* aspects of the social "equal billing," as it were, within their formulations of agency and practice. In this, the role that the actor plays in constituting practice could be thought of differently.

In the future, cultural studies' analysts must continue to recognize that agency is comprised of much more than the meaningful coherence of identity-based interpretations of the text or of the already-constructed social locations that provide their motive force. In addition to identity constructs, constructs of self, of self-reflexivity, of even more imaginative and playful processes of mind can be used to designate important and specifically social elements of practice that must be accounted for in the study of power. Precisely because these constructs name elements of practice that are understood to emerge *between* texts and identities, and are not bound (or enabled) by normative regularities, as texts and identities are believed to be, they can illuminate the postmodern condition of television use that much more adequately.

The lack of certainty regarding the role that the actor plays in cultural studies' conceptions of practice is also due to the fact that some analysts have aligned themselves much more closely with what is called poststructuralism. As a result, their references to the subjective dimensions of agency and practice are, at the very outset of inquiry, already more thoroughly absorbed within discursively based constructs than those of analysts whose work relies on conceptions of identity. In these kinds of accounts, analysts have dispensed altogether, it seems, with ideas of interiority or of a specifically *social* dimension of practice as something distinct, or separable, from the workings of discourse. They have pretty much abandoned, too, the strategy of talking in terms of a *person* who is understood to be capable of initiating thought and action, or who can be seen as responsible for the agency of their own practice. Nevertheless, analysts can continue to talk about television use, the use of other media, or practices more generally; only now, what they say is immediately couched in discursive terms. It is discourses and texts themselves that are understood to generate agency, to give form to practices, and to produce power effects. In the more "poststructural" of cultural studies' accounts, then, it is *discourse* that is without a doubt *always-already there*, serving as a kind of non-essentialist starting-point for speaking about people, about what they think, how they think, as well as what they do in social life.

Given the seminal work of Foucault, Derrida, and Deleuze in formulating what has come to be called a "poststructural" perspective on things, it is arguably the theorizing of Judith Butler that has been most influential in shaping the language of contemporary, poststructuralist-inspired accounts of practice in the field of cultural studies. Certainly, many theorists and cultural studies' analysts have taken up the terms of discourse and power in their work; but it is Butler, I believe, who has done so with deeper insight, broader vision, and more originality, frankly, than the rest. Consequently, her formulations of "performance," "performativity," "signifying practices," and so on have provided the preferred language for so many cultural studies' analysts who wish to designate agency as something *emergent from discourse*, and *not* from some essential qualities, or capabilities of persons. For Butler and the analysts who have followed her lead, it is the *repetitions* and *disjunctures* of discourse that are believed to generate agency, not an identity or a self that people possess. Identity, self, an interiority of persons, capabilities for thinking and action that are simply "given" – these constructs are, almost by definition, essentialist in origin, and, for that reason alone, they can no longer carry the theoretical significance that they once did. This is not to say, however, that Butler wishes to preclude analysts from talking about agency in terms other than performance, performativity, signifying practices, and so on; but it is to say that, if analysts wish to formulate any alternative conceptions of agency, then they must do so in a way that leaves them free of what she believes to be the traces of essentialist thinking.

While recognizing the ground-breaking quality of her work and the challenge it poses for sociologists who study culture, I am struck, really, by the similarity of language in her account of discursive practice and in more traditional symbolic interactionist and ethnomethodological accounts of the *social* construction of reality. For example, in *The Presentation of Self in Everyday Life*, Erving Goffman (1959) relies, like Butler (1995, 1990), on the construct of performance to capture the myriad ways that people, no doubt located socially by discourses of role definition and normative appropriateness, exhibit agency in the ways they present themselves to others in specific social situations. While Goffman is not really concerned with issues of power in the same way that Butler is, nor with deconstructing notions of identity or identity politics as she is, he *is* concerned with the indeterminacy of social interaction that is emergent from the very gaps and spaces of the normative order. Agency, even as it occurs in the repetitions of normative regularities, is of concern to both Butler and Goffman. But Goffman, unlike Butler, uses a language of interiority in elaborating his notion of performance. He speaks of a frontstage and a backstage in the presentation of *self*, with these terms, drawn as they are from a dramaturgical model, indicative of intentions, motives, and interests that people exhibit in presenting themselves in public. In Goffman's eyes, there is a mindfulness to performance, an internal process of thinking, of reflexive engagement taking place in people's minds, and much of this involves a working *with* as well as a working *over* of the very norms and expectations for performance which people believe to be operative in the interaction they are situated in. This mindfulness that Goffman speaks of is not some sort of unchanging essence – something rooted in the individual as a given of his or her individuality. Rather, Goffman is well aware of the changing and changeable aspects of performance and the multiple nature of people's presentations of self as they occur from one occasion to the next. Far from rooting this mindfulness in an unchanging essence, Goffman is explicitly concerned with showing the flexibility, the malleability, of self in the face of social structures and their normative requirements for appropriate interaction. In fact, it is Goffman's very reluctance to ground this notion of the presentation of self in any fixed or stable relationship to norms, roles, or social structure, that prompts others who work in the microsociological tradition of interactionism to question whether or not Goffman has gone too far in his attempt to articulate how the self is socially constructed. This is a concern that John Hewitt (1989), among others, raises in *Dilemmas of the American Self*.

I mention Goffman's work because I wonder, can the idea of performance as Butler and other poststructuralist or cultural studies' analysts use it be so easily dissociated from the interiority that Goffman speaks of? While performance certainly escapes the normalizing tendencies of discourse, and while it also escapes the stabilizing qualities of identity, I am not so sure that it must or that it should escape the interior processes of mind and emotion that Goffman speaks of. In fact, it would be problematic to say that performance, especially if it is to signify what it is that Butler wishes it to signify, could be so thoroughly divorced from the interior world of social actors. For Butler and others who see practice in thoroughly discursive terms, it is the very belief in the viability of a prediscursive I that constitutes the problem of subjectivity. In adopting Butler's framework or one similar to it for the study of television, it would indeed be difficult to speak about a person, an agent, an actor, who is capable of initiating thought and action, and, hence, who is capable of initiating practice, independent of discourse. But I am not so sure that Butler's critique of essentialism fits in Goffman's case. Because of that, I wonder, can such a notion of mindfulness be synthesized with ideas about discourse, power, and practice in order to advance beyond the limitations of these constructs in studying what takes place in the viewing culture?

Agency – whether it is called identity, nomadic subjectivity, signifying practices, performance, or performativity – is *both* discursively and socially constituted. Discourse certainly creates agency, the very possibilities for agency, even, but it does not create *all* of them. What is interesting about Butler's account, for example, is that many of her insights regarding signifying practice are typically couched in hypothetical terms: she often says things like, "If discourses are understood to do such and such, then practice may be understood to take the following forms, or to do the following things," etc. This is a language of possibility. It means that it *is* possible to formulate constructs of practice that are not entirely discursive.

Foucault (1985, 1986) also acknowledges that the possibilities for practice may extend beyond the discursive. In *The Use of Pleasure* and *The Care of the Self*, he accounts for "self-constitution" in Ancient Greece and in the Greco-Roman period in terms of a variety of forms of knowledge and practical understandings that free men cultivated in daily life. In *The Use of Pleasure*, Foucault says that practices of self-constitution were inseparable from the broader discursive regularities of Greek society and culture. This crafting of the self was a very personal and private domain of relations that one had with oneself, and, at the same time, it was constitutive of some of the most public moral and ethical actions on the part of these people. To speak about discourses of self-constitution was to speak about the inseparability of the public and private domains, because at this time, Foucault says, there were already-existent and agreed upon normative ordering principles at work in the process of self-constitution.

In *The Care of the Self*, Foucault's argument shifts ground due in part to his registering of changes between the classical period of Greek history and the later Greco-Roman period. For numerous reasons, the interpenetration of the public and the private in practices of self-constitution became problematic in Greco-Roman culture, which meant that, for Foucault, the individual was less in the grip of community standards regarding the moral and ethical bases of action. The relation of oneself to oneself, as Foucault refers to it, is no longer so thoroughly infused with kinds of normative ordering principles that constituted the interrelation of the public and the private domains in the classical period. He argues that, in the Greco-Roman period, practices of self-constitution became increasingly more autonomous from overarching, normative ordering principles that served, in previous times, to integrate individuals within public life.

In following his account of these transformations in self-constitution, it is sometimes difficult to determine whether Foucault is referring only to discursive shifts or if he is also attempting to identify or otherwise bring to the surface some sort of distinction between a language of discourse and a language of the social. Sometimes, he speaks in a language of self-constitution that is more thoroughly discursive, one in which changes in the practices of self-constitution at the individual level seem to register and record – indeed to locate – more significant discursive shifts in the broader society and culture. At these times, the languages of self-constitution seem to shift as discourses do, indicating that the private and personal patterns of self-constitution are being constructed in discourse, although differently, from one historical period to another. At other times, he uses terms that indicate a kind of interiority at work – people judge, monitor, and evaluate – in referring to what individuals do when they constitute themselves as subjects in discourse. And at still other times, particularly in *The Care of the Self*, Foucault's language of self-constitution embraces many of these same ideas about interiority but includes much more explicit references to the reflexive dimensions of people's actions, references that are, generally speaking, relatively absent in his work as a whole. At these times, he seems to be saying not only that individuals can make reflexive judgments regarding the representations and images that they routinely encounter and deal with, but that they should do so because this kind of reflexivity is crucial to people knowing who they are, how they are located, and how them locate themselves, in everyday life.

A most important part of Foucault's work consists of his registering of significant differences, changes, and transformations in the workings of discursive regularities. But, in his later work, especially, Foucault is also making a distinction between the workings of discourse and the workings of the social – with the social understood as, among other things, the mindful ways that individuals become engaged in their own lives on an ongoing basis. Foucault is talking about a distinctive *social* time or *social* space in which practices *emerge*. Discourse is certainly present, constituting the normative ordering principles for the various forms of self-understanding that he speaks about. But, unlike Butler, Foucault's language is not simply of discourse or the signifying system in the abstract (or in the concrete, for that matter). His is *also* a language of mind and symbolization, a language that speaks of capabilities for making judgments and thinking reflexively – about discourse, and about things social as well. I understand him to be saying that capabilities for mindful action – intellect, memory, judgment, reflexivity, and so on – exist right there in the midst of discursive regularities, and they are or can be equally constitutive aspects of the everyday practices of people. This is really a language of the *self*, one that Foucault uses in order to designate a particular aspect of practice, one in which people think and act in *social* terms, which means, I think, that they think and act in ways that cannot simply be subsumed under the markers of discursive power and resistance alone.

Butler's abstract and hypothetical terminology and Foucault's shifting language both highlight a more general question that recurs in cultural studies' accounts of practice: in talking about practice, how do analysts distinguish between what is discursive and what eludes or does not fit the discursive designation? Can we say that there is something in practice that is *not* discursive? – and not *essentialist*, either? I think we can. I also think that cultural studies' analysts have become so attached to their repertoire of discursive constructs that they have tended to lose sight of people as *social* individuals, including the fact that, as social individuals, people do indeed *develop* capabilities for initiating thought and action over the course of their lives. Consequently, analysts often fail to recognize that there is indeed something *social* that is *there*, *in* the reading, or interpreting of texts, or *in* the performance or performativity of practice, something that must be accounted for if they are to speak about power in empirically and theoretically convincing ways.

Make no mistake about it: where "the discursive" meets "the social" is, conceptually speaking, a very murky area indeed. This is due in large part to the fact that analysts can and do use discursively based and more socially based constructs in referring to an inchoate mixture of things public and private, things conscious and unconscious, and things thought, felt, and acted upon. This is particularly true when it comes to the study of television use, where discursive flows and interruptions in television programming are matched, if not exceeded, by continuous and sometimes very subtle movements of mind and emotion on the part of the people who watch.

My point is that this conceptual ambiguity and uncertainty regarding what is discursive versus what is social actually *opens up* the study of television use, the use of other media, or of practice more generally. Critical analysts are actually in an advantageous position, because now they can reconsider the use of a variety of more conventional and, in some cases, underutilized constructs that have been deployed outside of cultural studies over the years in order to address more adequately than they presently do the complex processes that constitute agency and give form to practice.

Looking across disciplinary boundaries, I find several accounts in which analysts formulate constructs of subjectivity in which elements of an *emergent sociality* figure importantly, but in ways that avoid the kinds of essentialisms that Butler, for example, has spoken about, while at the same time enabling ideas about discourse and power to remain significant, if analysts so choose. For example, Margaret Mahler (1975), in *The Psychological*

Birth of the Human Infant, draws from her reading of clinical literature as well as her own observations of infant and early childhood behavior, and argues that a constancy of care in the early caretaking relation is what enables the infant to develop patterns of constancy in representing both his or her own body and the objects that constitute his or her immediate environment. The inner world of representing emerges along with these patterns of constancy and serves as the earliest indicator of a developing sense of self. The social relations of caretaking continue to exist on their own, but a capability for representing has become a distinct aspect of what is social in the infant's life. Mahler certainly recognizes that these constancies – of care, of representing, of self – are not the only defining feature of infancy and early childhood relations. Yet, amidst the concerns in cultural studies with the dangers of essentializing agency and subjectivity, it is crucial to note that, for Mahler, these constancies are not simply given, there in advance, but rather they are understood as *emergent*, as socially constructed *developments* of early childhood experience.

In a similar fashion, Donald Winnicott (1971, 1965), another psychologist of early childhood development, demonstrates through his reconstruction of clinical practice, that, early on in the life of the infant, a constancy of care helps to bring about a sense of the body as a limiting membrane that then signifies the distinctiveness of this emergent person from the surrounding environment. Winnicott calls this "ego-boundedness" (1965). If the caretaker can continue to respond to the infant in ways that anticipate his or her desires and actions, then we witness what he refers to as the "use of the intellect": the first practical basis for the infant being able to develop and sustain a sense of bodily integrity (1965). Long before there is something called identity, there is, Winnicott says, a repeated use of the intellect to symbolize the absence of the living caretaker as a presence in the baby's mind. In Winnicott's account, this use of the intellect is linked with a number of other constructs: notably, a capability for symbolization, an activity that he designates as play, a further linking of both of these to something called the true self, and all of this to what he designates as "creative living" and "the life of the child" (1971). It is in play that the child's sense of self and a creative engagement with cultural life take shape. In Winnicott's account, as in Mahler's, visible actions and performances are linked consistently with internal processes of mind and emotion. And, perhaps most importantly, Winnicott, like Mahler, emphasizes the social construction of these capabilities for symbolization and play, *not* their essentialist origins in physiology or biology.

In both of these accounts, the practices of early childhood are understood to emerge as, or from, repetitions – the gestures and social relations of caretaking and, later, the speech that accompanies them. But, unlike what we find in cultural studies' accounts of practice, the repetitions of visible practices that Mahler and Winnicott write about are inextricably linked with the formation of an interiority, of an inner mindfulness, to people's experience, whether that experience is understood as something discursively situated, socially situated, or both.

In *Mind, Self, and Society* and *The Philosophy of the Present*, George Herbert Mead (1934, 1932) focuses attention on society, the self, and the temporal structure of self-reflection in elaborating his construct of *sociality*. He repeatedly points out that it is only because of the organization of social life that the self, and in particular, self-reflexivity, is possible. In *The Philosophy of the Present,* Mead says:

A society is a systematic order of individuals in which each has a more or less differentiated activity . . . [S]ociety can get into the separate individuals only in so far as he can take the parts of the others while he is taking his own part. It is due to the structural organization of society that the individual, in successively taking the roles of others in some organized activity, finds himself selecting what is common in their interrelated acts, and so assumes what I have called the role of the generalized other. (1932: 82)

For Mead, the self is composed of the "I," which he sees as its performative dimension, and the "Me," which he understands as the person's recognition of their construction from the outside – in terms of social roles, broader kinds of social placement in communities of various sorts, as well as the more diffuse ways in which people are typified by others in their everyday, social encounters. As Mead sees it, people routinely occupy at least these two different social locations – the "I" and the "Me" – simultaneously. It is this simultaneity of differing social locations that he refers to as the *sociality* of the self. Sociality, he says, is the capacity to be several things at once. The self as something that *emerges from* social life has the unique property of *not* remaining identical with itself; instead, he says, its emergence is predicated on a simultaneity of differences.

Sociality, then, designates both an awareness, an inner reflexivity, regarding one's constitution *by* objective social realities, and social action itself. In Mead's framework, practice would always include not only the performance, the action itself, but also this *internal* fluidity, flexibility, and reflexivity which enables people to *make* an object of their own and others' practice. The individual is mindful of others, of oneself, of how others see him or her, and aware also of the normative constraints imposed by social relations. He or she can make judgments, monitor thoughts, feelings, and behavior, and all of this occurs *in conjunction with* the outside world of discourse, not as something separate from or prior to it. Furthermore, Mead's construct of sociality has much in common with Winnicott's ideas about play and symbolization. In both cases the practices being referred to are understood as something *socially* constructed, the taking on of an identity is distinguished from the workings of self, and the act of symbolizing is understood as neither subjective nor objective, but something occurring *between* the two.

In all of these accounts, if there is anything pre-discursive, it is not so much a fully formed "I" that somehow stands apart from social situations, but rather the physiological and biological aspects of persons that are there at the start in the individual organism. Physiological and biological factors are very much a part of the naturalism that constitutes human beings, not unlike the life forces that Nietzsche (1968), Deleuze (1983), and others speak about, or the elusive yet enduring sense of desire or desiring that figures so prominently in Lacan's (1977, 1968) conception of subjectivity. Furthermore, to speak of this sociality in the ways that I have is to tell only part of the story of practice. Psychoanalysts would be the first to point out that this kind of sociality is always decentered by the splits, fractures, and disjunctures that characterize the relationship between conscious and unconscious life. A fuller discussion of these aspects of subjectivity and practice is not possible here. At this point, I simply wish to acknowledge their existence and the potential influence that they carry in qualifying the workings of this sociality as I have described it.

Conclusion

Sociality is emergent in practice and its distinctive features – symbolizing, imagination, reflective thought, an inner mindfulness – are not captured adequately in the language of discursive constructs, even those that purport to focus on the agency of reading, or interpreting texts, or of the performativity of practice. Oddly enough though, conceptions of this sociality are merely implicit if not altogether absent in cultural studies' accounts of subjectivity, agency, and practice. Analysts prefer, it seems, to subsume this interiority of persons, including the inextricable linkages it exhibits to whatever "outside" exists for people, under the markers of discourse and power. Yet, without the sort of conceptual specificity that a construct of sociality supplies for critical analysts, the language of power and resistance will remain unnecessarily vague, even when resistance is understood to *emerge from* power.

Returning to Butler's cautionary words about the use of a prediscursive "I," analysts can, if they choose to, use any number of constructs that refer to the social, to sociality, without risking a return to essentialist thinking. Within the very framework supplied by discursive constructs, ideas of sociality – interiority, mindfulness, reflexivity, self, and so on – can be used to designate an *emergent* aspect of practice that continues to afford people at least some degree of maneuverability, if not autonomy, in the face of power. Sociality emerges in a discursive environment, but is not reducible to that environment.

5

Components of a viewing culture

The social experience of people who watch television has not been conceptualized or documented adequately by social theorists, social scientists, or, more recently, by cultural studies analysts. In contrast to earlier sociological views, cultural studies does, in fact, accord television watching a legitimate place in its account of power, but it fails to adequately theorize the context of television watching as a new and distinctive cultural form. While cultural studies tends to examine texts as exemplars of ideology or discursive power, understanding them in terms of the social and historical conditions under which they are produced, I argue that, unless critical analysts generate categories of reception, of use, that can document the social function of television, the emphasis on textual reading among audience members remains incomplete and perhaps misses what is arguably most important about television use.

I use the construct of *sociality* to incorporate and move beyond ideas about discourse and textuality, and to systematically explore how television is used in ways that allow me to focus on more than just the dynamics of power and resistance, at least as they have typically been formulated in cultural studies' accounts. My strategy is to work through ideas about power by grounding them empirically in reconstructions of the practical uses that people make of television on a day-to-day basis.

The social world of television use is no doubt a complicated one. Its complexities – the differences in mindfulness that emerge there, the variety of ways that people construct social relations with others, as well as the ways that television fits with everything else that people do in their everyday lives – are certainly understandable as power effects, but not *only* as power effects. The language that we use to analyze and account for the complexities of this world must be able to say, with clarity and precision, what *else,* besides power and resistance, they are about.

Generally speaking, conceptualizing television use involves reconstruct-ing the practical ways that people who watch television situate themselves with the medium on a day-in, day-out basis. Contrary to appearances, tele-vision use is a multifaceted activity, one that is much more complicated than meets the eye. Assessing its meaning for people and the significance it carries in their lives involves nothing short of the analytical reconstruction of it as a distinctive kind of culture. I have referred to this elsewhere as "the viewing culture" (1994).

The sociality of the viewing culture can best be understood by proceed-ing in the following way. First, analysts must recognize that television is a powerful medium, that its power works simultaneously through multiple symbolic forms, and that the objective structuring of those forms can be documented empirically. There is a long line of work, both inside and outside of cultural studies, that understands power as a constituent feature of television, and this work must be incorporated into any analysis of the viewing culture. But, because people typically approach television practi-cally rather than analytically, the medium's power is not their primary concern, even though they recognize at times the influence that it has in their lives. For this reason, it is best that the reconstruction of their televi-sion use *not* begin by focusing directly on issues of power (or resistance). The second strategy follows from this idea. Analysts of the viewing culture must be cognizant of television's power, but they must then set aside power constructs in order to examine how particular kinds of viewers, whose lives are situated in particular ways, concretely construct their own meaningful relations with television. Once this reconstruction of the various kinds of routine practices that are involved in television use is underway, power con-structs can then be brought back into the picture by looking at how televi-sion and its symbolism works to construct the sociality of those viewing practices.

The turn to television

Typically, individuals must come to television from some other aspect of their lives, and, similarly, they must turn off the set and fit television back into their lives. This progression, from turning to television, to interacting with it, to leaving it and fitting it back in one's life is the basic cultural pattern in which viewers make their experience with television meaningful. When a person thinks about watching television, it is usually in a specific situation and often has something to do with what that person is thinking and feeling. Different things may go through different people's minds and they may feel a variety of things as they go about the business of situating themselves with television or in choosing to do other things. For various reasons, some of these situations, along with the thoughts and feelings that people have in them, recur regularly. Over time, particular situations, with their accompanying thoughts and feelings, serve as typical points of departure for watching television or engaging in any number of other activities. Turning to television, like turning to other activities, becomes a ritual part of people's everyday life. Because it takes shape amidst a multitude of factors that constitute the contingencies of daily living, the turn to television carries meaning on its own terms, quite apart from viewing itself. Furthermore, because turning to television becomes a habit, a ritual, it in turn shapes the contours of the broader context of people's lives. And, finally, it is this broader context of a person's life, including the place that television use has within it, that shapes in important ways the meaning of viewing itself.

To understand the meaning that turning to television has for people, analysts must consider more concretely just what is involved, socially speaking, in the situational contexts that give rise to television use. Since people do not ordinarily organize their lives exclusively around television; analysts must proceed by first stepping back from any inquiry into the turn to television *per se*, and instead gain some understanding of what it is that people do with the rest of their lives. Do they work? If so, what shift do they work? Does the shift vary or stay the same over time? If they are not compelled to do shift work, do they keep regular hours none the less? If so, what are they? What do they actually do at work? What are the pros and cons of the job? If people do not work for employers outside the home, how is it that they support themselves? – or, if this is not an issue for them, then analysts must inquire as to how they typically structure their day. Are they self-employed? Is their day structured around child care and household responsibilities? Do they attend school regularly? My research focused on working people, and as you might expect, work outside the home was certainly central to the way that they organized their everyday lives. But I also found that household work, child-care responsibilities, and the comings and goings of school-age children were independent factors that worked in conjunction with employment schedules to constitute people's everyday routines within the home. The interrelationship of work, family, and household routines is what structures the availability of free time for people, and in this way it constitutes an important, initial component of the structural contexts that can serve as a point of departure for their turn to television.

Once this more basic structuring of situational contexts is understood, the meaningful complexity of the contexts themselves must be accounted for. Even at this broad level of analysis, analysts do not want to focus exclusively on the turn to television because, in any given situation, people can just as easily turn to a variety of other activities, including hobbies, crafts, the use of other media, as well as visits with neighbors, family, or friends in order to relax and enjoy themselves. Once something of people's work, family, and household routines are known, analysts can then inquire as to which situations typically provide people with the opportunity to watch television or do any number of other things, too. What do people do before work, after work, before school, after school, before dinner, after dinner, late at night, on Saturday or Sunday afternoons? These are the more objective determinants of the situations that need to be accounted for. For any typical situation, determining the significance that turning to television holds for people is best accomplished by first accounting for where viewing fits amidst these other activities. In any given situation, it matters if people turn exclusively to television, if it is one activity chosen among other non-media activities on a regular basis, or, if it is turned to relatively infrequently.

As I said earlier, the power of television to shape people's experience must become a part of this analysis. Television is first and foremost an object of consumption. It is purchased in the market-place and, depending on the model, the make, and its specific features, the television set by itself can serve as a marker of status and consumer well-being. In comparison to friendships, family relations, hobbies, crafts, and even household chores and responsibilities, the turn to television, like the turn to radio, exposes people to discourses of consumption and orients them to the market-place, whether or not they are persuaded to buy products or identify with the imagery being sold. The simple questions of how often and for how long television is turned to, are important indicators of the ways in which discourses of consumption are extended into the private and personal space of the home. By situating the turn to television amidst the routine choices that people make in carrying out their daily activities, the analyst is able to document how television works differently in different people's lives to extend these discourses of consumption into their meaningful experience.

Beyond this recognition that television use exists as one among many activities, analysts face the far more difficult task of documenting the mindful and emotional qualities exhibited by viewers at different stages of their turn both to television and to other activities; and, beyond that, they must also be able to assess where it is that people end up, mindfully speaking, after they have become involved in watching television or doing other things. Are people typically feeling tired, bored, anxious, alert, relaxed, or some other way when they turn to television in any given situation? Do they typically feel the same, similar, or different when they turn to any of a variety of other activities in these same situations? Furthermore, we need to know more about how people decide to watch television and do other things. How mindful are they in turning to television or to other activities at different times? Television viewers that I have interviewed often display or express knowledge of having engaged in decision-making processes that range from sheer habit to highly reflective ones as they orient themselves to television and to other activities. Is the turn to television or to other activities done out of habit, for escapist pleasure, with an eye toward a playful kind of interactive engagement, or perhaps to engage oneself more seriously in whatever it is that one chooses to do? By documenting the mindfulness involved in turning to television and comparing it with the mindfulness exhibited in turning to other activities, the more concrete conditions in which people bring television into their lives can be analytically reconstructed. We gain insight into the meaning of television use that simply would not be possible if we were to focus directly on viewing or if we were to examine only the turn to television, without examining how it is situated amidst other activities. Examining the specific, mindful ways that people typically turn to television and other activities can tell us something about how their capabilities to act as a self are realized differently in their everyday lives.

Since turning to television is not all that people do in their time away from work, school, child care, and household responsibilities, analysts also need to assess where it is that people typically end up in these different situations by comparing the mindfulness of their involvement in television viewing and other activities. Different activities may have differing potentials when it comes to how mindful people can be while they take part in them, and some charting and profiling of this is in order if we wish to comparatively analyze the meaning of television use. When it comes to activities, I have found it to be especially important to determine whether or not the participation is active or passive, if the person can control the pace, if he or she is able to integrate their participation from one occasion to the next – that is, if the activity has a developmental course – and the degree to which the person is able to be reflective and gain insight about themselves, their society, or their environment. Taken together, participation, pace, developmental course, and possibility for insight are important dimensions of any activities, and their documentation will enable a comparative analysis of the actual activities, including television viewing, that people routinely become involved in.

Television interaction

Once television is turned to as an activity, the real-life context that may have shaped the turn does not recede completely into the background. Yet, the attention of viewers tends to be focused on television imagery. Despite the apparent simplicity of much television programming and the taken-for-granted nature of the set's presence in people's homes, the viewing culture is, in fact, a quite complex social world. In attempting to determine the meaning of viewing *per se*, there are numerous factors to consider, including the ways in which the different symbolic forms of programming work in constituting the mindful and emotional quality of viewing relations, and how the meaning of these viewing relations, may be constituted differently depending upon whether or not people watch alone or with others.

In discussing the turn to television, I pointed out that it was necessary for the analyst to recognize the structuring role that television often plays in exposing people to discourses of selling and consumption on a scale and with a repetitiveness that is unmatched by their involvement in other activities, save perhaps for radio listening and shopping itself. This is true, too, with what I am calling viewing relations: the analyst must be able to determine something of the power that these particular discourses have in ordering and organizing people's mindful and emotional experience. But analysts must do more than that, too. In order to consider how television works once people have turned to it, they obviously need to focus more directly on their viewing relations. And it is important that they do so by first accounting for the complexity of the symbolic forms that comprise programming, since the meaning of viewing is constituted in large part by the mindful involvement that people have with these symbolic forms.

The symbolic forms of programming

Discursive symbolism

In the first place, there are numerous levels of what we might term a "persuasive logic" that typify the marketing strategies of various individuals, groups, and corporate entities. For example, there are the advertisers, politicians, televangelists, and direct marketers whose symbolism ranges from hard-sell pitches to the more comforting imagery of national brand advertising manufactured by Madison Avenue firms; there is the image-making and rhetoric of politicians; the personalities that bring infomercials to life; the promotional pitches for upcoming films and television shows; and, most recently, the seemingly never-ending stream of goods and testimonials that comprise the home-shopping networks. The strategies may be more rational, relying primarily on words to convey the correctness of purchasing decisions, or more emotional, relying instead on the feel of visual imagery to suggest in subtle and sometimes unrecognizable ways the pleasure and satisfaction to be had through association with the product. Symbolically speaking, the net effect of all of this strategizing is to make it possible for viewers to experience varied encounters with the goods and imagery of selling on a continuous basis.

Then there are the conventions of story-telling to consider. Typically, it is realism along with genre, plot, and characterization that serve as the most important focal points of people's attention, since these are the features that are most salient in the representation of social action as if it were real. They provide the symbolic basis for a wide range of people's interpretations of programming, including what in the scenes, stories, and characterizations they find to be plausible as well as what they deem worthy of criticism. In a typical home, television programming provides people with a wide range and increasingly eclectic mix of story-telling conventions that are now available on upwards of forty channels simultaneously. At all levels – scenes, characterizations, plots – story-telling conventions can be more or less formulaic, depending upon the degree to which marketing considerations predominate over craft concerns in shaping programming. Story-telling conventions are intertextual as well, frequently making reference to depictions of plot and characterization found in films, previous television programs, and in the production of celebrity more generally. This layering of possible meanings in the symbolism of story-telling conventions adds up to rather complex depictions of social life in which the reference points for meaning–making on the part of people can shift quite easily from the real to the intertextual to the real over the course of any particular viewing session. Both persuasive messages and story-telling conventions refer to ideas about social life that unfold temporally as action develops in programming.

Presentational symbolism

In using the term presentational symbolism, I have adopted Suzanne Langer's (1957) term to focus attention on how images may evoke or signify meaning without relying on the linear or temporal development that we typically associate with the workings of story-telling conventions or persuasive messages.

One kind of presentational symbolism is the esthetics of visual imagery. The work of creative people, including the writing of dialogue, the appearance and performance of actors, the impression made by visual images, including the effects of lighting, composition, camera angles, and color contrasts, as well as editing techniques that result in various kinds of juxtapositions and movements of visual images – all of this presents itself to the people who watch as a distinctive kind of symbolism. It provides an objective basis in people forming a range of mindful and emotional relationships with programming. But these mindful and emotional relationships do not necessarily exhibit the unfolding of meaning that we typically find in people's encounters with either persuasive symbolism or the symbolism of story-telling conventions. From the standpoint of the people who watch, the esthetics work by way of a spatial rather than a temporal logic. The unfolding of social action is not needed for programming to become meaningful. Visual imagery works along the lines of what Walter Benjamin (1968) described as the "shock effect" of the film: emotionally powerful encounters that stimulate people's imaginative powers, perhaps leading to brief moments in which many different meanings are superimposed, one upon the other, as they call to mind multiple associations they may have with imagery.

Another kind of presentational symbolism consists of depictions of cultural life in which meaning may be more visual than ideational. This includes visual imagery that may serve as a premise for scenes of social action within a show; as a more visually oriented starting-point for the plausibility that is necessary if viewers are to involve themselves in a story; or simply as looks or actions that are repeated across different genres of programming and across different programs within genres and are recognizable as such by people. For example, the combination of furniture, decor, layout, and architecture of home interiors lends a decidedly upper-middle-class quality to the settings of shows. Similarly, the combination of mannerisms, modes of dress, hair styles, and facial features, among other things, conveyed in the image projected by a good many characters on television, signifies the middle and upper-middle classness, the conventional gender distinctions, and the heterosexual orientation of the characters that populate these shows.

By referring to these kinds of depictions of cultural life as "presentational," I am attempting to clarify how the symbolism of programming works in ways that do not seem to demand the same kind of attentiveness that we typically associate with the interpretations of persuasive messages or story-telling conventions. While each depiction of cultural life or impression made by visual imagery may be traceable to the intentions of creative people, including a show's producers, or to programmers, the broader patterning of these depictions and impressions need not be intentional, and yet the patterns do exist, objectively, and can be documented empirically as a form of symbolism available for meaning–making by the people who watch. These patterns of presentational symbolism are closer to what Deleuze (Deleuze and Parnet, 1987) and others have called "assemblages":

the patterns of cultural life that are produced unconsciously and thereby emerge from a place beneath or beyond intentionality. For Deleuze and others, these patterns take their place in the realm of what is cultural.

Commodity forms of symbolism

Finally, there are what I term the commodity forms of symbolism that serve as the most direct extensions of a marketing logic in programming. In the business of television, network executives and programmers are most concerned with maintaining and expanding market shares for their product. By doing so, they generate increases in advertising revenue. It is, after all, this interest in profitability that drives the delivery of programming into the home. But, in order for profits to accrue, this economic interest must be translated into the cultural currency that we encounter as programming. In the process, distinctive symbolic forms emerge that become part and parcel of the meaning making process for people who watch. First, there is the flow of programming that generates a continual circulation of imagery. Second, there is the segmented programming structure, composed of 15–, 30–, and 60-second commercial spots as well as half-hour, hour, and two-hour program blocks, that works by breaking up this flow of programming. Taken together, flow and segmentation generate disjunctures in the symbolic field of programming, where, unlike the discursive symbolism of persuasion and story-telling conventions, the movements and combinations of imagery do not develop normative continuity; and, unlike even presentational symbolism, the logic of these movements and combinations work to destabilize whatever cultural coherence may be depicted in the symbolism of visual images themselves. Third, conventions of story-telling are repeated again and again in different programs and then circulated on a daily (syndicated shows), weekly (network series), and season-long basis across numerous channels. This results in a distinctive, manufactured quality to the symbolism of programming that viewers can certainly distinguish from the rendering of real-life in the story-telling conventions themselves. Like flow and segmentation, this symbolism of repetition also derives from a marketing logic, which means that it does not necessarily work to order social experience in normative ways. When they become mindfully engaged with these commodity forms of symbolism, people make meaning by disengaging themselves from the real world that television purports to represent and instead rely on their practical knowledge, gained through repeated exposure to television and other media, that programming is a world of manufactured, manipulated, and manipulable images.

Television programming, then, is symbolically complex, and it can mean different things at different times to different people. Yes, it is composed, as we would expect, of persuasive messages of different kinds as well as the various conventions by which the stories of television are told. These discourses, as they have come to be called, serve as points of departure for a variety of viewing relations. In ranging across different channels it is commonplace for people to encounter different scenes, characterizations, and story-lines and to interpret them differently, depending on both the depictions themselves and what people bring to them in terms of social knowledge. In short, despite the mainstreaming tendency of these discourses, viewing is a symbolically rich and highly ambivalent activity. But these discourses, even in all their complexity, are not all there is to the symbolism of television programming. There is the presentational symbolism of programming, which is itself multi-layered and serves as a point of departure for the construction of a rich and complicated imaginative world on the part of people. And then there are the commodity forms that impart a manufactured quality to programming and generate discontinuities and disjunctures in the symbolic field, all of which exist quite apart from discourse and even the workings of presentational symbolism. Each of these symbolic forms can be documented as distinctive patternings of programming, and each works differently and simultaneously to constitute a multiplicity of viewing relations. Analysts of television must account for this symbolic complexity in their attempts to document the meaning of television viewing.

Viewing relations

Once the symbolic complexity of programming is understood, analysts face the difficulty of documenting how viewers actually situate themselves with television and make use of this symbolism. I have found that a wide range of mindful and emotional relationships with imagery are possible and, in fact, probable. Viewing can occur in solitary situations and in group situations. In solitary situations, people can or cannot become mindfully engaged with any and all of the symbolic forms of programming. At one extreme, they can relate to television as an object, using it simply for background noise or to have some company in the house while they do other things or otherwise occupy themselves. Or they may intermittently attend to what is on the screen, using the flow of programming to follow only the most exciting scenes of a program, and then quickly turning their attention to other things unrelated to television. People may watch what is on the screen, but they are not really thinking too deeply or getting too involved in anything they see. With the flow enabling them to just watch things go by, they may focus attention on the presentational symbolism and create meaning with visual images in a variety of ways – some related and others unrelated to the depictions at hand. They may watch a good portion of a single program in this way, alternatively spacing out and returning to the visual imagery or even the action as it develops on the screen. None of this, mind you, could be considered attentive viewing. People can become more mindfully engaged with the specifics of the story-telling conventions, they can get interested in the plot, the action of scenes, or with the characters themselves. They can be attentive enough to recognize how things are put together, or they can follow the scenes or what the characters do and concern themselves with why things come out as they do. In instances such as this, people are more consistently focused on the discourse of programming. At the other extreme, they can become so involved in the story, the action, or with the characters, that the depictions seem real to them, leading them to feel as if they are there, in the situations and a part of what is happening. In some cases, people may be attentive enough to make connections between what they are watching and things they have watched on TV in the past, or things they have seen in films, or even things they have had happen in their own life. Sometimes, this leads them to think reflexively about their own lives and, as a result, they feel enriched or more knowledgeable about themselves or their world. It is important to bear in mind, though, that people do not simply accept everything that they see, even when they watch in what appears to be attentive ways. They may be mindful of what is on in different ways. Sometimes they may merely recognize the implausible and make a mental note of it. At other times, if something that they feel strongly about does not make sense, they react to it verbally or with gestures to make their distance from the depiction that much more explicit.

Viewing also occurs in group situations where the same range of viewing relations that we can find in solitary viewing can occur; only now, their occurrence is complicated by the fact that interaction among people is an ongoing feature of television use. At one extreme, there are situations in which the relationship of each person to the television set is of primary importance. In these instances, the meaning of viewing is to be found by analyzing the separate, mindful relations of each person with the symbolic forms of the programming they encounter. And here we can assume it is the story-telling conventions that are most pertinent to their mindful involvement; although it is possible that they might find the presentational symbolism or even the repetition of programming more interesting to watch. At the other extreme, interaction among people can be so thoroughly integrated with their attention to programming that viewing becomes a highly organized social world in which people can play what one viewer aptly called "the game of television." This begins with viewers settling in to watch a favorite show or one that they like to see regularly. With the program serving as a focal point for their attention, different viewers can voice their opinions about what they are watching in order to elicit comments from the others and initiate some discussion. Then, the give and take of conversation (some of it highly critical) around specific scenes or characters' actions – and, usually, it is the story-telling conventions and the "real world" they depict which interests people most – enables shared meanings to emerge. Most of the time, however, the meaningful quality of group viewing lies somewhere between these two extremes. In some instances, people may all be gathered in the same room to watch, but each in their own way may be sufficiently distracted by other thoughts or by continued involvement in other activities of various sorts so that they pay less than full attention to what is on. Or, people may be gathered with the intent to watch a particular program closely, but it may turn out that the program does not hold their attention. In situations such as these, numerous scenarios are possible, depending upon how well the people know one another, their respective moods, and whatever else they may decide to do, to name just a few of the more important factors to be considered. Sometimes, sporadic commentary about television or other matters may emerge and take on a life of its own as people use the flow of programming or the presentational symbolism as something to fall back on during lulls in the conversation, or when they want to disengage themselves from social interaction. At other times, one or another person may leave the room to attend to other things then return to focus once again on what is on the screen, hoping that things had changed enough for the program to now hold their attention.

It should be clear from this discussion that the task of understanding the meaning that television viewing has for people can become quite complicated. So, too, can the task of specifying how the power of television works in constituting their mindful and emotional relationships with programming. People's presence of mind is constantly shifting while they watch. Still, the analyst must be able to determine if it is television or people themselves who are responsible for maintaining this presence of mind. Generally speaking, significant changes in people's presence of mind must be understood in relation to the workings of the different symbolic forms that I have mentioned. Discursive symbolism is not the sole determinant of the meaning of their viewing experience.

Leaving television and fitting it back within daily life

Beyond people's turn to television and their interaction with programming lie the issues of what they think, feel, and do as a result of using the medium.

First, there are behavioral effects of viewing to consider. Analysts need to account for the seemingly small and insignificant ways that our behavior may be transformed as a consequence of what we encounter on television. How do depictions of characters and celebrities become incorporated into people's daily routines? How do such depictions alter the meaning of people's actions? This world of behavior and behavioral change does not lend itself easily to documentation because it is sometimes too personal, too close, too much about who people are becoming for them to reveal it to the analyst. Furthermore, the television-driven world of behavior can easily shade into fantasy, where the lived reality of things becomes more imaginary and sometimes that which separates the two realms is not so easily identified. But what is more easily identified is the conversation that people have with others, when they are no longer watching, about what they have seen on television. Conversation may sometimes lead people to reinterpret what they have seen or heard. Over time this talk may change the very way that they watch television – not only what they watch, but, more importantly, what they find believable or worthy of criticism. So, the analyst must be able to determine whether or not people talk regularly, with the same people, about what they watch. Do they talk about the same shows? Is it important for them to discuss their favorite shows or favorite characters on a regular basis? What sorts of story-lines or characters' actions typically elicit their commentary and provoke the most enthusiastic kinds of talk? What does "critical talk" consist of? If talk about television does not take place regularly, it may still occur, only it may be more random and infrequent. If so, what does that talk consist of? Is it focused on favorite shows, is it limited to comments about special shows such as sporting events, award shows, political debates, mini-series, and the like, or is it some combination of the two? Questions such as these mark only a beginning of an inquiry into the meaning of people's conversations regarding television.

Television can figure importantly in the ways that people think about and deal with problems or issues in their own lives. Do the ways in which particular characters deal with fictional situations, such as marital or family problems, job stress, relations with supervisors, alcoholism, drug use, and so on become incorporated into the ways in which people who watch handle similar situations in their own lives? If so, what is it, specifically, about televised depictions that resonate with their own lives? Similarly, do they witness depictions of "real life" on television that serve as clear indicators of what *not* to do if they are confronted with the same or similar circumstances in their own lives?

Leaving television and fitting it back within daily life also encompasses the formation of attitudes and opinions that emerge from television use and that people may carry around inside their heads and draw upon in making sense of themselves and their world, especially the world beyond their own day-to-day experiences. People certainly think about their world, the social relations they are a part of, the people and places they come into contact with, including what they see on television and in other media. They develop attitudes and formulate opinions on a wide variety of things. When it comes to television, analysts have to document how viewers think differently, and how what they already think is supported as a result of what they watch. When viewers accept particular television presentations of, say, inner-city police or criminal lawyers as plausible, does this have a direct bearing on how they understand inner-city police or criminal lawyers in the real world? It seems problematic to focus only on specific interpretations people make while watching television and then to extrapolate these interpretations to stand for some more diffuse knowledge that they have of the world – say, of inner-city police or criminal lawyers. To depart from such a strategy of documentation would mean to deal more directly with how it is that specific interpretations or even more stable and consistent patterns of interpretation based on viewing favorite shows or recurrent themes in programming are actually fit by people into their everyday lives. Some of what people interpret may become meaningful in actual behavior and some in fantasy. But if attitude and opinion research offers us any indication, there may be yet another realm in which some of what people watch takes on meaning as more diffuse and free-floating ideas about the world that are simply stored in their preconscious or unconscious mind. These ideas may surface when real world occurrences or encounters with the media or both provoke people to recall the "televisual knowledge" they have stored away and use it to elaborate the meanings associated with such occurrences and encounters in their own minds. Armed with a prior understanding of the symbolic forms of programming, and knowledgeable regarding the viewing habits of people, including their favorite shows and characters, the analyst can then identify the kinds of depictions that resonate most with particular people and, on that basis, attempt to reconstruct how these more diffuse, free-floating ideas about the world take shape in their everyday lives.

Conclusion

Television use involves a complex process of meaning–making, one that is mindfully and emotionally constituted in a variety of ways, ranging across the three components that I have mentioned – the turn to television, interaction with programming imagery *per se*, and leaving television and fitting it back within daily life. Understanding how television is situated in people's everyday lives necessitates that we analytically reconstruct their use of the medium in all its complexity. In considering the turn to television, analysts need to know how a person's responsibilities structure everyday life and create the opportunities for turning to television in the first place. Typically, these responsibilities include work, school, child care, and housework. Analysts need to know the situational contexts that typically serve as a point of departure for television use. This includes documenting the feelings people have in these situations, their mindfulness in turning to television and to other activities, the activities themselves, as well as their mindful potential. In analyzing the second component, television interaction, analysts should proceed knowing that there is more to programming than discourse. The presentational and commodity forms of symbolism work along with discursive symbolism in providing an objective basis for people's continual movements in and out of a variety of viewing relations. Analysts need to know what these viewing relations are, what typifies the movements between them for different people, and when and how the television constitutes the meaning of these viewing relations, and to distinguish this power from the directive role that people's identities and sense of self play in giving meaningful form to their viewing. And, finally, with regard to the third component, leaving television and fitting it back into daily life, analysts need to know how television imagery becomes situated in people's everyday lives. They need to reconstruct the act of turning off the television so as to better understand the emotional complexities that attend to it. They need to know both what people do differently as a result of their viewing as well as how what they do, if not noticeably different from what they have done in the past, is nevertheless solidified as a result of watching television. Furthermore, analysts need to understand people's talk about television, whether or not they find what they watch helpful in dealing with personal problems and issues, the ideas they formulate about the "real world" as a consequence of watching television, and the daydreams and fantasies that might be stimulated by television use.

I refer to this complexity of meaning that is involved in people's day-to-day television use as the sociality of the viewing culture. In talking about this sociality, it is crucial that analysts account for television's power by identifying the different ways that it can work: as an object of consumption, discourses of persuasion, story-telling conventions, visual symbolism, flow, a segmented structure of programming, and as a repetition of manufactured images. It is in all of these ways that television can shape the sociality of the viewing culture. Certainly, discourse is powerful. But understanding the sociality of the viewing culture involves much more than accounting for power and resistance.

PART III

Documenting the viewing culture

6

Methodology and the turn to television

Understanding the sociality of television use requires that the analyst provide some systematic way of exploring what *typically* goes on, socially speaking, when people become involved in the various activities that constitute their daily, weekly, and monthly routines of relaxation and enjoyment in the home. My strategy of empirical research into television use, beginning in the late 1980s, was to reconstruct people's social experience with television across the different, yet interrelated, phases that constitute what I call the *viewing culture*, with the purpose of doing research that stayed as close as possible to the lives of the people involved. The phases of television use that I began with are (1) the turn to television, (2) interaction with television imagery, and (3) leaving television and fitting it back into daily life. Now, a decade later, this still seems an important way of understanding the significance that television use holds for people. By looking at television viewing in the context of everyday life, one is led to re-examine many of the claims that cultural studies' analysts often make regarding the workings of the medium's power. This chapter attempts both to explain why one needs to look at television's influence in this context and to actually examine some of these influences. After some important preliminary discussion of methodological concerns, I focus on empirical research that looks only at the initial phase of television use, the *turn* to television, and discuss in some detail the significant patterns emerging from my research.

Before discussing the turn to television, two preliminary sections in this chapter examine some methodological concerns of my approach to empirical research. In the first section, "Social relations and the power of television," I argue that empirical accounts of use are indispensable to the theorization of television's power effects. In the second section, "Accounting for television as a social experience," I explain my overall approach to looking at television culture and how the ideas of *ritual* and *qualities of mindfulness* figure importantly in understanding the activity that is the turn to television.

In the third section of this chapter, "Patterns of turning to television," I present the results of my documentation of the viewing culture, which emerged from watching television with working people (participant observation) and reconstructions of their viewing experiences provided to me in interview accounts. Again, this documentation is limited to what I found regarding just the first segment of the viewing culture – the turn to television. It is in this section that I detail how people bring television into their lives and the implications of their doing so, especially with regard to power effects.

The fourth and final section in this chapter, "Power relations and the sociality of simultaneous viewing," is an elaboration on a group of people discussed in the third section. This large group of people I interviewed has a particular way – as it turns out, an important way – of watching television: what I refer to as "viewing while pursuing other activities simultaneously," or "simultaneous viewing," for short. This is such an important group that I wanted to focus in greater detail on the nature and implications of their viewing habits as they relate to the power effects of television. I conclude this section, and the chapter, with an analysis of the functional use of television for simultaneous viewers in the after-work time period.

Social relations and the power of television

With the construct of discourse, cultural studies analysts have attempted to understand how television orders and organizes people's social experience. While it is the desire for entertainment and pleasure, they say, that often draws people into the world of television, it is the discursive power of television that, over the long run, is most salient because it provides them with normative guidelines for thinking and acting in their everyday lives. Embedded as it is in the very language of television imagery, this discursive power works in sometimes very subtle ways to constitute practice.

Despite the insight afforded by such a perspective, when it comes to day-to-day television use, ideas of discursive power (and resistance) remain abstract, operating, as they do, a step or two removed from so much of what people actually do when they watch television. As a result, discursive constructs fail to grasp adequately much of what is *socially* complex about television use.

A more appropriate way of documenting the social complexities of television use is to acknowledge the discursive power of television (perhaps even carrying out detailed, preliminary analyses of its objective structural features), but then to set aside such ideas and proceed by reconstructing people's *use* of television as a part of the routines of relaxation and enjoyment that constitute their everyday lives. In this way, analytical attention can be focused on how television shapes these routines, but without losing sight of the sociological complexity of the routines themselves.

In carrying out my field research and in conducting depth interviews, it was my intention from the start to account for the social relations that were a part of people's television use. Virtually all research perspectives acknowledge (even if they do not focus on it) that *what people do with one another can mediate the power of television* in important ways, in some cases amplifying it and in other cases deflecting and qualifying it. In my interviews with television viewers, from early on and repeatedly over the course of an interview, each person would mention other people – family members, housemates, friends – with whom he or she often shared time away from work. Of course, the individual accounts varied quite a bit in their specifics, but the *social facts* of home life were a constant across all the accounts. Elements that were important included: whether the informants were cohabiting or lived alone; whether they had children; whether they typically watched alone or with others; the kinds of conversations they had about television or while the television was on; their hobbies, including clubs, classes, team sports, or group meetings they regularly took part in, and so on. As I expected, much of people's individual experience was in fact *social*, and I felt, and still feel, it was crucial to capture all of this, since it would figure importantly in any analysis of their television use, especially when it came to questions of power.

I not only documented the social interactions and the group life that often shaped what happened in the home, but I also focused on capturing individual thoughts and feelings, both when these individuals were with other people and when they were alone. The fact that what people think and feel happens *inside* does not make it any less social than what people say to or do with one another. A good deal of the mindful encounters that people have with objects in their world, such as with television and with other people, can be *socially constituted*, without it ever having to find outer expression, either in words or actions. In other words, these thoughts, feelings, and actions exist in relation to other people. As a social activity, television use is typically constituted as a relation, one in which the people who use it have a certain separateness, or distinctiveness, with regard to the object, television, and to the other people that use it with them. At the same time, they remain connected to the television and to other people who may be using it with them. It is this simultaneous separateness and connection that makes it possible for there to be an inside, a mindfulness, to people's use of television or, for that matter, for there to be an inside or a mindfulness to any of the activities that comprise social life.

To speak about a sociality of television use is to acknowledge that the inner mindfulness that people have when they are engaged with the medium is just as important as the more conventionally understood, outward indicators of social life when it comes to providing cultural form to their experience. This is particularly true, I think, when we are dealing with a technology that works in as private a way as does television. Typically, it is this inner mindfulness, this inner world of emotional experience, that is often ignored in scholarly explorations of the viewing culture. As I said, it was my intention from the outset of this study to make sure that I documented it and retained some sense of its significance in my analysis of what people do with television. Consequently, in this chapter, I pay particular attention to the mindful approach taken by the people I interviewed during their turn to television.

Accounting for television as a social experience

In turning to television, people provide an opportunity for the discourses of power that are inscribed in the medium to enter their homes and become a part – in some cases, a very important part – of the social world that they create, inhabit, and sustain there. It seemed, from my earliest television research, that virtually everyone who watches television is aware of the regularity (or irregularity) with which they turn to the medium. Because of this, I thought, if given an opportunity, a television viewer could indeed reconstruct a good deal of what they think and do to bring television into their lives on a regular basis. It is this sense of *typicality* in people's turn to television that served as my starting-point in reconstructing what people do with television.

When it came to working people, this framework for reconstructing the sociality of television use had to be grounded, obviously enough, in the particularities of *their* lives. Typically, the first opportunity people who work a conventional "day shift" have for turning to television comes after work, when they make the transition to their home life. Their time at work is not, strictly speaking, their own, and it ordinarily does not provide them with the opportunity for watching television or doing anything else, really, that involves the kinds of relaxation and enjoyment that are characteristic of what they do with their free-time. The world of work has a variety of meanings for working people, but one common meaning it carries is that work represents a meaningful counterpoint to home life, which, in turn, typically takes shape around one's work life. Whatever it is that working people typically do at home, it is safe to say that it is punctuated by their routines of going to and coming from work. It is for this reason that I began my discussion of television use with the working people I interviewed asking them about their work – its routines, its pressures, and its rewards. From there, I focused attention on what they typically did when they left work. This was my entry point into their everyday lives, and it was one that seemed to make sense for them, given their routines of work and relaxation.

Based on my preliminary research, a significant portion of my interview schedule focused on the reconstruction of this transition from work to home life, and I was especially interested in understanding how people typically structure this transition time with regard to their use of television. But, in order to understand what it meant for them to turn to television, I needed to reconstruct the *place* of television in their everyday lives during this transition time. This meant that, in the interviews, I had to account for how they typically oriented themselves to (thought about) television and other activities. I also had to account for what they watched, how they watched, as well as what they usually did besides watching television at this time, including how they typically did those other things. (I did not complete interviews with anyone who said he/she never watched television.) Furthermore, I had to do all of this *without* presupposing that television occupied any special, or privileged, position for these people. In short, I had to capture, in descriptive accounts, the full range of sociological factors and social–psychological processes that are typical for people as they made their transition from work to home, day-in and day-out. Because I was especially interested in workday routines, I asked my interviewees to describe to me what they typically did, and the processes they went through both during this transition time and during the eventual passage into the evening period. I also asked them to reconstruct something of their weekend routines and the role that television played there, but our conversations during the interviews tended to focus mainly on the work week.

Mindfulness: an analytical treatment of interiority

In addition to identifying activities my interviewees were involved with and who was included in them, I found it was important to be explicit in documenting the *mindfulness* with which they went about doing their activities. As I said earlier, one of my major concerns was to treat this inner social world as carefully as most analysts have treated the outer one. In the real time of the viewing culture, people do not ordinarily make distinctions between the phases of their activities. They are not generally in the business of analyzing their own television use, or their own participation in other activities. Nevertheless, people do pass through mindful phases during their activities. They orient themselves mentally to what they are about to do, based on whatever it is they are presently doing, and then, once they have actually turned to a particular activity, they enter a new phase, one in which they become mindfully engaged in the activity itself. In passing through the phases of any activity, people are mindful – they think – and their mindfulness undergoes changes and transformations. This mindfulness, then, constitutes a most important *interior* dimension of social actions and activities. Through prior field research, use of viewer diaries, the completion of preliminary, open-ended interviews, and more informal conversations with people who watch television, particularly working people, I found that it made sense to distinguish between the mindfulness with which people turned to activities, including television, and the mindfulness of their participation in activities themselves. That is, how people think *in orienting themselves to* activities is not necessarily the same as where it is they end up, mindfully speaking, *while engaged in* the activities.

In order to systematically investigate the mindfulness in the turn to television (and to other activities) I asked working people in my interviews to provide an account of the typical course of their after-work routines. Precisely because work followed by the transition period (with all it entails) was part of what these people did every day, I thought that they would, when asked, be sufficiently familiar with their actions to be able to reconstruct them in the context of an open-ended interview. Included in the interview were inquiries regarding the variations that they, as people who worked, might typically experience. I asked about feeling tired after a hectic or stressful day at work, for example, versus feeling relaxed and energetic after a good day at work. As our conversations proceeded, I was certainly interested in having them reconstruct the broader context of their television use, including the activities that preceded, followed, and occurred simultaneously with television viewing. But I was especially interested in having them tell me in detail about the processes they went through at particular periods after work so that I could gain some insight into their mindfulness at these times.

I approached the particular problem of documenting working people's turn to activities using the idea of a *continuum of mindfulness*. Points that I established along this continuum are: *habitual*, the least mindful way of approaching activities, where people are acting out of habit or, in effect, orienting themselves to doing things in an unthinking way; *escapist*, a slightly more mindful approach to things, where people typically have at least some awareness of a desire to be freed up, mentally, emotionally, physically, or socially, from their present situation (not acting simply out of habit); *playful*, an orientation to activities not only where people are getting away from what they were previously doing or feeling, but also, more importantly, where they are thinking in terms of separating themselves from what they were doing, and, by virtue of this separation, turning to something else in a creative or imaginative frame of mind; and, finally, *reflective*, the most mindful of the qualities, when people monitor and evaluate their present thoughts and feelings, trying to anticipate how they might think or feel if they were to choose one activity over another, and in general, trying to be conscious of where and how the activity might fit into the larger context of their free-time activities.

When it came to documenting the mindfulness of people's actual involvement in activities (as opposed to the act of turning to them), I identified four dimensions of social action that would be applicable to a wide variety of activities and, at the same time, allow meaningful comparisons to be made between them. In the first place, I wanted to know whether people participated in a more *active or passive* way in the activities that they chose. Second, I thought it important to know whether or not people typically had *control over the pace* with which their activities proceeded. Third, I wanted to determine whether people become engaged in activities in such a way that one occurrence was connected to and built upon the last, so that, over time, the activity could be understood by them to have a *developmental course* to it. And, finally, I was interested in knowing the *possibility for insight* that various activities held for people; that is, whether or not, and to what extent, their participation in activities provided them with insight about themselves, about others in their world, or about the broader environment in which their lives were situated.

As you might expect, the qualities of mindfulness characterizing people's turn to activities and characterizing their involvement in activities varies greatly. Assessing qualities of mindfulness is a difficult analytical task, in part because mindful participation depends on so many things, including, obviously, interviewees' backgrounds, the kinds of work they do, the situations they typically find themselves in after work, the way they think and feel in those situations, their living situations, the kinds of responsibilities they have there, the activities that are available to them, and so on. Furthermore, I have found that the "same" activity can be perceived very differently by different people. For example, the mindfulness of television viewing is not something that remains fixed across different social contexts or across the different uses that people make of it. For someone who tunes into a favorite show, and views it alone in an uninterrupted manner, paying close attention to the development of the story, day after day, or week after week, watching television can be a very mindful activity indeed. The same can be true when people watch favorite shows together, as a family or as a household, and place a priority both on following the action closely and on spending time together. In contrast, for someone who uses television as background noise or for company and only pays intermittent attention to what is on while doing other things, it is safe to say that watching television is a relatively "mindless" activity. In this kind of viewing, there is little, if any, sense of a developmental course to the activity; the people involved are not really very active in making what they see meaningful, and there is less of a chance (compared with other ways of watching) that they will come away from television with much insight, with regard to either themselves or others.

By asking working people to provide an account of the typical course of their after-work routines, I was able to reconstruct the broader context of their television use, including the activities that preceded, followed, and occurred simultaneously with it; and by asking them to recall something of the mindful way in which they typically went about these activities, I was able to understand something of their inner process of mind as well. With these constructs of mindfulness in place, I was able to assess whether or not working people turned to television with a particular frame of mind that recurred from one occasion of use to the next. I was also able to assess whether they approached other activities in the same way; and, if they did not, I was in a position to know how they did approach other activities, mindfully speaking, and I attempted to determine why this was the case. Perhaps most importantly, this kind of documentation enabled me to compare people's mindfulness in turning to television with their mindfulness in turning to other activities. Similarly, I was able to compare where it is, mindfully speaking, that people ended up as a result of having turned to television versus their having turned to other activities on a routine basis. As a result, it was possible for me to move beyond an understanding of television use as something isolated, and see it instead as something thoroughly *situated*.

Transitions and ritual

The nature of the transition from work to home life, and vice versa, in the lives of those I interviewed, can be seen in terms of ritual. As ritual, these periods of transition have a practical significance that extends beyond the phenomenological moment. The transition actually contains, within itself, something of the broader patterning of one's television use, among other elements of one's life. These transitions or rituals also contain the insight and recognition that people have, and carry with them, regarding the *social* nature of what they do – at work, with television, in other activities, and so on. The reconstructions that were provided in the interview accounts symbolize, quite literally, the ritual nature of the turn to television. They tell us about this first opportunity that working people have for bringing television into their lives, but they are about much more than that, too.

These rituals of coming from and going to home and work, along with the patterns of mindfulness and the actions that emerge from them, have become an enduring part of the weekly, monthly, and even yearly routines that constitute the lives of those I interviewed. Each person coming home after work must make decisions regarding what to do and how to do it. As people go through this, they live in the moment, of course. But, while their transition from work to home is made anew each day, it is also, in some sense, already structured by the practical knowledge they have gained, not only of having turned to television or other activities before, but of having participated in these activities many times and of having to leave these activities behind and resume their lives at work once again. The ritual then contains and expresses the entire cycle of television use in their everyday lives.

The rituals I found in my research surrounding the turn to television after work provide a means of exploring the workings of power within the world of the viewing culture. In other words, the turn-to-television rituals allow us to look at specific ways the power of television worked in the lives of those I interviewed: the ways the sociality of television use and participation in everyday activities counterbalances or mediates television's power effects. Together, an understanding of ritual and the construct of mindfulness become important as a means of reconstructing television use and understanding the complicated mix of forces in everyday life.

Generating accounts

The reconstructions of everyday thoughts, feelings, and actions that people provided me with should not be treated naïvely as facts, as *things* divorced from the context of their production. This analysis of television came about not only as a structured response to theoretical problems, but also because I posed particular questions to people, structuring our conversations in ways that were no doubt out of the ordinary for those involved. These were not people who usually talked to sociologists, journalists, or others inquiring about things as mundane as their television viewing habits. Many things beyond my control – and theirs – may have been going on in the interviews, coloring responses or diverting attention from the intended objective. And it is normal for people to forget some things and to reconstruct other things selectively, or in ways that may change from one occasion to the next. These reconstructions, then, are flawed in all the ways that interview accounts usually are. Nevertheless, even with all their potential flaws, these accounts offer evidence of much that is valuable and important regarding the use that working people make of television, and, correspondingly, the use that television makes of them. It was the ordinariness of their television use that I was after. Perhaps because of this (I hope) they experienced less of the distance and of the sense of difference that is normally inscribed in the research process.

With the documentation provided by this empirical research, especially the information related to mindfulness, it is possible now to interrogate notions of standardization and normalization by examining the ways in which this power operates, shaping working people's everyday experiences. This data provides an empirical reference point, a kind of evidence, really, for thinking through ideas about television's power. With this reference point, power becomes no longer simply an abstraction (albeit a useful one), but, rather, something concrete. The interview and participant observation data allow for an understanding of the extent to which the people in this study were able to direct and control what they did with television, and hence the extent to which they could call into question, circumvent, or simply ignore its power.

Patterns of turning to television

I interviewed 60 people from two workplaces in Northern California. In total, 37 were women, 23 were men, 50 were white, 3 were Filipino–American, 2 were Chinese–American, 2 were Mexican–American, 1 was Puerto Rican, 1 African American, and 1 identified as Portuguese. Although, certainly, research ought to be pursued to show patterns among race, class, and gender groupings, what I found most important in these interviews, in relation to power effects, given the exploratory nature of the work, were viewing patterns.

From the interviews I found three significant patterns of television use in the turn-to-television phase that, when considered carefully, complicate the models of power and resistance that have figured so importantly in recent media research. Those who always turn to watching television after work bring to consideration both television's power to establish meaningful parameters for their social world, and each one's capacity as a self that counterbalances the power television exercises in their lives. Those who turn to television "less mindfully" allow us to see the ways television's power works to standardize ways of thinking over time, as well as how such viewing practices imply a counterbalancing set of mindful activities. A third group, those who turn to television while pursuing other activities simultaneously, provides evidence that television's power is undercut by its merely intermittent attention to it, as well as considerations regarding television's role in habituating viewers to seek mindless companion activities.

Turning exclusively to television

There were clear lines of influence attributable to television arising from the interview accounts, but not at all to the extent that I had expected. Out of the 60 people I interviewed, only 3 said that they came home from work and *always* turned to watching television, as opposed to turning to any other activities. For these three viewers, because of the way they watched television, it had the power to set the meaningful parameters of their social world at this time of day. They were drawn into a mindful relationship with the discourses of programming for periods of time, but these power relations were mediated by the existence of alternative social experiences in their lives and by alternative mindful orientations to television viewing at other junctures.

The three people who turned to television viewing after work at all times were three married men. All were white. One was a fork-lift operator, another a mechanic, and the third a machine operator. Two of them worked the early evening shift, getting off work at 11. P.M., and one worked the night shift, getting off at 6. A.M. What was common in their accounts was the fact that they were typically tired after work, and, because they worked late shifts, no one was usually awake to talk or share time with them when they came home. As a result, each had established a similar routine of turning to television to make the transition from work to home life at this time.

By turning to television every night after work, these men allowed the mainstream world of television imagery to enter their homes. Once they were situated with television, it served as the primary focus for their meaning–making activities. This lasted – again, every work night – for anywhere from an hour and a half to two hours, from the time they came home until they decided to go to bed. Because they did not do other things during this time, they did not ordinarily have the opportunity to become engaged with other sources of information, with other ideas, or in experiences other than those that were provided by television. Alternative ways of seeing that might emerge from use of other media sources or from participation in other activities were lost to them at this time. They were, in a sense, unable to engage their minds or stimulate their imaginations in ways that extended beyond the horizons of television's image worlds. As a result, over time, television came to have a certain power in their lives. It is the power to set the *meaningful parameters* of their social world. This is, really, an indirect kind of power; power by default. Television could set the agenda at this time, every night, because other things could not and did not.

The power of television works in the lives of these three men in a more direct way, too, by structuring their interpretive processes. (This will be discussed in greater detail in chapter 7, "The practice of viewing," because it is part of how power works normatively.) Because these three people turn exclusively to television after work, and because their viewing involved focusing attention on the text and sustaining that kind of attention throughout the time they spent with television, they were, in comparison to others, more susceptible to the power that television has to order and organize the ways they make their experience meaningful during this time. Unlike many other people who watch television after work, these men did not move about the house while the television was on; instead, they actually sat or lay down and watched what was on. All three preferred to watch in an uninterrupted manner. Of course, they were not always able to watch in this way, because television did not, from moment to moment, provide them with sufficiently interesting or compelling material. But it was this kind of involvement that they looked for. They wanted to be able to pay consistent attention to what they watched. Even if they did not always watch closely, they were mindfully and emotionally engaged with the social action as it unfolded before them on the screen.

In Rob's case, he said that he usually watched *The Tonight Show* and *Nightline*, "bouncing," as he referred to it, "back and forth between the two"; when he found something entertaining, he would "stay with it." Phil said that he usually turned to either *The Tonight Show, Barnaby Jones* reruns, a late night movie, or *The David Letterman Show,* flipping between them until he found whatever seemed most interesting, and then "staying with one thing to pay attention to" as he put it. For Don, it was re-broadcasts of auto racing and golf on ESPN that he most liked to watch; when they were on, he "kept watching." Because they chose not to do other things while they watched, these men were, compared with others, more likely to continue paying this kind of consistent attention to what was on. Typically, each of them said that they would watch for anywhere from an hour and a half to two hours, or until they started to fall asleep, then they would move off to bed.

Rob, Phil, and Don were drawn into a mindful relationship with the *discourses* of programming. At the very least, they were observers of social action. They reflected on what they saw and heard, and they regularly made judgments of various kinds with regard to the social action that unfolded before them on the screen. It was common for them to imagine themselves, they said, if only momentarily, in the places or as the people that they saw on television. As they watched, they would play with the idea of what it might be like to enter into relationships that the people on television had with one another, to live out these people's lives. This is what it meant for them to be *mindfully engaged* with television after work.

But, because it was late and they were typically tired, they were not looking to be critical of television at these times. In fact, all three said they wanted to find something entertaining to watch, something that they could continue to follow. These ingredients allowed them, more often than not, to attribute legitimacy to what they saw and heard on television, and in doing so they were drawn into the power that televisual discourses have for ordering and organizing their mindful experience. Of course, there were times when they would fail to find television's depictions of social life plausible. (They would move on or flip channels.) When this occurs, the discursive power is, by definition, suspended, and its legitimizing functions deferred, for the moment at least. (The role of such questioning and criticism will be taken up in the discussion of viewing relations in the next chapter.) These three men turned to television after work precisely so that they could enter into the world of television imagery uncritically, with a willingness to accept what that world had to offer them. Remember, they wanted to be mindfully and emotionally involved in such a way that they could believe in what they saw and heard. As a result, for these people in this situation, it was television that had the power to shape a good deal of what they took to be "real."

The discursive power of television carried over beyond the bounds of the after-work period for these three men because all three watched television as a part of their before-work and weekend routines of relaxation and enjoyment. It was a continuing influence in their lives.

This was perhaps most evident in Phil's case, because he sat and watched *I Love Lucy* and *Perry Mason* reruns before work, "enjoying them enough," he said, to "stay pretty involved in the shows." In Don's house, the television was typically "just on," from mid-afternoon, when his son came home from school, until the time he went to work, around 9.0 P.M. Early in the day, he would play with the baby while his son watched cartoons or other children's programs, and, a little bit later, when the news came on, he would "catch bits and pieces of things." When his wife came home, he finally had time, he said, to "settle into some of my favorite shows," which typically included *The Wizard,* science-fiction movies, and ESPN programming. On weekend evenings, he settled into his routine of watching ESPN, especially boxing, sci-fi movies, or a rented movie with his wife. In Rob's case, the time before work, like the time after work, was often a time for watching television. From around 11.0 A.M to 1.0 or 1.30 P.M., he and his wife (and his kids, if they were home) watched game shows together, "playing along" with the contestants. At noon, he and his wife sat down to watch *All My Children,* a soap opera that they both had been watching since 1970. On the weekends, the television was often just turned on in the morning, and, starting with *World Federation Wrestling,* it stayed on through midday old movies and afternoon sports, and he checked in from time to time, sometimes sitting to watch, but otherwise, doing things around the house. On other occasions, Rob watched specific sporting events, devoting his full attention to them.

Alternatives to television viewing (at other times)

Although both before work and on the weekends television continued to order and organize their experience, it was not always the sole source of their meaning–making activities at these times, as it was during the after-work period.

Phil, who usually watched *I Love Lucy* and *Perry Mason* attentively, sometimes did not, and instead he did household chores while at the same time "coming in and out of" what was on television. Even though Don spent a good deal of his television viewing time focused on the text, he also took time, while the television was on during the day, to play with his daughter, and, in the evening and on weekends, to talk with his wife. In Rob's case, if the story-lines of *All My Children* were uninteresting, he got up and did other things, and on weekends, with the television simply left on, he routinely took care of "other things around the house," like housecleaning, yardwork, paying bills, and so on. He, too, watched intermittently at these times.

Furthermore, during the day, before work, at work, or on the weekends, each of these men, in their different ways, did other things besides watch television.

Phil ran regularly, at which time he said he concentrated on his workout or just cleared his mind of things; he also found the time, every couple of days or so, to read parts of the *San Francisco Chronicle* at work, or magazines, such as *Sports Illustrated,* when he was at home; and on the weekends, he visited with his kids from a previous marriage, or he window shopped with his current wife and his stepdaughter, as they found this to be a relaxing way to spend time together. Rob read the *San Francisco Chronicle* and the *San Jose Mercury News* on his breaks at work; at home during the day, in addition to watching television, he sometimes read science fiction, fantasy, and history books; he also listened to talk radio as an alternative to television; and, sometimes, he simply slept for an hour or so before work. On the weekends, he regularly spent time with his wife and kids. Typically, they did things outdoors, like going to the beach or for walks; they shopped, or went to flea-markets; and he also worked on household projects by himself. Don did not read the newspaper, or magazines, and he seldom read books, either. But, on the weekends, he and his family visited regularly with his parents, or his wife's parents; he worked on his own or friends' cars; he played around with the kids at home; and he did yardwork.

Newspaper and magazine stories, the ideas found in books, the differing perspectives heard on talk radio, the ways of seeing things, as well as the give and take that are an integral part of conversation and interaction with others, all of this enabled these men to become mindfully engaged and to make their experiences meaningful outside of the television context. Although newspapers, magazines, radio, and even books are certainly forms of *mass* media, their content is not shaped by marketing and ideological restrictions in the same way, or to the same degree, that the programming of commercial television is. For this reason, they served as *alternatives* to television and provided these men with images, ideas, and information with which to understand something of themselves and their social world in a different way from that typically provided by television. Conversation and interaction with others did much the same thing, but in ways that were, for the most part, much more removed from the commercial and ideological influences that are a part of media discourses. When they talked with their spouses, their children, or with co-workers and friends, these men became mindfully engaged in other discourses, besides television, and, because of that, they regularly had the opportunity to see themselves, others, and their world differently. Exposure to this wider range of ideas constitutes an important part of the sociality of their television use.

Beyond this exposure to alternative images and ideas, there is the *mindful form* of their orientation to and involvement in activities, including television, to consider. The daily social experience of watching television is realized in different ways for each of them.

Rob takes the *least* mindful approach, turning to television out of habit, he said, seeing it "as a way of winding down after work," and as something "to just have on in the background" before work and on the weekends. But when it comes to Forty Niner games, or other noteworthy sporting events, he takes a much more mindful approach to television, actually planning ahead of time to watch, which means not only organizing in his mind what *else* he would or wouldn't do, but also anticipating it as kind of a stimulating and playful activity. Don also flips on the television when he comes home from work, but he said he does so with the idea in mind of getting away from work, a seemingly small and momentary kind of recognition on his part, but one that is not evident in Rob's account. Don is more mindful of escaping the feelings left over from work, it seems. And he, like Rob, takes a more mindful approach to television on the weekends and in the early evenings before work, looking forward to boxing, *The Wizard,* or rented movies as a potentially more playful and stimulating experience as well. Phil takes this kind of more-mindful approach to television from the very start. He seems to separate, in his mind, the feelings that carry over from work and the playfulness and pleasure that he wants to get from being entertained. He takes this approach to watching *I Love Lucy* and *Perry Mason* before work, too.

Mindful orientation to television

Although I do not want to underestimate the habitual nature of turning to television, the interview accounts of all three of these men indicate that, both individually and as a group, there is significant variation in their mindful orientation to television. Aside from Rob's automatic and unthinking initial approach, all three men at different times linked the idea of getting away from (escaping) feelings associated with work with the idea of using their minds or stimulating their imagination (play), or else they clearly stated that this sense of using their minds or stimulating their imagination was there from the start of their thoughts associated with watching television. These ideas – of escape and play – were often closely linked in their minds, and together they became associated with their looking forward to television viewing as a pleasurable and even thought-provoking experience. In effect, by orienting themselves to television with such ideas in mind, these men are representing to themselves something of where it is they have *come from*, mindfully and emotionally speaking, and where they would like to *move to*. Their linking of these ideas, or, more simply, their holding ideas about playfulness or imaginative use in mind, is momentary, but it is the existence of such qualities of mindfulness, not their duration, that matters most. In distinguishing thoughts they have at home from whatever thoughts and feelings that they might have carried over from work, these people are in effect creating a mindful space that then enables them to anticipate their own imaginative involvement with television and to envision, however briefly, what they might want to watch and the ways they might want to feel when they watch. Acting in this more mindful way is different from acting out of habit, which is what Rob did on many occasions, and what the majority of the people I interviewed said they typically do when they turn to television or to other activities after work. (I discuss this group in the section, "Turning to television less mindfully.") Unless it is contrasted with a more automatic or unthinking approach, this anticipation of a certain playfulness, this envisioning of an imaginative use of one's intellect, cannot be fully understood on its own. Like the act of watching television itself, this quality of people's orientation *to* the medium is an integral part of their ritual of use. Furthermore, their mindful approach to television is often on a par with the approach they take to many other activities they become involved in.

The anticipation of playfulness, the desire for stimulation is something that Rob, for example, looked for when he oriented himself to (thought about) listening to the radio, taking up household projects, going shopping or to flea-markets, or taking walks with his family; it was something that Don envisioned when he prepared to work on cars, play around with his kids, or visit with family; and it was something that Phil had in mind when he went running, visited with his kids, or went shopping with the family.

By persisting through their *repeated* involvement with television and other activities, this quality of mindfulness plays an ongoing role in distinguishing what is *social* about the way that these particular people continue to bring television into their lives.

Not surprisingly, this quality of mindfulness extends beyond their orientation and into their actual involvement with television, and with other activities, as well. As I said earlier, when these men became mindfully involved with what they watched, they were at times both accepting and critical of the shows. They also frequently imagined themselves, if only momentarily, in the place of the people they saw on television. Furthermore, the fact that these men sat and watched some programs in an uninterrupted manner, and paid close attention to social action, means that their viewing often had continuity to it. And the fact that they sometimes followed shows over time, as Rob did with *All My Children* or Phil did with *I Love Lucy* and *Perry Mason*, or that they kept up with their favorite sports teams from game to game, as Rob did with the Forty Niners, means that this continuity is able to develop over time. This degree of mindfulness is also a characteristic of the conversations and interactions that are an integral part of their walks and visits, shopping, and hobbies that they undertook with others. It also figures importantly in their solitary activities. The specific activities besides watching television that these men pursued, day-in and day-out, and how long these activities, including television viewing, lasted, varied a great deal, of course. In doing any and all of these activities, they had thoughts and feelings, evaluated courses of action, judged the plausibility of ideas and actions, and, at times, took a reflexive stance on things. This is what constitutes the mindfulness of living everyday life for them.

Television's power mediated

Woven through all of this is television's power: the power to establish meaningful parameters for the social world of these men and the power to give meaningful form to the interpretations that they make of programming. Television's power is working, it is doing these things *to* them, and yet, it cannot be separated, really, from the degree of mindfulness that characterized their viewing activity. Their mindfulness is not reducible *only* to the workings of power, even when oppositional interpretations are included in the definition of power. Beyond viewing *per se,* we have seen that the mindful ways they turn to television and other activities, as well as the mindfulness they exhibit while involved in other activities, counterbalance the power that television exercises in their lives. In addition to being something that is constituted in and through power, this degree of mindfulness is indicative of a sociality that gets created and is sustained when people use television, a sociality that is evident in many other things they do as well. More than that, though, it is indicative of the workings of a *self*, of a person who has the capabilities to act, to judge, and, most importantly, to make an object of his or her own social conditions, including, of course, television use. There are times television does have the power to fill or otherwise constitute a person's mindful experience. But at other times it does not and it cannot, precisely because this sociality extends into areas beyond the reach of television on an ongoing basis, even while television remains an important part of one's life. In the case of these three men, the emergence and continued existence of this sociality or of their sense of self should not be conflated with the interpretive process. The sociality in their lives is the other side of television's power in their lives.

Turning to television less mindfully

In much of the critical commentary about television, analysts come to the conclusion that television has the power to *standardize* people's mindful experience. This is certainly the case in critical theory accounts, particularly in the work of Adorno and Horkheimer (1972), and Marcuse (1964), where the mind*less*ness of television use – indeed, of media use more generally – is understood to carry rather debilitating consequences regarding the fate of democratic culture and possibilities for social change. In some ways, this is an old argument, but it is one that still merits some attention. More recently, such fears about the way that some people use television are empirically substantiated in research undertaken by Kubey and Csikszentmihalyi and reported in *Television and the Quality of Life* (1990). The authors found many people consistently reported that television viewing was a passive activity for them, and that it required little concentration on their part compared to a variety of other leisure time activities. They also found that some people turned to television to ease the discomfort that they felt in experiencing "unstructured time," and that the medium helped them to, in the authors' words, "maintain psychological stability." Furthermore, they argued that the persistence of heavy viewing can cause further intolerance for unstructured time, leading people back to television, and, in the process, solidifying television's hold on their mindful and emotional experience.

Television is, among other things, a medium that can be watched, *just watched*, day after day. The imagery simply flows. By just watching, people can register and recognize social meanings in what they see and hear without necessarily having to monitor, evaluate, or judge what it is that passes before them on the screen. It is often argued that television relieves people of the responsibility for having to make their experience meaningful, and in doing so it fosters a kind of mind*less*ness. People do not have to participate actively, control the pace, develop continuity, or gain insight as they watch. Television is a force that can slowly and gently lessen what is mindfully required of people in order for them to see themselves as involved in something or doing something. It has the power to provide people with the pleasure of *not* having to think about what they do. Over time, this less mindful way, or "mindless" way, of watching television can extend, quite insidiously, to the very way that people come to orient themselves to the medium in the first place. When this happens, television has the power to provide people with the pleasure of not having to think about *how* they are viewing and thinking of television. This is a way that some people become habituated to television. This is what I mean when I say that television has the power to standardize people's mindful experience.

Eight of the people that I interviewed reported a pattern of television use in which such a power effect is evident. These eight regularly turned to television viewing after work, but not every night after work, as with the previously examined three men. When these eight people turned to television, their turn was characterized by "less mindfulness" than when they turned to other activities at this time. This less mindful turn to television is what distinguished them from the others I interviewed. These eight people included four women and four men. Five of them identified as white, while Annie identified as Puerto Rican, Jose as Filipino–American, and Frank as Chinese–American.

Each of these eight people worked a regular day shift, and their after-work routines included a number of activities that varied from day to day, depending on their situation and mood. Each of them typically approached their activities with different qualities of mindfulness and they participated in different activities, too. Because they did not turn exclusively to television after work, television did not have the power to establish discursive parameters for their worlds in the same way that it did for Rob, Don, and Phil in the previous section. It is precisely because these eight people did not usually watch television in a focused way in the after-work period that television's power did not work to structure their interpretive process in quite the same manner as it did for the earlier three. But television's power did work in the lives of these eight in a different way: by standardizing their way of thinking about doing things over time.

The less mindful turn to television that emerged from the accounts of this group of eight is, at least on the surface, indicative of a standardizing kind of power effect. All of these people said that their turn to television after work had become patterned in such a way that it involved less of a presence of mind than the way that they typically did other things at this time. This occurred in different ways. In the majority of cases, these people turned to television, they said, simply out of habit.

Marjorie, a production manager at a publishing house, came home, turned the television on, and proceeded to do her household chores. Ray, a designer at the publishing company, did much the same thing. So, too, did Annie, a clerk in the shipping department at Lipton, and Jose, a warehouseman there. And, in a slight departure from this basic pattern established by the others, Janine, a production editor at the publishing company, said that it was her husband who often turned on television out of habit, but she heard it while she cooked in the kitchen, and, even though she initially saw herself as alone with her thoughts in the kitchen, the fact that the television was on was enough for it to have become a part of her routine, too. This occurred for her, as it did for the others, without any awareness of what she was missing, emotionally or mindfully speaking, or what she was getting herself into by having the television on.

In describing this particular after-work routine, neither Marjorie, Ray, Annie, Jose, or Janine made any mention, really, of the momentary kind of *looking forward* to television that characterized a more playful approach to doing things; nor did any of them remark about a desire to get away from thoughts or feelings associated with work, as did many other people. Rather, the language of their accounts indicated that turning to television was just something that they did after work. Although among them the shows watched, the time they spent watching, and the level of their attentiveness varied, they all had a routine in which television was turned to in an unthinking way.

But this is not the only set of circumstances in which television represented something less mindful to do after work in my interviews.

Mitchell, a production manager at the publishing house, generally turned to television and kept it on while he prepared dinner, ate, and read through the newspaper; but, rather than just turning it on, as with the others just discussed, he approached it, he said, with the idea of it being something stimulating, something playful, something that would occupy his mind for a while after work. The same was true of Carol, an acquisitions editor where Mitchell worked, and Frank, a maintenance mechanic at Lipton. Both of them, when they turned to television, did so not just out of habit, or to get away from things, but rather, like Mitchell, with the idea of engaging their minds in an interesting or stimulating manner for a while. Carol sometimes looked forward to watching the news in this way. In

Frank's case, watching television was something fun to do with his two young boys; an opportunity for them to "exchange ideas with one another," no matter what they watched.

Mitchell, Carol, and Frank each turned to one or two activities after work in the same way they turned to television, but for each of them there were still other activities to which they turned more mindfully – in a reflective manner.

Although Mitchell generally turned to television in a playful manner after work, he also turned to phoning friends or going out for drinks after work in a less mindful way than he turned to reading fiction. For Carol, turning to television held the same preparatory weight as turning to playing the piano, but was a less mindful turn than preparing to go to bible class or playing racquetball with friends. Similarly, Frank turned to television in the same way he turned to spending time with his children, but he turned more mindfully to doing projects around the house.

In contrast to their turn to television, all three of these people turned to at least some other activities after work in a more mindful – reflective – way.

For each of these eight people, turning to television represents a step down, mindfully speaking, from the way that they typically oriented themselves to doing other things after work. It is the consistency of the less mindful turn to television that emerges as an important feature of their continued contact with the medium through the years. Over time, it seems, turning to television had become ritualized in such a way that these people implicitly understood that watching television, relative to the other things that they regularly did, required less of their mindful and emotional energy.

As an analyst, I do not wish to dispute the empirical existence of television's power working to standardize mindful experience; nor would I want to argue, at a more abstract, theoretical level of analysis, that television was not capable of producing this kind of power effect. But, having said this, it seems to me that such a standardizing effect, to the extent that it does, indeed, occur in these people's lives, is by definition, *counterbalanced* by the *more* mindful turn that they routinely made to other activities. To say that people turn to television in a less mindful manner than they turn to other activities is also to say that they turn to other activities in a *more* mindful manner than they do television. Tautological reasoning aside, the evidence of a standardizing effect only makes sense because there is, at the same time, the equally evident patterning of a more mindful turn to other activities, as well as the actual involvement by these people in other activities besides television. Even when a kind of standardization of thinking may be produced by television as one of its power effects, such an idea of power cannot by itself explain all that is significant about the way that television works in people's everyday lives. When ideas about power are formulated without any explicit consideration of variations and differences in mindfulness, we are often led to see resistant, or oppositional *interpretations* as the most likely limit, or alternative, to power. Such critical interpretations represent a kind of practical knowledge that people who watch television have by virtue of their social positioning in the broader culture, and, when it is the power of the text that is at issue, critical interpretations offer evidence of a limit to that power in establishing meaningful parameters or in structuring interpretive processes.

But such formulations of resistance or limits to power are not very helpful when it comes to issues of standardization, because, in this case, we are talking about television's power to structure the *very capability* of people to be mindful participants in their own lives. This is not a question of whether or not people who watch television make this or that interpretation; rather, it is a question of their ability to be mindful enough to engage in interpretative activity of any consequence. This is where the construct of mindfulness becomes important, because it enables significant comparisons to be made regarding the formation of a person's thinking across an entire range of activities that constitute daily life. In this way, the standardization of thinking that may occur as a result of people repeatedly turning to television is not seen in isolation. Instead, it is viewed in relation to other patterns of mindful activity (including interpretive activity) that are also an ongoing part of people's lives.

All eight of the people who watched television "less mindfully" after work regularly turned to other activities, besides television, after work as well.

Marjorie worked in the garden; Annie played tennis; Ray biked or shot baskets; Janine did volunteer work or walked her dogs on the beach; Jose went out to dinner with his family or carried out different household projects; Frank worked on projects around the house; Carol went out to dinner, played racquetball, or attended bible-study class; and Mitchell read fiction. In almost all cases, they said that they turned to these other activities in a more mindful way than they turned to television. For example, Ray looked to biking and shooting baskets as a way to "just get away, to get my mind off things for a while," and Annie approached playing tennis in much the same way. Janine thought about walking the dogs the same way that Jose envisioned eating dinner out for a change: with a certain kind of playfulness in mind, looking forward to the stimulation, the engagement that these things would provide for them. When Marjorie was going to work in the garden, when Janine was going to do volunteer work, when Jose and Frank undertook household projects, or when Mitchell read fiction, each of them said they deliberated with themselves a bit before coming to the decision to do these things. They thought about what it was that they wanted to do with their time, about how they were feeling, and about the options available to them. Sometimes, they weighed in their minds the pros and cons of becoming involved in this or that activity, including how they thought they might end up feeling if they chose one thing to do as opposed to another, before they actually decided what to do.

Compared to watching television, these kinds of activities represented much more of a mindful and emotional commitment on their part, and this was reflected, it seemed, in the mindfulness with which they approached these activities, too. Even though their approach to these activities, like their approach to any and all activities that they pursued, had become ritualized, the ritual itself had, over time, taken on and maintained its own distinctive mindful qualities.

Of course, their everyday, after-work routines did not always conform to this pattern in which television was turned to less mindfully than other activities. There were instances in which people turned to television, and other activities besides television, in the same way.

Jose sometimes approached listening to music in the same *un*thinking way that he went about watching television while he and his wife fixed dinner and took care of the kids after work. And, in one type of situation, it was Carol who said that she actually turned to television in a *more* mindful way than she typically went about fixing dinner and listening to music.

In one sense, these cases are exceptions to the broader, more consistent pattern of television's standardizing effect; but, on the other hand, they offer further evidence of the variability that constitutes the mindfulness of everyday social experience.

In the evening, television continued to play a role in all their lives, but it did so differently, again reflecting the fact that variations in mindfulness are intrinsic to their use of television itself, apart from other activities.

For Frank and Jose, watching television served as the primary way that they spent time together with their families. In Frank's case, interestingly enough, he said that, compared to the after-work period, he approached television in a *less* mindful way in the evening. He, his wife, and their two boys watched a wide range of programs together – from nature shows on PBS, to family oriented network shows, to old movies on cable. This was their way of spending time together as a family; over time, they had simply fallen into the habit of it. But this did not mean that there was not much that was mindful about it. For example, when he and his two sons watched *Eight Is Enough,* they discussed moral issues that might have been raised, not in any self-conscious way, but simply as a practical part of understanding the show. They often came away from watching, he said, feeling that they had learned something together and that what they had learned was perhaps applicable to how *they* related as a family. Typically, after the boys went to bed, Frank and his wife continued to watch together, with shows like *Cagney and Lacey, Hill Street Blues,* and the various network news magazine shows comprising the usual fare. While his wife was typically less attentive to what was on than he was, this did not really matter to Frank, because, like the viewing they both did with their sons, this was simply a time to be together, to talk and interact, to share experiences with one another. This was what "family time" with television often meant.

In Jose's case, television was a primary evening activity for his family, but not the only one. They usually sat and watched together (although it was as likely for the kids to sometimes watch television in another room), and, for him, with the exception of *Amazing Stories* and Boston Celtics games, it was more important that they were together than that they watched specific shows. Sometimes, while watching, he thought about or actually started "drafting out" projects that he planned to complete around the house, like building the backyard fence or remodeling the kitchen. Besides television, he said that he and his wife spent at least one night a week "just talking, with the television off," and this served as a way for them to "get caught up on whatever things we had of mutual interest, like the kids or the house." In addition, Jose also played music regularly, which meant that, at least one night a week, he got together with his musician friends "just to create music together." And all of these things, Jose said, he approached in a playful way, looking forward to them as something that would be stimulating and fun to do. This was a significant move *up*, mindfully speaking, from the more automatic way that he typically turned to television after work.

For Annie, who lived alone, the television typically stayed on right through the late afternoon and on into the evening; it was something that she just did out of habit. Occasionally, she focused her attention on a show, or a segment of a show, but otherwise she used it as a background while she talked on the phone, ate, cleaned up, or otherwise did things around the house. On Tuesday nights, things were a bit different, because her favorite shows were on: *Who's The Boss, Moonlighting,* and *Jack and Mike.* In contrast to just having the television "on," she oriented herself to these shows in a more mindful way, looking forward to the pleasure and imaginative enjoyment this provided. She watched these shows more mindfully than when she watched television at other times, too. She stopped whatever else she was doing and stayed involved "all the way through." Mitchell, who also lived alone, said that television was his "primary form of attention" in the evening. He said he had many favorite shows – *LA Law, Cheers, Hill Street Blues, MASH, Family Ties, Cosby,* and *Moonlighting* among them – and he came to these shows with the same playful orientation that he took to television and other activities after work. But Mitchell said that there were also evenings, or certainly parts of evenings, when the television was turned off and he read fiction instead; or, on still other occasions, he went out with friends or co-workers, perhaps to a movie, or to a bar where they talked and just spent time together.

For Carol, Marjorie, Janine, and Ray, television played a less prominent role in their evening free time than it did for the other four. In Carol's case, between her evening class at a local community college, the studying she had to do for it, and the time she spent reading fiction, playing piano, and listening to music, there was little time left over to watch television. She preferred music to television as a background while she read or studied, and what little television watching she did do was, like almost everything else, the result of a deliberate choice on her part. She said that she looked through the television listing in the Sunday paper to plan out in advance which shows she would watch for the week; and when the time approached for one of these shows to air, she looked forward to it as a time for relaxing, but in a mindfully engaging manner. Marjorie was also quite deliberate in deciding how to spend her evening. Typically, she read fiction, wrote letters to friends and relatives (in England), or wrote in her journal, and, as a lesser option, she decided to watch specific shows on television, preferring *Mystery* and other BBC dramas over the typical network fare. Interestingly enough, Marjorie turned to television in the evening in a considerably more mindful way than she did after work, when she just came home and turned it on. In Janine's case, she typically read, or spent time talking or watching television with her husband in the evening. Television served as a kind of "fall back" activity for them, something to do if she tired of reading, or if she or her husband did not have the energy for talk and interaction alone. She and her husband had favorite shows: among them were *Cagney and Lacey, Hill Street Blues, Moonlighting,* and *LA Law,* and if a San Francisco Giants baseball game happened to be televised, well, that too became a "favorite." Like Marjorie, Janine said she turned to television more mindfully in the evening, indicating, once again, that people approached television differently at different times, depending on the situation and their mood. Janine also attended Alcoholics Anonymous meetings, and sometimes she did volunteer work in the evening, too, with both of these activities adding further to the diversity and depth of her mindful experience outside of work. Ray turned off the television after dinner and chose to read or paint in the evening, seeing both of these activities, but especially painting, as ways to use his time creatively. Oftentimes, the stereo, rather than the television, was on while he read or painted. He interspersed his television viewing with more sustained periods of reading or painting, and on those occasions when he brought work home, watching television served as a kind of respite from its mindful demands as well. Typically, Ray started out doing these other things, and, when his attention began to waver, he simply turned to television, watched for a while, then turned it off and took up his reading, or painting, or work again. He also had favorite shows, such as *Cheers, LA Law,* baseball games, and boxing matches, and he looked forward to watching these, anticipating the pleasure and stimulation that they provided for him. In both cases, either as an escape from more demanding activities, or as a playful activity in its own right, watching television was for Ray a *more* mindful activity in the evening than right after work, when, he said, he turned to it simply out of habit.

Notwithstanding all of the significant variations in the amount of time these people spent watching television, or the kinds of programming they preferred to watch, it was clear from the interview accounts that the act of watching often provided opportunities, even if they were only momentary

in nature, for reflecting on the significance of stories, events, or issues, sometimes critically. And sometimes it provided simply an opportunity for these
people to imagine themselves differently. When they watched television,
they were often engaged in a process of *symbolization*, a formative process,
and they were often involved in the exercise of *capabilities of self*. When
these people treated television as a mindful activity, watching television
became an activity that had continuity to it. As viewers they were able to
gain insight into themselves, others, or their world as a result. All of this
routinely occurred amidst the workings of television's power, whether that
was the power to establish parameters of meaning, the power to structure
the interpretive process, or the power to standardize thinking.

The same possibilities for symbolization existed in their mindful involvement with the wide range of activities in which they reported participating
regularly in their lives. Typically, these other activities, things such as
reading, writing letters, talking with family and friends, and painting,
enabled them to be active, to control the pace, to develop continuities, and
to gain insight as well; perhaps even more so than was the case with their
television watching. The simple fact that *all* of these people *regularly*
became involved in other things, besides watching television, is evidence
that a mindful counterweight to television's standardizing effect did, in fact,
exist in their lives.

Furthermore, the fact that these people turned to other activities, and in
some cases to television as well, in a playful or a more reflective way indicates they were capable of moving beyond an unthinking approach to
things and capable of a somewhat more mindful approach to getting away
from thoughts and feelings carried over from work; an absence of either of
these capabilities could be associated with the standardizing effect that is
often associated with television. These people, however, were able to see
themselves as desirous of becoming involved in activities in a way that
would stimulate their imagination, and require a continued presence of
mind on their part.

In conclusion, then, although a standardization of thinking may be produced by television as one of its power effects, it is an effect that always, at
the same time, needs to be contextualized amidst constructs of mindfulness. It is this mindfulness, in all its varied forms, that comprises the *sociality* of television use. This sociality – of turning to television and watching
it, of turning to other activities and becoming involved in them – is an indispensable part of what actually constitutes the evidence for standardization.
However persistent television's power effects may be, that degree of persistence can be matched by the sociality of the viewing culture, and, because
of this, it is not so easily subsumed under the markers of discursive power

effects. As we saw with Rob, Don, and Phil, the three men who turned exclusively to television after work, this sociality is, really, the other side of television's power. At the same time that Frank, Jose, Marjorie, Janine, Mitchell, Ray, Annie, and Carol have become used to a "relatively mindless" (i.e., less mindful that other activities) use of television, they also continue to constitute themselves in more mindful ways, both by turning to and becoming involved in other activities besides television on a regular basis. In addition, a few of them do this by sometimes turning to television itself in more mindful ways. When people act mindfully in these ways, they act *as a self*. By acting as a self, they complicate analytical assertions that simply equate one's turn to television with a standardization, or leveling, of that person's thinking processes. The interviews, along with my direct observations, indicate that these viewers are *aware* that they typically turned to television less mindfully than they ordinarily turned to other activities, and, thus, that they recognize their own involvement in the medium's power effects.

Turning to television while pursuing other activities simultaneously

Approximately twenty-five of the working people that I interviewed did not typically separate their turn to television from their turn to other activities in the after-work period. Instead, they said that they turned to both television and other activities *at the same time*. This way of watching television represents one of the most significant, and unanticipated, findings that emerged from my research. I have come to refer to this particular use of television, viewing while simultaneously pursuing other activities, as *simultaneous viewing*. In analyzing this particular use of television, I argue that power works here in different ways at the same time, which is, in part, what constitutes the mindful complexity of simultaneous viewing. Because these people paid intermittent attention to television, the medium did not establish meaningful parameters for them, as it did for the three who turned to television exclusively after work. But television's power does play a role in structuring their interpretive processes, a role in which the workings of discursive power shifts from the more elaborate representations of social action found in story-lines and broader narrative trajectories of shows, to the shorter, hyper-ritualized scenes of social action within programs. Interestingly enough, this results in a dissociation, rather than a centering, of meaning–making on the part of television viewers, which raises important questions concerning the hegemonic role of television in people's lives. Television also works to habituate people to expect, and seek out, a relatively mindless kind of involvement in activities during simultaneous viewing. This is similar to the standardizing effect that I discussed in the previous section of this chapter ("Turning to television less mindfully"), although the standardizing effect works differently here, since, in simultaneous viewing, television is turned to at the same time as other activities, rather than being turned to less mindfully than other activities. Yet, even with these power dynamics operating as they do in these people's lives, they by no means constitute all that is socially significant in their everyday lives. Again, as I have shown in the previous two sections, it is through the formation of a sociality in the turn to television that the power effects are contextualized and in many instances limited.

Ten of the twenty-five people in this category of simultaneous viewers said that they almost always turned simultaneously to television and other activities after work, and doing other things unrelated to television was for them, at this particular time, very much the exception rather than the rule. Of course, on occasion, they came home from work and did things without the television on; or, alternatively, they visited friends or family, or went shopping. These things happened sometimes. But typically, they said, they came home from work, and if the television was not already on, they turned it on and kept it on while they, and perhaps other members of their household, proceeded to do a variety of other things that had become part of their after-work routine.

For example, Barbara, a senior editorial supervisor at the publishing house, turned the television on as soon as she came home, and watched the local and national news as she went about preparing dinner and taking care of things around the house. Pam, a clerk at Lipton, did much the same thing. By the time she came home, either her husband or one of her sons would have already turned on the television, so it simply was there for her as she prepared dinner, took care of household responsibilities, and talked with her sons and husband. Similar patterns were reported by the others, too.

In addition to these 10, there were 4 others whose patterns were practically the same, but who made a point in the interviews of telling me that alternatives to this simultaneous viewing routine existed for them in theory, but instead, when it came time to choose, they turned to the simultaneous viewing pattern.

For example, Deana, a laboratory technician at Lipton, said that she had the time to shop for herself after work and sometimes thought about doing so, but usually she did not. Similarly, she thought about reading instead of watching television when she came home, but usually she did not do this either.

It may be that by reporting that they considered but did not actually engage in other activities, this was a way for these people to rationalize, to me, the interviewer, their seemingly mindless use of television: they *could* do other things if they wanted, but they chose not to. The other ten made no mention of these other possibilities for mindful involvement.

This brought to 14 the number of people for whom simultaneous viewing was their primary, if not exclusive, after-work activity. This group constituted approximately one-fourth of the people that I interviewed. For these particular people, turning to television in this way had become a habit; they just did it automatically, without thinking, when they came home from work. Furthermore, in establishing this particular pattern of television use, these people excluded other, discrete activities from their daily routine. As a result, there was no mindful counterweight, in the form of other, ongoing activities, to the role that television played in their lives at this time.

Another 11 of these 25 people said that they, too, turned, simultaneously, to television and other activities after work, but with one notable difference compared to the 14 just discussed: these 11 *also* turned, with some regularity, to other activities besides television during this time. They did this, they said, in the same mindful way that they turned to simultaneous viewing, which meant that, at the outset, they did not ordinarily envision their involvement with television differently than they did these other activities. This was not the case, for example, for the six people who, in one way or another, turned to television *less* mindfully than they turned to other activities.

For instance, Paula, a telephone operator at the publishing house, ordinarily had the television on while she prepared dinner and tidied up around the house, but she also sometimes took walks, or read the newspaper or magazines instead; Nan, a machine operator at Lipton, usually watched television with her boyfriend as they relaxed and prepared dinner together, but sometimes she visited with friends or went shopping instead; and for Kurt, who worked on the loading dock at Lipton, simultaneous viewing was his "routine of choice" after work, but he also became involved in one or another of his ongoing household projects with some regularity. Similar accounts were offered by other people as well.

The particular activities differed from person to person, but the fact that each of them turned to other activities, besides simultaneous viewing, was a constant across all eleven interview accounts. Even though these people, too, watched television while simultaneously doing other things, this kind of viewing did not occupy the same prominent and constant position in their lives as it did in the lives of the 14 people who always viewed simultaneously after work. In contrast to the 14, these 11 *regularly* became involved in activities that did not revolve around the world of television or become broken up by it on an ongoing basis.

Frequently occurring activities

For all 25 of these people (a little less than half of the people I interviewed), this way of spending time after work had become *automatic* for them. There were numerous activities that typically took place in conjunction with television use, and this varied from person to person, depending, for the most part, on whether they lived alone or with other people. Living with family or roommates often complicated the simultaneous viewing routine, because, every activity was now, at least potentially, a socially interactive one. In general, though, the hustle and bustle of household life was considerably greater when family members or housemates were present, which meant that a person's involvement in any particular activity was more likely to be interrupted, which, in turn, meant that people were more likely to experience shifts in mindfulness as they moved back and forth between various levels and types of activities.

For those who lived alone, interaction with others was not typically a part of their simultaneous viewing routine, unless, of course, they talked on the phone with family or friends, which was, for some people, a common occurrence. For the most part, the people who lived alone enjoyed a greater freedom in structuring their daily routines.

Virtually all of these people said that they typically took care of the more mundane household chores or responsibilities they felt needed to be done. These things included preparing dinner or a snack, washing clothes, straightening up the house, vacuuming, taking out the garbage, sorting through the mail, paying bills, and working on various small "fix-it" jobs around the house. Many, if not most, of the women I interviewed felt a greater sense of responsibility, if not of need, for attending to the day-to-day work that kept the household functioning smoothly. Whether by design or by choice, it was they, more often than the men, who cooked, cleaned, washed clothes, etc. In contrast, the men spoke of doing yardwork, or working on projects of various sorts around the house, things such as woodworking, replacing tile, and painting, that were a step removed from what had to be done everyday. (This is not to say that many of the men did not at times also assume responsibility for cooking or cleaning or doing housework, because they often did. These kinds of gender-defined household roles are evident in many of the interview accounts.)

Next on the list of most frequently occurring activities was casual conversation with family members or housemates (and this included, for some people, talking on the phone). People said that they typically moved in and out of casual conversations, and, sometimes, these casual conversations might deepen into more serious discussions having to do with such topics as work, their children's school activities, their housemates' social lives, paying bills, the pros and cons of making a major household purchase, or other issues pertaining to family or household relations. Occasionally, some of them said, time was set aside for more structured kinds of discussions or social interactions, such as helping their children with homework, or talking through a more immediate issue or problem which might have come up with a family member or housemate and that needed to be dealt with right away. In addition to conversation and social interaction, some people (though fewer in number) also used at least some portion of this transition time after work to read the newspaper or page through magazines, sometimes doing so while they sat and watched television.

Use of television during simultaneous viewing

With regard to the actual use of the television during simultaneous viewing, people reported watching and listening to news (both local and national), game shows, syndicated reruns of prime-time network programs, and, to a lesser extent, talk shows and previously recorded programming (usually soap operas). The segmented formats of news and game shows, in particular, were quite compatible with the demands of simultaneous viewing. Compared to typical television drama or situation comedy formats, the news typically presented short and, for the most part, unrelated news items that viewers either followed or ignored as they saw fit. Although the structure of game shows resembles the traditional narrative structure, the game shows are segmented into a succession of puzzles, or games within a game, and people reported that they could pick and choose what they wanted to watch here as well. The fact that the rules of the game are relatively simple and known in advance by those who watch meant that they could follow the dialogue and interaction of the participants in these shows with less attention than, say, a soap opera or a drama. This was true, too, although perhaps not to the same degree, for the reruns of prime-time programming that some people watched after work. Taken together, news, game shows, and prime-time reruns constituted 85 percent of the programming that people tuned into when they became involved in simultaneous viewing after work.

For some people, such as Ellie, a forklift operator at Lipton, or Tom, a building mechanic there, the television was on while they prepared dinner, sorted through the mail, cleaned up a bit around the house, and ate. For others, like, Erica, who does data entry at Lipton, or Phyllis, a senior production editor at the publishing house, the television was on while they cooked, snacked, took care of various household chores, talked on the phone, and read through the newspaper. For others still, like Paul, a production editor, or Deana, a laboratory technician at Lipton, the television was on while they did all of these things and talked with their spouses, too, trading stories about their respective days at work, or other topics. And, in Deana's case, life was fuller, still, after work, because she regularly took at least some time to talk with her two children, perhaps helping them with the day's homework assignments.

Duration of simultaneous viewing

Simultaneous viewing typically lasted anywhere from an hour and a half to two, or sometimes two-and-a-half hours, as people moved back and forth, continually, between watching or listening to something on television and doing any, or all, of these other things. Cooking, cleaning, talking, reading, and so on – all of this went on, from their point of view, at the *same* time. Most people said that they held to this routine until just after dinner time, when they, and usually others in their family or household, too, faced a decision, of sorts, as to what to do with the rest of their evening. None of them did exactly the same things, in the same way, everyday. No doubt, there were variations in their routines. In fact, in the interviews, they sometimes found it difficult to reconstruct what typically transpired from moment to moment in any single situation of simultaneous viewing, or, for that matter, in one situation as opposed to another. The time that people typically spent in one or another activity, how particular activities succeeded one another in time, how, when, and why people shifted their attention from one activity to another, how their mindful involvement varied from one activity to another, how and when they brought their participation in any of these activities to a close – all of this was, for them, generally unpredictable.

Patterns of mindfulness

Although it was difficult, if not impossible, to define a single, mindful pattern that dominated during simultaneous viewing periods, there were, nevertheless, regularities evident in this kind of television use. After careful consideration of all of the interview accounts of people's turns to television, as well as a systematic review of field notes pertaining to my observation of and participation in the viewing culture, I found that the regularities comprising simultaneous viewing were perhaps best described as occurring along a continuum of use. The continuum ranged from intermittent viewing to focused, interpretive viewing.

At one end of this continuum, television played more of a background role for people as they carried on with any number of the things that I have mentioned – cooking, cleaning, eating, talking, reading, and so on. People followed what was on television, but in an intermittent manner. Oftentimes, they listened more than they actually watched. On occasion, a particular news story, or an exciting moment in a game show or a sitcom rerun caught their attention, and they stopped what else they were doing and focused on what was on television. At moments such as these, they were drawn into the representational world that television provided for them, and they did so in a way that approximated the kind of mindful involvement that they typically exhibited when they watched television in a more careful and focused way, which was usually later in the evening. (This was similar to the more focused kind of viewing that Rob, Don, and Phil exhibited when they used television after work.) These were interpretive moments, and sometimes they found things plausible, sometimes not. In either case, at this end of the simultaneous viewing continuum, the more focused, interpretive moments passed rather quickly, because people's attention usually shifted back to their involvement in another activity, whether it was cooking, cleaning, snacking, talking, or something else. After all, people who were using television in this way, were not that intent on sustaining these kinds of interpretive moments to begin with. Even so, most people indicated that, even after they turned their attention back to doing other things, they continued to keep an eye, or ear, open to what was on television, so as not to miss anything exciting or important that might have come up. At this end of the continuum of simultaneous viewing, the actual time spent watching, or listening, to television was clearly outweighed by people's involvement in other activities. But, because the television stayed on, programming could always be heard, if not watched, and this alone made it possible for their involvement in the other activities to be interrupted at any time. Consequently, people could, also at any time, immediately be *there*, in the image worlds of television, with all the power that they carried for organizing their meaningful experience.

This kind of simultaneous viewing was exemplified in the daily routine that Patricia, a secretary at the Lipton plant, maintained for herself and her family after work.

Married, with a son, Patricia said that "the TV is already on when I come home, because my son is watching." After settling into things, she said that she usually just proceeded to cook and clean and her son continued to watch cartoons or *Sesame Street*. At some point, she said, her son began his homework, and she helped him with some of it while she continued cooking and attending to her other household responsibilities. Amidst all of this, she usually switched the television to the local news, since her son was now occupied with other things. "Having the TV on," she said, "helps me to relax." Patricia said that she liked the local news and soap operas because, as she put it, "I can follow [them] without having to pay much attention to what's on. Things are simple enough that I can understand what happens [without paying much attention]. I can miss parts of shows and it won't bother me." Usually, she watched the news, but if she remembered to tape *One Life To Live*, her favorite soap that was on earlier in the day, she popped it in the VCR and had that on instead of the news. Typically, Patricia moved in and out of paying attention to what was on television, as she continued cooking, cleaning, and talking with her son, and later with her husband when he came home from work. Sometimes, she said, "if I get a break from my housework, I'll sit down and read the newspaper." It was not a problem for her to "follow the TV and read the newspaper"; "I can do both," she said. By the time her husband came home, she had usually finished with her soap opera, and the television was switched back to the news, since that was what he preferred to watch. This routine went on from 4.30 P.M.or so until around 7.30 or 8.00 P.M. In Patricia's house, the television typically stayed on through the later afternoon and into the evening, although this simultaneous viewing gave way to a more focused kind of viewing, as she and her husband (and sometimes her son, too) settled down to watch prime-time programs for rest of the night.

At the other end of the simultaneous viewing continuum, watching television seemed to be the primary concern, and preparing dinner, fixing things to eat, taking care of things around the house, or talking to other people were all activities that fit around television viewing. As a result, the time that people spent watching outweighed, by a considerable margin, the time and energy they devoted to the other activities that were a part of their after-work routine. Typically, people said that they sat and watched for considerable stretches of time, perhaps paying attention to an entire portion of the news, such as the sports or weather, or following a game show or sitcom segment through to its completion. During the commercial breaks they got up and attended to one or another thing that also occupied their attention (typically, cooking or eating), or they stayed put in front of the television but turned their attention to other things, such as paging through the newspaper, or talking to people in a more extended way. This pattern of alternating attention between television and other activities continued, maybe for an hour or two, and people simply picked up where they left off, either with what was on television, or with whatever else they were doing, as they went back and forth between these things. Some people said that, even though their television set was in the living room, or the family room, it was situated in such a way that they could see what was on from the kitchen, or from the doorway leading to the kitchen, and this enabled them to continue watching while they prepared dinner, fixed something to eat, talked, or did other things. Others had smaller television sets in the kitchen, making it possible for them to simply shift their gaze to catch what was on the screen while they stayed involved in what else they were doing. When people watched in either of these ways, their viewing pattern shifted in such a way that shorter but more frequent periods of attention to the television were interspersed with continued involvement in these other activities, as opposed to when they sat and watched shows, or portions of shows, right through. But watching television was still the most mindfully engaging activity they were participating in.

Dave, a security officer at Lipton, usually came home, turned on the television, sat or lay down on the couch, and "relaxed for a while by watching television." His wife usually took care of most of the cooking and the other housework that needed to be done, and that, coupled with the fact that they didn't have any children, freed up Dave to watch television in a focused way for longer stretches of time than most people in the category were used to doing at this particular time. Typically, Dave watched local and national news and ESPN, switching back and forth, depending on the stories being presented and whatever sports programming happened to be on at the time. Because he enjoyed sports, he usually watched the sports segment of the local news all the way through, often doing the same with the weather, too. He preferred to watch baseball, golf, and tennis, and, if any of these sports were on ESPN, he stayed with them for a while. Dave usually picked up the newspaper and read through it while he watched television, and it was also common for him to carry on conversations with his wife, who was either in the kitchen, or moving about the house at this time. From time to time, he got up and went into the kitchen, either to talk with his wife or to help her with one or another aspect of the evening's dinner preparations, and then he went back to sit and watch television, and perhaps read the paper again.

This kind of movement back and forth, between these somewhat sustained periods of attentiveness to television and reading, talking, and helping out in the kitchen, continued for about an hour and a half, until 6.30 or so, when they sat down to eat dinner. The television stayed on through dinner, and, between eating and talking, both of them would catch bits and pieces of what was on. When dinner was over, Dave said that he usually helped his wife clean up for a while, and then he went back to the living room, lay down on the couch, and watched *Wheel of Fortune* and *Jeopardy,* two of his favorite game shows. Sometimes his wife joined him and they would watch these shows together for a while, until she tired of television and got up to do other things. Dave then either continued watching right on through for the rest of the evening, or he got up to work on one of his cars or other projects in the garage. Eventually, though, he came back into the house and took up watching television again, and his wife usually joined him at some point. Typically, they spent the rest of the evening together, watching television and talking.

A similar kind of simultaneous television viewing was also reported by Alicia, a budgetary analyst at the publishing house. She and her husband had established a routine in which they came home and watched the national and local news while they read the day's newspapers and talked together. Typically, they followed *The NBC Nightly News*, *The McNeil-Lehrer News Hour*, and the *Channel 7* local news from San Francisco on television, and *The Wall Street Journal, The San Francisco Chronicle*, and *The Salinas Californian* in print. She and her husband actually sat and watched the news with a critical eye, "paying attention," she said, "to what they're telling us about this country and the world." Both Alicia and her husband were somewhat distrustful of commercial television news, and they maintained a certain distance from its reporting on the world by monitoring and evaluating how news stories were put together, which sources were used and why, and how it was that news reporters and anchors framed issues and events. Alicia said she was particularly critical of the local news, primarily because of its sensationalism, and she watched it simply to keep up with what was going on in San Francisco, since she lived there at one time. In contrast, both she and her husband found *The McNeil-Lehrer News Hour* to be more "objective," and hence, more believable, than either of the commercial news shows.

Typically, she said, they would move back and forth between watching what was on television and reading about the day's happenings, and both of them often used the print version of issues or events to inform their criticisms of televisual depictions of the same things. While they were involved in reading and watching in this way, Alicia got up at some point and began cooking dinner, and even though she went back, sat with her husband, and continued to watch and read, she was now also involved in this fourth activity, and she had to monitor what was on the stove or in the oven while she did these other things. Sometimes, her husband pitched in and helped to prepare dinner, but most of the time this task was left to her to complete. From time to time, she might also go off to take care of household chores of one sort or another, and this added to the activities that she moved in and out of. For the most part, however, Alicia preferred to stay seated and watch the news, read the paper, and talk with her husband. If she became particularly critical of television's presentation of things, or if what was on was not interesting or newsworthy enough to hold her attention, she would turn her attention back to reading or talking with her husband. Since he was doing much the same thing, conversation was often interspersed with watching and reading; this was, in large part, what made simultaneous viewing a relatively mindful activity for Alicia. This routine continued for an hour to an hour and a half, and by about 7.0 or 7.30 they ate dinner. After that, Alicia made a conscious decision about what do with the rest of her evening. Usually, she read fiction or mystery novels, but she was also a fan of the PBS *Mystery* series and the *San Francisco Giants* baseball team, and if either that program or a game were on, she watched it instead of reading. This is how Alicia typically involved herself in simultaneous viewing after work.

Other viewers fall somewhere between these two ends of the simultaneous viewing continuum. Sometimes, as with Dave and Alicia, they engaged in periods of sustained attention to what was on television, at which time, whatever else was going on in their lives was clearly backgrounded to their viewing. At other times, they devoted their energies more wholeheartedly to other activities, as Patricia did, and it was television imagery that seemed to slip into the background. This was evident, for example, in the daily routine of Pam, a clerk at Lipton.

When Pam arrived home from work, the television was usually already on, because either her husband, or one of her two sons, had turned it on when they came in. Susan set to work in the kitchen, preparing dinner for her family, and, for about an hour or so, the television was, for her, merely a background to her cooking and cleaning up. Earlier on, her sons usually watched sitcom reruns, and she was less inclined to follow what went on, although she would listen and from time to time notice particularly funny lines or become aware of exciting situations that the characters had gotten into. At some point, either she or her husband switched to the news, and, even though she was still primarily in the kitchen, Pam said that she was more inclined to follow particular stories, and on some occasions, she came into the living room and watched what was on. Around 6.0 or 6.30, the family sat down and, ate, and amidst family talk at the dinner table, they watched *Magnum P.I.* reruns. After dinner, *Wheel of Fortune* and *Jeopardy* were on, and, at this time, with her cooking and cleaning up out of the way, Pam said that she usually sat down and watched these shows with her husband and their two sons. Conversation continued, and sometimes, she, like Dave, picked up the paper and read through it while she watched and spent time with her family. But, compared to late afternoon, when she pretty much listened to television from the kitchen, the early evening was a time for more focused viewing: even though she read and talked, she, along with everyone else in her family, followed what the contestants did. When these shows were over, Pam attended to her children's needs, perhaps helping them with homework or talking to them about their day, and, at that point, she, like many of the people I interviewed, faced a decision as to what they would do with the rest of their evening. Since she was very involved in the PTA and local school politics, Pam often attended meetings in the evening, which took her out of the house for the rest of the evening. At other times, she sewed, but, after a while, she came back to television and, with her husband, watched some of their favorite shows together. Generally speaking, though, if she didn't have a meeting, or she was too tired to take up one of her sewing projects, Pam sat and watched television, using this as a time to continue spending time with her husband.

Conclusion

The workers I interviewed used television, it seems, to create a kind of mindful space for themselves, one in which they did not have to think about any one thing or be *held responsible* for their thoughts and actions in the same way they typically had to do throughout the day (or night) at work. This is especially true for many of the women that I interviewed, since it was they, as opposed to the men, who took primary responsibility for cooking and cleaning, and therefore experienced in some sense a continuation of the work day, long after they left the world of paid employment. These people certainly experienced television's power effects. But, just as important, they turned the medium to their own advantage by creating a mindful and emotional space in which they were freed up, in a way, if only temporarily, from a felt sense of the various demands that were routinely placed upon them. These are not necessarily discursive acts of opposition to power as much as they are the formation of a sociality in the turn to television. The question of whether or not we, as analysts, privilege conceptions of television's power or opposition to it is in my mind moot. It is more important, analytically speaking, to focus on the indeterminateness of power and document the sociality of use that occurs beneath the threshold of oppositional interpretations.

Power relations and the sociality of simultaneous viewing

Simultaneous viewing of one type or another was a feature in the lives of virtually all those I interviewed. Watching television while simultaneously becoming and staying involved with other activities is actually a very complicated combination, more complicated than most other kinds of television use. The fact that it seems to have become such a prominent feature of so many people's lives after work (and at other times, too) requires that an analyst seeking to understand the sociality of television use systematically accounts for the mindful patterns across these situations. These mindful patterns comprise the shifting nature of people's relationships not only with television, but also with the range of other activities that typically accompany its use. Beyond the patterns themselves, the analyst needs to draw out the connections between the mindful relations and the broader context of people's everyday lives. In this way, both the power of television and the sociality characterized by its use in simultaneous viewing are best understood.

Television's power undercut

Because simultaneous viewing is such a complicated activity, it poses distinctive problems as a focus in the study of power. As I have noted, television's power works in different ways at the same time and not always in the manner that cultural studies' accounts have led us to believe. There are two ways in particular that television's power is undercut by the social relations that predominate during simultaneous viewing.

First, there is the issue of television's power to *establish meaningful parameters* for those who use it – to constitute the discursive horizons for their meaning–making activities. In the case of the first three viewers I discussed, Rob, Don, and Phil, for example, the discourses of television set meaningful parameters for them (and structured their interpretive process in certain ways, too), in large part, because they turned exclusively to television after work. With the group of twenty-five simultaneous viewers, however, because they moved back and forth between the television and other activities, the image worlds of television never quite had exclusive access to their mindful experience as it did for Rob, Don, and Phil. In this way, television was not able to establish such meaningful parameters.

Second, is the issue of television's power to structure a person's interpretive process – viewers making interpretations of programming, and television providing ways for viewers to make meaningful connections to the larger culture. In simultaneous viewing, the interpretive process is more fragmented than in viewing that focuses on the television text alone. Viewers find meaning in programming, but they do so by dissociating scenes, segments, or sequences of images from the meaning *developed* through the overall narrative. As a result, meaning emerges in less predictable ways compared to other kinds of viewing. In large part, this is because people were provided, through the commodity forms of symbolism, with a continual flow of imagery that was at the same time broken up into discrete segments at regular intervals on every channel (*flow* and the *segmented programming structure* were discussed in chapter 5). As a result, television imagery, even as it provides depictions of social life, also becomes something that is just there in the room with "simultaneous viewers." It is always available to them, and they can watch or listen for brief moments or more extended periods of time as they move in and out of doing other things. This continually accessible programming, coupled with the ongoing nature of the other activities, make it possible for an intermittent kind of attentiveness to emerge from such fragmented involvement with programming. In this kind of attentiveness, the movements of a story-line, the interrelations between different story-lines, the integration of characters' actions within story-lines, and, especially, the way that these representational forms come together to constitute the narrative significance of the show as a whole – all of the things that elaborate the deeper meaning of social action in programming – are much less likely to serve as a *centering* presence for people's mindful experience. It is not so much these deeper, more elaborated levels of meaning that this group of interviewees became mindfully involved with in simultaneous viewing, but, rather, the more clearly delineated, easily recognizable, and repetitive ones that the image flow and the segmented programming structure elevate to a potentially more prominent position in people's minds. So, it was shorter, more discrete segments of a show, or the hyperritualized scenes of social action taking place inside these segments, or various combinations or juxtapositions of such segments and scenes, sometimes drawn from different shows over a period of time, that this group of people paid attention to. When this happened, the importance of continuity and of the developmental quality of social action diminished, if it mattered at all. These are two features of sociality that are crucial in constituting the plausibility of television's depictions and in allowing discourse to play a formative role in shaping meaning by anchoring and stabilizing people's mindful experience. In simultaneous viewing, people's mindful experience with programming (or with other activities) does not have to be consistent, or integrated from one moment to the next, or, for that matter, over the broader course of the viewing experience. When people use television in this way, their thinking does not have to be anchored in the discursive regularities of programming to the same degree that it often is when watching in more focused ways. As a result, people do not necessarily come away from television with discursively coherent or stable ideas about social life, about the world "out there," or about their own life in relation to what was depicted in these image worlds, as they might have done if they watched a particular show from beginning to end. This is what I mean when I say that, in simultaneous viewing, television shapes people's interpretive processes in a fragmented manner; that it *dissociates* meaning while at the same time enabling meaning to emerge. To the extent that critical analysts attribute television's power in structuring people's interpretive process to the regularities of discourse, they may inadvertently underestimate the medium's role in bringing about this dissociated kind of social experience that is typical of simultaneous viewing. This more distracted way of watching requires that the analyst look inside the workings of television's discourses in order to illuminate the sociality of their use.

Television's power at work: habituation

Television could also be understood to have "leveled" the thinking of this group of twenty-five, and, over time, habituated them to a relatively mindless way of doing things. As a form of power, this is really very similar to the standardizing effect already discussed. Here, though, it is not so much the distinctiveness of people's turn to television as it is their turn to other activities that establishes the power effect (as it was for the six people who turned to television "less mindfully"). This could be said to derive from the fact that, among those who turned to simultaneous viewing, there was no such distinction at all between turning to television and doing other things, mindfully speaking. Rather, for them, it was the linking, over time, of a certain unthinking way of approaching television and other activities in combination that constituted the workings of power. This habituation resulted from their relying on television, in conjunction with other activities, to ease the transition from work to home life.

When television and other activities are turned to in the same, relatively mindless manner, it becomes difficult, if not impossible, for the analyst to separate out what is distinctive about television in people's social experience. In the interview accounts, I could not distinguish people's mindful and emotional expectations regarding television from their expectations regarding any number of other activities as they made the transition from work to their home lives. This was true both for the handful of people who did not become engaged in simultaneous viewing and for all the rest who did. It seems that the other activities – cooking, cleaning, and casual conversation being the most frequent – had, at least potentially, roughly the same power of attraction as television in orienting their thoughts and actions, and in establishing at least some sense of what it is they anticipated would happen once they were actually involved in the activities. As with watching television, these other activities had become routine for the people I interviewed: they were not the kinds of things that people looked upon as particularly noteworthy to begin with.

Despite this apparent indistinguishability in the mindfulness of the approach to television and other activities, the accounts indicate that the majority of these twenty-five people had become *habituated* to this relatively mindless way of watching television – simultaneous viewing. Of all the people that I interviewed who turned to television after work, those who turned simultaneously to television and other activities were more likely than any of the others to do so in an unthinking way – out of habit. In fact, the more exclusively that people turned to simultaneous viewing, the more likely they were to act out of habit in the after-work period. It was in the after-work routines of ten people who said they used television in this way almost exclusively after work that I found the clearest association between television use and relatively "mindless" behavior. This was an association that was repeated day-in and day-out, with little else occurring in that time period to counteract or qualify this apparent power effect.

Qualifying television's power: limits to habituation

In following the reports of mindfulness of this same group, who rarely watched television without a companion activity, as they moved into the evening period, the next morning (the next available period of free time for those who worked evenings), or the weekend, it quickly became clear that even these people, as habituated as they might have been to television after work, acted in more mindful and self-directive ways at other times. Eight of the ten who almost always viewed simultaneously after work either continued to watch television into the evening or, if they worked evenings, regularly turned to television in the morning and early afternoon before they went to work. Interestingly enough, almost all of them indicated that their orientation to television was more mindful at these times. They were looking for something stimulating or fun to watch, they said, something that would allow them to become imaginatively engaged and focus their attention for a while, unlike what they did while engaged in simultaneous viewing. They all had favorite shows that they watched every week, which enabled them to establish continuities in their television use – again, something that was absent in simultaneous viewing. Furthermore, all of these ten people became involved in various activities at times other than after work:

Tom sometimes read detective stories at night, and played golf, or undertook small projects around the house on the weekends; Erica read romance novels; George read and wrote poetry; Deana read historical novels and sewed in the evening, and on the weekends, she did yardwork and small "home improvement" projects; Pam went to school board and PTA meetings or went shopping; Paula went for walks, read autobiographies, or wrote letters in the evening, and on the weekends she worked in the garden; Kurt worked on household projects, read the paper, or cleaned his guns.

Even though these people repeatedly turned to television out of habit after work, they continued to act in more mindful and self-directive ways, both with and without the television, at other times throughout their daily and weekly routines. Even for these ten people who were the most thoroughly ensconced in a pattern of relatively mindless viewing, habituation was for them a process, not a state of mind.

There were other people who were less exclusively oriented to simultaneous viewing after work, and, because of that, they were more distanced from the medium's habituating effects. Unlike the exclusively simultaneous viewers, when these people described themselves as feeling relaxed as opposed to tired or stressed, after work, their orientation to things was significantly more mindful. People in both of these groupings, then, continued to watch television after work, most of them simultaneously, too. And yet, their approach to things at this time was significantly more mindful than those who became involved in simultaneous viewing alone. Here, the very fact that there were variations in mindfulness means that a more complex sociality was taking shape as well.

For both of these groupings of people – those who participated in simultaneous viewing after work and those who did this at times but also turned to other discrete activities regularly – individually oriented and socially mediated activities were a routine part of what else they did, in addition to watching television, after work. They read books – science fiction, romance novels, and non-fiction – as well as newspapers and magazines, and all of it provided them with an opportunity to think inside the social worlds represented there, sometimes reflecting on what they read, and, perhaps, drawing parallels to their own lives, or the lives of people that they knew. In a less self-conscious way, reading enabled them to try out imagined roles, or, more simply, to sense what it may be like to live in some other time or place. Furthermore, book reading in particular was an activity that typically develops from one occasion to the next, providing the reader with a kind of mindful continuity that is, for the most part, absent in simultaneous viewing.

The same is true of conversation, another activity that was a typical companion activity of the after-work routine for these groups. Sometimes, their conversations centered on run-of-the-mill kinds of things, such as what they wanted for dinner, what to buy, what to wear, and plans for visiting family or friends later in the week. These kinds of things surfaced somewhat randomly and they usually passed quickly from people's minds, too. At other times, the talk and interaction in the home was reported to be deeper and more meaningful. It was not uncommon for some people to say they became engaged in conversations about work, co-workers or supervisors, the progress of their children's schooling, and so on; and, when that happened, it provided them with at least some insight, however momentary it might have been, about themselves, others, or their world. For example, Nan, a packer at Lipton, usually sat and talked with her co-workers at the end of their work day. In addition to the more obvious development of friendships that occurred in this activity, some if not most of the time, these casual conversations provided her and her co-workers with some insight into the situations that they confronted at work, including the power relations intrinsic to the work process. They sometimes discussed such things as which of their supervisors were more responsive to problems with their machines, how supportive other workers (and supervisors) were to their complaints or to ideas about correcting problems with a machine, and the pace of line production on particular shifts. But, whether conversation was superficial or deep, it, like book reading, afforded people with opportunities for *developing* their relations with one another, and enabled them to experience meaningful continuities in their lives. This was true, I think, even when conflicts and tensions surfaced, because they, too, developed over time, and were integral to the ongoing nature of people's sense of themselves.

Besides reading and talking, there were a variety of other things that people did, too. They took walks (alone or with others), worked in the garden, made phone calls to family and friends, had drinks with co-workers, played with their children, went to meetings, played softball games, repaired cars, ate out, or went shopping. In all of this, they were active participants who controlled the pace of what they did, unlike what typically happened in simultaneous viewing. Conversation was often an integral part of these activities, and this alone allowed people to develop their relations with others and experience a continuous sense of themselves, as they did when they read or simply talked at home. But, even as solitary activities, they were often highly mindful, because they exhibited continuity and a developmental course as people connected, in their minds, one occasion of their participation to the next. People had the opportunity to monitor and evaluate what they were doing as they did it; they also created a mindful space in which they could think about other things, unrelated to their participation in the activities themselves, and, in this way, gain insight about themselves or their world.

Kerry, a designer at the publishing company, said that painting and drawing, as opposed to simultaneous viewing, provided her with a means for creative expression in the after-work period, because when she paints or draws, she said, she is engaged in a *continual* process of translating ideas to paper (or canvas), testing them out, evaluating their outcome, and then redirecting her efforts accordingly. Similarly, Kim, a secretary at Lipton, said that she routinely played with her baby daughter when she came home, and that for her this involved noticing the developments of her daughter's muscular co-ordination and her use of words. Beyond that, she said that the shared intimacy of this mother–daughter relation made it mindfully and emotionally fulfilling.

Compared to simultaneous viewing, all of these activities were, to different degrees, of course, more mindful: people participated in them more actively than they did in simultaneous viewing; they were more likely to control the pace of their involvement, something that they did not do with television at this time; they were also more likely to carry with them a sense of development as their discrete instances of involvement often built upon one another over time; and, as I said, people were able to gain insight about themselves and their world to a greater degree in these activities than in simultaneous viewing. Even though these people had become habituated to watching television in a relatively mindless way, they continued to act in more mindful and self-directive ways in other activities after work, sometimes choosing to do so rather than simply falling into the habit of watching television. And, like those who were more exclusively oriented to simultaneous viewing, these people who pursued other activities, too, thought about and became involved with television in a more mindful manner in the evening. So, here again, I am led to see habituation as a process, rather than a state of mind.

Among the people who turned with the same degree of mindfulness to television and to other activities, but who did not do so simultaneously, their television viewing itself exhibited a continuous quality that resembled their involvement in the kinds of activities that I just described. Like most people who engaged in simultaneous use, these people watched the news (both local and national) and, to a lesser extent, game shows and sitcom reruns. But they also watched programs that they had recorded previously, and they were much more likely than simultaneous viewers to use the remote, too. So, both they and simultaneous viewers watched what they wanted to watch, but in very different ways and with very different mindful consequences. These non-simultaneous users of television usually sat and focused their attention on the television when they watched, and this attentiveness was sustained over the course of a show. With recorded programming, they controlled the pace of their viewing: they stopped a show at particular points, they re-viewed scenes, or they skipped through commercials and picked up the program again. Similarly, with the remote, they flipped between stations in a deliberate way in order to sustain the kind of focused attention to the show (or shows) that they most desired. Compared to simultaneous viewers, these people watched what they wanted to watch in a more controlled manner, which brings story-telling conventions, especially the development of narrative action, to the center of their viewing experience. Their television use exhibits more continuity than that of simultaneous users, and it provides them with more opportunities for gaining insight from what they watch as well.

In one case, a father spoke of sitting down with his son and daughter to watch *Eight Is Enough*, a family oriented drama that, at the time, was in syndicated reruns. Typically, he said, they followed what happened in order to "get" the message, or messages, that the show was putting across to viewers. This enabled them to become involved in discussions centering around the moral issues raised in the show, not in any overtly self-conscious way, but as a practical part of making meaning from what they watched. As a result, they often came away from the show feeling that they had learned something, *together*, and that what they had learned was perhaps applicable to how they related with one another as a family. Watching television, then, was an integral part of their shared "family time." This was no doubt a highly mindful – and emotional – activity for them, one that, at the same time, brought them inside television's image worlds, often enabling the discourses of programming to become their way of seeing things.

In this sense, their television use was actually very similar to that of Rob, Don, and Phil, and to the six people who turned to television less mindfully than they did to other activities. This discrete form of television viewing occupies a kind of middle ground, mindfully speaking, between the more mindful alternative activities that they regularly participated in and the less mindful, simultaneous viewing that had become an ongoing part of other people's routines of relaxation and enjoyment after work.

Qualifying television's power: habituation without television

One-third of the people I interviewed (twenty) said that they did not use television at all after work, although they did use or watch television at other times. The findings related to this group very clearly qualify assertions regarding the workings of television's power in people's everyday lives. Compared to those who did turn to television after work, these particular people were much more likely to become engaged in different, successive activities, and, in doing so, to shift the mindful way that they proceeded to do things. By not turning to television after work, they prevented the medium from establishing meaningful parameters for them at this particular time. Consequently, they did not become habituated to television, nor were the discourses of programming able to structure their interpretive processes at this time. These twenty people were free from the various power-effects of television during this apparently important transition time, and, partly because of this, it seems they fashioned a distinctively more mindful approach to doing things as they moved out of this transition time.

The members of this group said that they came home from work and turned first to the more routine activities, such as cooking and cleaning, that nearly everyone attended to at this time. They reported doing this out of habit, requiring little, if any, conscious decision-making on their part. Many of the people who turned to television after work did much the same thing. But these twenty people had established this habitual routine without resorting to television, and, by doing so, they cast doubt on assertions that tend to single out television, across the board, or the mass media more generally, as being primarily responsible for people having become habituated to doing things in "mindless" ways. In fact, the people for whom television was not an option after work (but for whom it was an option at other times) turned to cooking and cleaning out of habit more frequently than simultaneous users of television. If anything, then, they were more likely to have become habituated to taking an unthinking approach to things at this time. But this habitual turn was merely the beginning of their after-work activity period.

Beyond television's absence from their routines, this group of twenty described finishing up, or moving out of, this cooking–cleaning phase and then turning to other, more mindfully engaging activities in the same after-work period. The activities are familiar ones by now: reading books, newspapers, and magazines; sewing, working on various hobbies, talking, or otherwise spending time with their family, friends, or housemates. As previously described, compared to cooking, cleaning, and even television use, all of these activities are more "mindful," especially in terms of providing a continuity of involvement, a sense of developmental course, and the possibility for insight. These twenty people moved beyond the routine nature of their turn to cooking and cleaning and oriented themselves to the other activities in more playful or reflective ways. In fact, when their initial, unthinking approach to the more mundane activities is ignored, the way that they pursued the other activities after work was the most mindful of the sixty people that I interviewed. This progression from less to more mindful ways of doing things after work was reported by only *two* of the people who said that they turned to television at this time, and neither of them became involved in simultaneous viewing.

Television was simply not compelling for these people after work. Like those who did use television, these people, too, wanted to "catch up" on what went on in the world while they were at work. They chose to do so, however, by reading the newspaper, talking with friends, family, or housemates, instead. All but two of them turned to television in the evening (or, alternatively, the next morning), pointing out that they had favorite shows that they watched regularly and others that they tried not to miss. In comparing the mindfulness with which these people *first* turned to television, which was in the evening, to the mindfulness exhibited by those whose first exposure to television was after work, I found that those who held off using it until the evening were least likely to say that they acted either out of habit or with ideas of escape in mind. Put another way, beyond the after work period, when these people turned to television as a way to relax and enjoy themselves, they did so more mindfully than any of the people that I interviewed. The fact that these particular people *did not* turn to television in the after-work period, when most others did, a time, it seemed, when everyone's capabilities for mindful involvement in things was lowest, indicates that they had come to exercise a greater degree of self-control than any of the other people that I interviewed regarding the conditions under which they allowed television to enter their lives. Because of this, when they turned to television, they did so, as I said, in more mindful ways than the others I interviewed. Their interview accounts offer documentation of a sociality of television use that qualifies, in yet another way, how it is that we understand the power of television to work in people's everyday lives.

Conclusion: functional use of television after work

Simultaneous users of television in my study made certain choices in order to set up situations in which they did not need to maintain a high degree of mindful attention toward any one object that they became involved with after work. Whether it was cooking, cleaning, talking, television shows, or other things, none of the activities required close attention. By using television while simultaneously doing other things, people have, in effect, created a new activity, one in which the continual movements back and forth between watching, or listening, and doing other things allow them not only to shift the focus of their attention but also to shift ground, mindfully speaking, between an activity (television viewing) which is generally receptive in nature, with no control over the pace, to other activities (cooking, cleaning, conversation, reading, etc.) that tend to require more active participation and allow for control over the pace. Active participation and the control over pace is continually interrupted and then reversed. It is this interruption and reversal of their mindful involvement that comes to define the continuity of simultaneous viewing.

Simultaneous viewing carries with it, then, a distinctive sociality, one that seems well suited to assisting people as they make the transition from work, where their minds usually have had to be focused on particular things outside themselves, to home life, where they have the opportunity to reorient their mindful and emotional experience back to themselves or their relationships with family and housemates. Although it sounds like a relatively simple adjustment to make, in actuality, shifting one's gears between work and home requires a certain space and time in which people's mindful and emotional experience can find a new and different grounding, one that enables them to re-establish control in their own lives. This kind of adjustment is further complicated by the fact that, if those I interviewed are representative, most people continue to be faced with work responsibilities of one sort or another (usually cooking and cleaning) when they arrive home from work. By providing people with a ready-made but constantly changing imaginary space that they can move in and out of at will, television in some sense frees people from these continued responsibilities, and, more generally, from having to sustain a more focused kind of mindful involvement in any particular activity. All of this leads me to understand the social logic of simultaneous viewing less as habituation than as a *functional use* that people make of television in order to ease this transition from work to home life, especially when it involves the continuation of work in one way or another. In using television for this purpose, people seem to be calling into question the need, so prevalent in our culture, to remain constantly productive by using their time efficiently, with clear goals or outcomes in mind. What is functional for them, at this time, is to disrupt the normalcy of productive activity.

The simultaneous viewers I spoke with expressed an awareness of their own (and others') motivations for becoming involved in this kind of television use in the first place. The language of their interview accounts indicated this and supports this functional use interpretation. When they said such things as "television is just easier than doing anything else," or "with television, I do not have to think too much about anything," or "television gives me something to fall back on when I am tired after work," or "with television, I do not have to think about *one* thing," they are seeing television, not as something that has become inscribed in their experience out of habit, but, rather, as an object, as something separate from themselves. Furthermore, they recognize that other people, too, see television in this more distanced way. In doing so, they become mindful of a ritual significance of their own and others' simultaneous television use. Indeed, they become aware of simultaneous viewing as a distinctive form of their cultural practice. Even though simultaneous viewing has become "habit" for people, and even though, over time, they have become "habituated" to it, this does not mean that they do not at the same time operate with an awareness of it *as* a habit, and, in doing so, maintain, to some degree, a knowledge of their own habituation to television as something socially constructed and therefore *changeable*.

This functional use of television carries with it unintended consequences. One of the most significant of these has to do with the effect that this kind of viewing has on the continuity and developmental course of people's involvement in other activities. Although this was not an issue when it came to preparing dinner or taking care of household responsibilities, it did become significant for some people when their intermittent attention to television interrupted, or displaced, the progressively interactive potential of conversation and social interaction with family members or housemates and, to a lesser extent, the continuity and developmental course of their reading, sewing, or other household projects and hobbies. When it comes to this issue, the interview accounts indicate that people had mixed feelings, and that they often held on to contradictory thoughts and feelings about it. On the one hand, conversation or social interaction in the after-work period was looked upon as just another activity, like preparing dinner or taking care of household responsibilities. In this sense, those I talked to did not really want to become too mindfully engaged in talk and interaction. They often felt mindfully and emotionally drained by the demands of their work day, and they simply did not have the energy for attentive participation in any activity, let alone conversation and meaningful interaction. At times like these, television came into play by taking their minds off such talk and interaction and substituting in its place the possibility for a more disengaged kind of involvement in its image worlds. On the other hand, many of these same people who used television in this functional way also said that they sometimes felt guilty about not being able to be more attentive and focused when they were talking and interacting with one another around the house. They were quite open in acknowledging that if the television were not on as much as it was at this time, they would probably have had more time – more "quality" time at that – for talk and interaction with others. But, practically in the same breath, they would go on to say that in the past they have been unwilling to alter their routine and give talk and interaction without television, or alternatively solitary activities, a more prominent place in their lives after work. Thoughts about the virtues of more and better communication are one thing; the reality of having to live everyday life, and meet the demands and responsibilities that it places upon people, is another. Some people even commented, jokingly of course, that they were not so sure that actually having more time to talk and interact would be a good thing. Better to leave well enough alone, they seemed to be saying. All joking aside, it appears that some people wish to be able to remain somewhat disengaged from the demands of more mindful involvement at certain times in daily life, in particular in the transition from work to home life and, in some ways, television and simultaneous viewing makes this possible.

7

The practice of viewing

This chapter focuses different kinds of viewing relations that typify the experience of those I interviewed and observed. There were two phases of participant observation in my research. The first occurred over a two-year period prior to my conducting depth interviews and did not involve any of the people who participated in the interviews. After initiating contact with a few people who worked at the University of California, I used a "snowball" sampling technique to include friends, acquaintances, and co-workers of those with whom I first watched. I tried to some extent to enlarge my sample, and, frankly, I was limited in doing so. It was difficult to find people who were willing to let me come into the privacy of their homes and just watch television with them. It certainly helped to be "referred" to new people by others that they knew and trusted. Over a period of time, there were eight settings in which I became familiar enough with the people involved to return repeatedly, if not regularly, to "hang out" with them for a while and just watch TV and talk. I supplemented these private observation situations by frequenting various bars and restaurants where at least some of the patrons were attentive to what was on television at least some of the time, and I made it a point to watch one or another "special" sporting event – such as the Super Bowl, the NCAA Basketball Tournament, the NBA Playoffs, and so on – in such public settings. The second participant observation phase involved watching television with some of the people that I interviewed. After the interviews were completed, and after telling them of my interest in observing, several of them invited me back to their homes on other occasions, and, as in the first phase, we watched and talked through a typical evening of prime time, or sat and tuned into game shows and the daytime soaps, depending on the situation.

The observations made and the insights gained from the first phase of participant observation were translated into the open-ended format of my interview guide. The initial interview questions focused on topics such as favorite shows, how people distinguish between "good" and "bad" shows, what constituted "good" and "bad" television, the relevance of various features of programming, such as the story-line, character interactions, setting, genre, and so on. From that point on, people were free to take the interview where they wished. As they developed and clarified their thinking about one or another aspect of their viewing habits, I was able to spontaneously pose new questions based on what they said in order to draw out their thinking on the matter at hand. This format provided the opportunity, really, for significant and unanticipated findings to emerge.

In addition to the use of these methods, a smaller number of people also provided "diary" accounts of the more personal and private aspects of their television use. And, throughout the research phase of my work, I routinely undertook a more casual questioning of people, across a variety of naturalistic settings, with regard to their viewing habits. It is from this variety of empirically based accounts that my reconstruction of viewing relations is made.

Plausibility

People who watch television routinely make judgments regarding the plausibility of programming. When they find something to be plausible, it usually means that one or another aspect rings true with what they take to be their own experience, and, because of that, such programming usually merits their sustained attention. Such judgments concerning plausibility are indicative of a meaningful form that people give to the activity of watching television, one that, while it certainly resonates with what is discursively significant in programming, none the less involves a transformation of the pre-existing symbolism of programming into a more practical, meaningful aspect of people's everyday lives.

In distinguishing plausible from implausible programming, people usually relate what they are watching to one or another aspect of their own lives or to things that they have seen and heard elsewhere. In doing so, they supply a referent, or referents, to the television discourse. So, despite the fact that in finding plausible programming people often locate themselves, at least mindfully, inside the discursive structuring of television's representational world, they are at the same time establishing connections between that world and their own as a way of making that discourse meaningful. Even though people who watch television may do so in ways that indicate they are subsumed within the discourses of television, the fact that they make plausibility judgments indicates that they also creatively transform what television provides for them. In making plausibility judgments, viewers select from an array of programming choices, and, in doing so, they establish a mindfulness to their activity, one that is not simply based on their acceptance of discourse as it exists.

When people identify plausible programming, they are, in effect, saying that they know that the world of television is essentially a fictional one, and yet they are making the choice to become mindfully involved with its imagery in a way that is not simply oriented around escaping thoughts of their own real-life circumstances. The interview accounts and the commentary that often accompanied viewing indicated that when people look for plausible programming they do so with the understanding in mind that what they watch *could* be real. For the vast majority of people, to attach the label "plausible" to something that they are watching is to say that it is close enough to real life to merit their sustained attention. This is quite different from their saying that it *is* real life or, alternatively, that they are watching it for its entertainment value alone, and whether or not it is believable is irrelevant. To label programming "plausible," or "believable," is to indicate a form-giving quality to one's activity, one that extends the logic of the sign system outward to the real world.

Throughout my research, there was overwhelming evidence that people who watch television do not simply accept programming as some kind of realistic reflection of the world. Quite often, and usually at the very start of my interviews, people would tell me they knew that the world of television was *not* real, indicating a very basic kind of mindful and emotional distance that people were placing between themselves and the social world of television *in toto*. This is probably also a defensive nod to the widespread perception that watching television is a waste of time. Yet these very same viewers were quick to acknowledge that television was indeed a low-cost and convenient source of entertainment, an easy way for them to become emotionally and imaginatively involved in worlds beyond their own on an everyday basis. After all, critics of television notwithstanding, the use of television for relaxation and enjoyment in leisure time is perhaps one of the most frequently documented facts emerging from the literature on media use and effects.

In recent analyses of the audience, this knowledge that viewers have about the "unreality" of programming is often linked with the construct of *formula* to explain the ritualistic nature of television use and, especially, with the pleasures that people derive from watching it (Ang, 1985; Fiske, 1987; Radway, 1984). The repeated viewing of what turns out to be remarkably similar programming, with its predictable characterizations and storylines, is what establishes the pleasure of the text. In this view, what is enjoyable is closely linked with ideas about television programming as something that is *not real.*

Ideas about formula and pleasure can explain much about what draws people into television programming, but they also explain too little. But, by focusing on the plausibility judgments of people who watch, we are able to see – much more clearly than through the lens of formula and pleasure – the mindful and emotional process that people become involved in as they attempt to disentangle the "real" from the "not real."

A "real-life" orientation to programming persists for many people as they turn to television, despite the fact that they readily acknowledge the separate-from-reality nature of the medium and its programming. This quality of being separate from reality is what people understand as the *entertainment* basis of television. Despite their working knowledge of television's *unreality,* people continue to turn to it to derive something more than merely entertainment. The people that I interviewed and watched television with made distinctions in this entertainment experience, and an important part of the distinctions they made involved their continuing to look for programming that in some way rings true with their own everyday experience of the world; a world that they know in common with others – family, friends, co-workers.

I use the term "plausibility" to identify the kind of criteria that people apply in selecting programming that they believe is realistic enough, or that rings true with their experience enough, so that they can involve themselves in it and continue to watch. I saw this in three areas: plausibility in characterizations, in situations and story-lines, and in the unpredictability of the story-line.

The most frequent form that plausibility judgments took in my research was expressed in the desire that people had for programming that provided them with "human," or "believable" characterizations. In the interviews and in conversation while watching, people used different phrases to convey what was essentially the same basic idea: that the characters in the programs they watched should exhibit the emotional attributes of real people on a consistent basis. For example, one viewer referred to programming as being plausible when it expressed "the complexity that you find in human beings." Others look to characters who "have feelings" and who are "vulnerable" as being more plausible than those who do not have such qualities. And still other people referred to the "three-dimensional" nature of characters as a requisite quality for their being plausible, because that meant that these characters expressed "some of the depth of feelings or emotions" that they expected to find in real people. This quality of human characterizations is articulated in a particularly eloquent manner by a mail clerk at the publishing house when he discussed the lead character Mike Hammer in the show by the same name:

[Mike Hammer] represents a number of qualities that I find noble . . . loyalty to his friends, standing up for the underdog . . . also being a working man, how I don't trust the rich financial types. He pulls them down to size . . . it is really a kind of violent stance in a way, but you relate. The underdog and the loyalty to his friends . . . is something that I find missing in the materialistic society of the 80s and that gives me a warmth. Even though it's written to a certain shallow extent, you can also feel something between him and his friend who is a police captain, or between him and his secretary. You feel there is a warmth there, there's an understanding there, there's a loyalty, so you get good traits from it, good qualities.

Similarly, a regular viewer of *The Cosby Show*, pointed out that she and her husband continued to come back to this particular show because:

While the parents and kids being so well dressed and everything is not true for most families, a lot of the interaction between Cosby and his wife [is] very typical of what [her husband] and I feel. It's really true, it's true for our experience. It's one of our favorite shows because there is something human going on that makes us think about . . . look humorously at our own situation. There aren't many TV shows that have that human characterization thing, and in preference, I would always choose that.

As it is articulated through the words of these viewers, judgments about plausibility in terms of human characterizations sounds very similar to what Ien Ang, in *Watching Dallas*, refers to as the "emotional realism" of television melodrama (1985: 41–47). The fans of Dallas who wrote letters to Ang, like the people I interviewed, were able to bracket certain stereo-typical and unrealistic aspects of the roles played by television characters, and focus their mindful attention instead on the reality of emotional experience conveyed in character's actions and interactions.

A second way that people identified plausible programming was through their judgments as to whether or not the situations or stories depicted could actually happen in "real" life. This is the most directly narrative-based aspect of the plausibility judgments I found. During the interviews, people who regularly watched one or more daytime soap operas pointed out that they knew, or knew of, others who faced circumstances very similar to those depicted in the shows. This way of thinking about plausibility was not limited, however, to daytime television. For example, another regular viewer of *The Cosby Show* said:

I like *The Cosby Show* because . . . they are letting them be who they are and finding the humor in that . . . When I see a kid say something on *The Cosby Show* that I've heard my sister, who is twelve years old say, I am thinking, "this is very funny," even though at the time it pissed me off that she said it.

Another *Cosby* fan echoed this sentiment when he said that "what they portray is so close to real life – I mean, those situations happen in real life. There was one last Thursday where the son was going to shave his head to be in a rock band. I mean, that is something my brother would do." Similarly, a regular viewer of *The Golden Girls*, commented that:

The characters are so funny because they are so real. There really are women like those three women and their mother; there really are situations like that. Some of them are stretched a bit, but they [the characters] are down to earth, and that's why the show is so interesting to me. They're characters, and they are so clearly delineated, and yet they are in the same situation as me, being unmarried and looking for the guy and having to get together and deal with each other and all this stuff.

Similar sentiments extended to more dramatic, action-adventure programs, such as *MacGyver* and *The Wizard*. In these shows, the seemingly fantastic ability of the heroes to ingeniously escape from impending danger or catastrophe week after week was none the less understood as plausible. In such cases, the viewers themselves often had sufficient working knowledge regarding the operations of mechanical or electrical equipment that enabled them to feel what the characters did was within the range of what they or others they knew could, or would, do in similar situations. For example, one viewer regularly watched *The Wizard* in large part because he liked the fact that:

The little inventions . . . that he comes up with are really believable because they fit the situation. He likes to use a lot of those remote-control robots, airplanes, and stuff, and you know that anybody can come up with that. It's real, it gives you ideas, like if I ever get into remote-control type things, I would know what to do. When my little boy gets older, I plan to get one of those remote-control sand buggies.

A third aspect of plausibility is less closely tied to the actions of characters or the unfolding of social action in situations or stories; instead, it is based on what people see as the *unpredictable* quality of programming. For many people, *not* knowing how social action will proceed, or how things will turn out in a scene or show, corresponds to situations in which they or others they know may have found themselves; where the outcome of their actions, the actions of others, or of the relations they became involved in cannot be anticipated in advance. Not knowing the outcome is more plausible than knowing what will happen. It is this aspect of plausibility judgments that allows even what otherwise appears to be "formulaic" programming to be seen as plausible.

This quality of unpredictability cuts across different genres of television programming. The people I talked with found it in soap operas (both daytime and prime-time), game shows, local news, live sporting events, dramatic series such as *Murder She Wrote, LA Law, Hill Street Blues,* and *St. Elsewhere,* as well as in more reality-oriented shows such as *Divorce Court, The Judge, True Confessions,* and *The People's Court.* In fact, this aspect of plausibility was the one that was most frequently mentioned by viewers. For example, one viewer said that "what I like about *Perry Mason* is the intrigue, not knowing, and to see how he unveils the bad guy. You have to maintain your attention and I like that." Another viewer said that she enjoyed *Hill Street Blues* precisely because "you couldn't always predict how these characters would act." Similarly, still another viewer said that her enjoyment of *The Cosby Show* came from the fact that "I do not know what the kids are going to do next." An editor at the book publishing company regularly watched dramatic shows on the Arts and Entertainment Channel because, she said, "these shows are not predictable . . . I am left wondering what will happen. There's a real sense, as in real life, [that] you do not know how things are going to turn out." She went on to contrast this unpredictability with the predictability of network television by saying that "if it had been *Mistral's Daughter* [a network mini-series running at the time] we would have known in the first five minutes that she [the heroine] was going to die . . . and she was going to look beautiful doing it." Evidence of the fact that people link their desire for plausibility with unpredictability in programming also emerged during the time I spent watching television with people and observing. As viewers became interested in a story-line or situation, I found it quite common for them to wonder, out loud, about what might happen next, what a character might do, the possible impact that a character's actions might have on others, and so on. This indicated that they found things believable enough to follow for the time being.

It was clear from the interviews and my observations of viewing that these three different aspects of plausibility complimented one another and sometimes came together in many ways to solidify the appeal of particular shows for people. When this occurred, it was much more likely that viewers would focus their attention on the text and maintain that kind of attentiveness over the course of the entire show. This layering of the different aspects of plausibility in a single show figured importantly in whether people designated a show among their favorites. *Hill Street Blues, LA Law, Family Ties, 60 Minutes, Jeopardy,* and *Wheel of Fortune* were mentioned again and again by many of the people that I interviewed as favorites – the ones that they watched regularly or tried not to miss. I found this to be particularly true of *The Cosby Show.* Many regular viewers of this show said that they thought the situations presented seemed "real" to them, the characters expressed a range of human emotions that often seemed to approximate the complexity that they – the viewers – understood to be like the emotional life of real people, which, in turn, lent a quality of unpredictability to the way that social action unfolded on the show. Many times, they said, they simply did not know what might happen next.

The fact that plausibility judgments in my research came together in favorite shows, coupled with the fact that such shows were watched by many people (as was the case with *Cosby*), suggests that at least this particular aspect of people's mindful participation in the viewing culture can be shaped by the "mainstreaming" tendency of television programming. While people's judgments about plausibility cannot, and should not, be taken to stand for the actual unfolding of their interpretive process as they watch television, the fact that, at different points in time, people who are different in so many ways, and whose programming preferences may otherwise diverge in significant ways, have chosen to center their judgments regarding plausible programming on the same shows is, I think, precisely what George Gerbner (1977) was intent upon uncovering when he wrote about the mainstreaming effect of television.

As important as it is, this kind of mainstreaming influence that is operative in this coalescing of different aspects of plausibility judgments in the same widely popular shows is not all that is significant in the ways that plausibility as a concept works in the viewing culture. Certainly, this process of coalescing represents one of the more cohesive and stable dimensions of the way plausibility judgments work when people watch television. But there are also other, less cohesive ways plausibility judgments work in the rituals of day-to-day use. Programming that was deemed plausible by some viewers in my research was seen by others as quite predictable and formulaic. Generally speaking, I found that, from person to person, there was often considerable variation in the programs that were identified as plausible, even when the same criteria of judgment was in use. For some people, plausible programming extended from reality-oriented shows such as *The Judge* and *True Confessions* to a variety of family-oriented situation comedies, such as *The Cosby Show*, *Family Ties*, and *My Two Dads*. For others, plausible programming encompassed selected family sitcoms, such as *Cosby* and *Family Ties*, and extended to police and detective dramas such as *The Rockford Files*, *Hill Street Blues*, and *Simon and Simon*, while reality oriented shows or prime-time soap operas did not enter the picture. For still other viewers, the range of plausible programming extended from prime-time soap operas such as *Dallas* and *Knot's Landing* to some of the more innovative, dramatic programs such as *LA Law*, *St. Elsewhere*, and *Hill Street Blues*. Some viewers found game shows such as *Wheel of Fortune* and *The Price is Right* as totally implausible, with one viewer in particular saying that he just "cannot get into them at all," while other viewers found these same game shows plausible as exemplified by a viewer who said they were "interesting . . . because you don't know what the outcome is, and you can guess and try to figure things out."

Among the people that I interviewed, it seems that, in addition to whatever mainstreaming influences there were at work in shaping plausibility judgments as seen in common judgments of plausibility centered on particular shows, there was, at the same time, a concurrent dispersal of these judgments across different programming choices. In other words, while, in some instances, positive judgments coincided, in other instances they diverged significantly. This divergence of plausibility judgments stems, in part, from the simple fact that at any one time, as well as over time, there are a multitude of shows to choose from when it comes to making plausibility judgments. When this vast range of programming possibilities is combined with the myriad factors involved in the turn to television, it is no wonder that the specific shows that viewers deem to be plausible, along with whatever patterns may have developed in their making such judgments, would be unpredictable, defying any straightforward or consistent kind of classification. It is no doubt true that, aside from ratings, people who watch television have little, if any, direct say in the decision-making processes that put programs on the air in the first place. In this sense, corporate decision-making is unmistakably undemocratic, which is one reason that the mainstreaming tendency represents evidence of the commercial power of television to shape experience. Yet, at the same time, people continue to supply reference points of their own and make plausibility judgments in unanticipated ways. In contrast to the mainstreaming tendency that I spoke of, this dispersal of plausibility judgments constitutes one of the more pluralistic aspects of individual's participation in the viewing culture.

I also noticed, in many of the interview accounts, a significant shift occurring in the way that viewers described how they arrived at their judgments regarding plausibility. In addition to comparing characters, stories, and situations with their own real-world reference points, many viewers also juxtaposed one show with another, or a show with a film, or a television character with a movie actor, etc., in arriving at their sense of what was plausible. One viewer described what he found plausible in *The Cosby Show* by comparing it to *Family Ties*:

That whole set up [of *Family Ties*] jars me. To me, it's like a star vehicle for Michael J. Fox . . . It just rings false to me, in terms of the interaction of the characters. I admit it is amusing, and I think that it is still a cut above the *Three's Company* type of show – that is the absolute pit [of TV] . . . It's like skimming off the obvious, whereas *Cosby* digs a little deeper into situations, and goes for something a little more buried down.

Another viewer revealed very clearly this intertextual way of arriving at plausibility judgments when he offered an account of how he distinguished between different family-oriented shows:

I approach *Cosby* different than I approach *Our House*. [In] *Our House*, they're hitting the reality of today's society, and they're hitting it hard. It's designed to deal with the problems that are busting up families, and they are showing how to make it through, and I like that, whereas [with] *Cosby*, I don't really see them dealing with too many problems . . . not the real problems. They're trying obviously to look for the laugh, and you've got to understand that when you're watching. *Cosby* is at one end and *Our House* is at another in terms of how they deal with problems . . . and *Family Ties* is probably more toward *Cosby*, but somewhere toward the middle.

Similarly, another viewer discussed how she distinguished *Family Ties* from other situation comedies that she watched regularly (including *The Cosby Show*, *Cheers*, *My Sister Sam*, *Newhart*, and *Kate and Allie*):

Family Ties is more contrived. I think that the other shows take very real relationships and they find the humor in them. On *Family Ties*, for instance, the father is always a dupe, um, which on the Newhart Show . . . [it] kind of falls into that too. There is enough humor in real roles, and real life characters that when you take a character and somehow almost parody them inside themselves, it is not as funny to me. To me, on *Family Ties*, that show would be funny if they just let the father be a liberal and the kid be a right-winger . . . you do not need to make the father into a dodo besides. That goes too far for me. So I'm not as interested in the situations that they come up with on *Family Ties*. The kid – there's a little kid that they have added to the show. One thing that drives me nuts on TV is when they have a small child speak as if he is an adult. That's probably why I like *The Cosby Show* because they write the kids as kids.

Still another viewer's words echoed those of many others when he said that in watching television, "I want to see real stuff." But, interestingly enough, in his account of *LA Law*, this sense of "the real" was established by using intertextual comparisons.

LA Law is better than *Knot's Landing*. It's better because there are new characters, they're realistic and believable, they are not overly melodramatic . . . they don't bring in some foreign power to change the story-line like they did on *Knot's Landing*.

The use of intertextual criteria for making plausibility judgments did not altogether replace the real-life criteria people used. Rather, those I interviewed often moved back and forth between the two realms as they tried to determine what was "real" and, hence, worth watching. For example, one viewer used the sign system of television in the interview as often as he did real-life criteria. Here he discusses how he judged the plausibility of a wide range of prime-time programming. Notice that the intertextual criteria seem to lack the sense of definition provided by the real-life criteria.

At one time I was into *Dallas*, but they killed people off and brought them back and killed them off. They fall into the same old rut, like any daytime soap. There's only so much they can do, and then they have to start repeating themselves. It gets old. J.R. goes out and has an affair with a lady this week and then he goes out and has an affair with another lady next week. Sue Ellen is an alcoholic this week and then next week she's going off and drying herself up. Week after week it's just too much. *Knot's Landing* and *LA Law* is on [sic] at the same time, and *LA Law* is a little more interesting than *Knot's Landing* . . . and like *Dallas* is still on Fridays competing with *Miami Vice*. I'd rather watch *Miami Vice* even though it falls along the same lines as *Dallas* because eventually it repeats itself. They change characters, but they are always dealing with the drug end of it and you know, there's only so much they can do, whereas with *Sting Ray*, you know it's a different situation. This week he's [the main character] supposed to go on a cruise and do something on a boat. On *Sting Ray*, every week it's something different. It centers around the guy who plays *Sting Ray*, but every week there are different people. [The] same is true with *McGiver*. *Air Wolf* is another one that is like that.

Similarly, another viewer, who works the evening shift at Lipton, described the differences between some of her regular shows by moving back and forth between intertextual and "real" referents.

With *The Judge* and *True Confessions*, it is a little harder [to guess the outcome] because . . . I do not know . . . it just seems like you have to listen to the whole thing on *The Judge* to really figure out which way he's going to go, and sometimes, you know, he'll usually go pretty much with the way that I would go one way or another. But with *Divorce Court*, after you've heard the plaintiff and the defendant, that is it, you do not need the witnesses . . . you can just go . . . oh well, she's going to get it for adultery, and he's going to get it for cruelty, so it's [sic] going to divide this and that. On *The Judge*, you never know what is going to happen, 'cause each case is different, but on *Divorce Court*, it's always oh, he's good, she's bad, he screwed around on me, she screwed around on me . . . the same thing. It's not enjoyable to watch because you just know. It's like listening to a record 20 times. After a while it gets boring.

And again, the intermixing of these different criteria, especially the intertextual relationship of film and television, is brought out very clearly in one viewer's account of the popular television crime drama, *Hunter*. In commenting on the believability of Hunter, an experienced and street-savvy police detective, he relied on a comparison to movie characters:

I like Hunter's attitude toward what he's doing, you know, with the violence. He seems like a Clint Eastwood type cop, a Dirty Harry almost, but every once in a while you can see glimpses of this more humanness.

This shift from a "real-life" to an intertextual basis for making plausibility judgments is, like the mainstreaming of plausibility judgments itself, an important indicator of television's power to shape the mindfulness of people's involvement in the viewing culture. In both cases, people are making judgments regarding whether or not, and how, programming rings true with their experience. But, when plausibility is determined using comparisons with the world of televisual and filmic representation, what people understand as "real" has become, almost imperceptibly, a step removed from what they take to be their own experience. Or, putting it another way, what people take to be their own experience is increasingly centered in the world that television (and film) provides for them.

Certainly, the world of film and television imagery is a world that people experience in a first-hand way; it is clearly, for some, an important part of what they do in their everyday lives. Nevertheless, this should not obscure the fact that this shift in referents, from the previously experienced to the previously viewed, indicates a point at which mass-mediated sign systems begin to infringe upon and erode these more traditional, often interaction-based, sources of meaning for people. With such a change, instead of extending outward, away from the world of television or other media, the criteria for an individual's judgments become enframed within the representational world of television (or mass media) itself. Their previous viewing experience (for the most part with television, in my interviews, but with film as well) provides them with imagery that then serves as a reference point in itself against which to evaluate and judge the plausibility of the shows and characters and story-lines that they continue to encounter when they watch. I found that people continued using ideas of plausibility, or believability, even after the real-life basis gave way to an image-based frame of reference, and even after the point that programming, apparently, bore no relation to their own real-life experience. Because of this, a tension emerges from the mindful experience of ordinary viewers, a tension between previously experienced and previously viewed referents used in making plausibility judgments. Viewers can and do continue to make their viewing experience meaningful using both kinds of plausibility judgments.

As is the case when real-life criteria are used, television's power to mainstream the making of plausibility judgments is operative here, too. But now, television also has a hand in shaping the very ideas and images that people rely on for making those judgments in the first place. When the mainstreaming tendency works in conjunction with this use of intertextual criteria, people receive a "double-dose" of its influence. Yet, at the same time, a dispersal of meaning that characterizes the making of plausibility judgments when real-life criteria are used is at work here, too; and perhaps it is even more pronounced, since the use of intertextual criteria can involve people in a more diffuse and transitory process of meaning–making.

Regardless of the referents being used, plausibility judgments are the single most important factor in enabling people to maintain what I call *narrative-based* viewing relations (discussed in the next section). Whether it is by virtue of their paying consistent attention to the development of social action over the entire course of a program, their looking for human characterizations, their belief that something they see could happen in "real-life," the unpredictability of social action, or some combination of these factors, when people find programming plausible, they are more apt to stay mindfully engaged with programming and avoid the distractions of other activities, and, to a lesser extent, of other people, in the viewing culture. When programming is deemed plausible, it is more than likely that people will become mindfully and emotionally engaged with it on the terms that television provides. Yet, in making these judgments, people act reflexively. They recognize various meaningful aspects of the social worlds put before them, and they evaluate, in one way or another, the validity, or truth value, of what happens in those worlds. This recognition and evaluation are momentary yet crucial aspects of the reflexive process. In moving back and forth between them, people who make plausibility judgments are continually positioning and repositioning themselves with respect to television. In deciding what to watch or what not to watch, they give meaningful form to their activity. They act as selves, and, because of this, a sociality emerges from the making of plausibility judgments, one that cannot be reduced to the particular contents of the judgments themselves, nor to the mainstreaming or dispersal of meaning associated with them.

Understood in this way, plausibility judgments, in addition to whatever else they might be, are indicative of a kind of imaginative and emotional distancing on the part of viewers. They constitute part of a complex, multilayered symbolic world that people inhabit in the viewing culture, the dynamics of which are not adequately accounted for by notions of power and resistance alone.

Narrative-based viewing

In narrative-based viewing relations, people imaginatively constitute the developmental quality of narrative action and, in doing so, they embrace the discourse of programming as they make meaningful connections to the larger society. If programming remains plausible, people will stay mindfully engaged and avoid the distractions of other activities and, to a lesser extent, of other people, while they watch. I have identified two kinds of narrative-based viewing. In the first, people focused their attention on various ways that the realities of programming were represented – the quality of the writing, how lines are delivered, the directing, editing, lighting, or camera work, or "production values" more generally – as a basis for their mindful and emotional involvement while they watched. I call this "viewing at the representational level of social action." In the second, people focused on the realities themselves, and treated developments there not as something *represented*, but as something they took to be real. I call this "viewing at the 'real' level of social action."

Viewing at the representational level of social action

In this kind of narrative-based viewing, people recognized that what they were watching was an artifact, a product of the work of writers, actors, directors, editors, and others who are responsible for the creation of programming. They indicated this in the interviews and in the spontaneous commentary that routinely emerged during my participant observation. Typically, people commented on the technical or esthetic qualities involved in the depiction of social action as it unfolded in particular scenes. This included how the scenes were written, the way that a particular actor might have played a scene, the angles and movements of the camera, the editing, the lighting of scenes, or even the set design of a show. One viewer provided an account of how she watched *MASH*, her favorite show. Her account is typical of many others in which people indicate that *how* things are represented was an important dimension of their mindful and emotional involvement with programming. Regarding *MASH* she said:

They've done a nice job of making each character a caricature of real life – the woman in the army, the chaplain in the army – and I really just enjoy what character development they've allowed them . . . I giggle all the time at the stupid things each character and the person that they are is allowed to do. Frank Burns is such a jerk and he's great at it, and you get to sit there and look at him and say you're really a jerk – and he is, he's a wonderful jerk. Frank is a caricature of a real jerky kind of person.

There's a writing level [too]. The writers of the script are also working at what they are doing as writers. I do get back to as far as whose written that line and why. Frank is going to deliver a line to Alan Alda, and the writers have to make sure that Alan Alda is going to deliver a line back to Frank that's totally in character with Alan Alda. So I'm watching this dynamic to see how this reaction is going to take place . . . that Alan Alda is going to come back with something that is not going to be nice, but you're still going to laugh, and is it a line that is going to poke fun at Frank the person or the caricature of Frank.

Other viewers echoed these sentiments in their interview accounts as well. One person pointed out that in *Moonlighting* "the characterization is very important" in making it an "intelligent and witty" show. Another, a regular *Cosby* viewer, in describing why he liked this show said that "whoever writes the scripts does such a good job. Everything is smooth. The progression resembles something that has gone on in real life." Similarly, another viewer distinguished "good" from "bad" shows in terms of the way they were written, too, saying:

I always look for good writing, good plot . . . good tension, good character establishment and building, and a good realistic dialogue. When there is narration, is it artfully done . . . the structures of just good drama and literature [*sic*].

Still another viewer articulated very clearly the factors that, for him, went into making a "good" show:

A strong story-line is a pretty consistent draw for me, whether it's *Cheers* or *Cosby* or a drama. If there's a strong story-line I tend to appreciate it more. Intimately related with that is good writing – how the characters are written in and woven together. As an English major and a closet screenwriter, the writing is an important element. You can get into a whole conversation about TV being a boob tube and being an opiate of the masses and sitting in front of it and gawking, but that's where I think good story-lines and good writing are important because they are the things that get you stimulated and thinking about it.

By watching television in this way, these people understood the realities of programming as a construction, as something crafted by the people who work in television. As I just described, this understanding is sometimes conveyed in comments about specific shows, or about particular characters and story-lines within a show; at other times, it is revealed in language that moves beyond the more topical aspects of their viewing and articulates a broader and deeper idea of television's constructedness. Whether limited to internal comments or going beyond to see relations between shows, what these accounts indicate is that people became involved with the realities of entertainment programming, but in a distanced kind of way. Their practical understanding of programming as an artifact comes between the naturalness of television's depictions of social life and the power of these discourses to order and organize their mindful and emotional experience, even if, and when, they are ultimately accepting of such depictions as "real." As we can see from the role that plausibility judgments have in television culture, people act as selves, even when their thoughts and actions are productive of power. They give a *social* form to their viewing, which means that their mindful experience, while certainly productive of discursive power, is, at the very same time, constitutive of a capability to act beyond or different from that power, and without having to "oppose" it in any explicit way. The simple recognition by television viewers that what they watch is constructed is itself an indication that their world of mindful and emotional experience is much more complicated than is usually acknowledged in cultural studies accounts that focus on reading strategies alone.

Viewing at the "real" level of social action

In a second kind of narrative-based viewing, people ignore or fail to notice the "constructedness" of television programming, and instead take up mindful and emotional positions inside the time and space of the "realities" depicted there. The knowledge that they have of television as being *not* real, while certainly demonstrated at other times, is absent when people become more directly involved in the stories and in the emotional lives of television characters developing over the course of a show. They identify motives for characters' actions; agree with or perhaps second-guess their actions; antic- ipate different outcomes regarding characters' actions, scenes, or the story as a whole; or they speculate about the potential consequences of actions taken by those they see on television. Thoughts and emotions such as these take place *within* the world that writers, actors, directors, editors, and so on have constructed. For example, one viewer accounted for her favorite char- acters on the popular soap opera *Days of Our Lives* in the following terms:

Mike and Robin are exciting because they are in love together and she married someone else because she's Jewish and Mike's not Jewish, but she loves him and . . . so it's kind of exciting because they keep seeing each other on the side and all of this kind of stuff. Mike's . . . neat because I mean he jokes around a lot and then again he'll turn around and be serious, but he's more of a joker than anything else.

Another viewer regularly watched what she and others sometimes referred to as "reality-oriented" shows, such as *The Judge*, *True Confessions*, *The People's Court*, and *Divorce Court*. During the interview, she said that some shows were better than others in terms of allowing her to lose herself in the social world that was on show:

The Judge [a show in which civil cases are litigated] . . . to me it seems like reality, it seems like normal. Like if you were in that situation, what you would do? [With] *The Judge*, each case is different. Sometimes it will go right along with how I would do it, sometimes it will kind of go both ways, and sometimes it will go totally off the wall from something I would do.
    [With] *Divorce Court* . . . it's like . . . well . . . "I caught him sleeping with her, or he beat me, or" . . . that gets boring for me because it is the same thing with different

people or different names. You can usually say, "well, he's going to win or she's going to win" within the first couple of minutes and then usually I'm right. [With] *The Judge* it seems that you have to listen to the whole thing.

Still another viewer, a long-time fan of *General Hospital*, identified quite nicely the fine line that existed for her between viewing in a way that takes into account television's constructedness and viewing in a way that focuses more on the story itself. In her interview, she pointed out that *General Hospital* was one show that she is "stuck with" for fifteen years because, she said, "it was always on at a time that was appropriate for me to be watching, and you do get hooked into the characters – you watch them age, and get better with their roles." But she went on to say:

I feel that I know the characters as characters. I don't think of the actors and actresses as really being that person. I can probably slip into the fact of them being real people every once in a while – it depends on how good they are doing their role. There was a scene last week that had me sobbing and crying. It was about surrogate parenting, and I think I got away from the character there. They became real people with real problems.

Other viewers seem to negotiate this same fine line in their viewing, too. One woman began watching *Dynasty* in its first year and has stayed with it since. She did so, she said, because:

they were real people ... Blake Carrington was the big guy, but he was also human, loving and caring – he could still be an asshole in the board room, but he loved his wife and they had a relationship. She was sensitive and vulnerable and had feelings about other people. They were real; they were like real people.

When people watched in either or both of these ways, they were, compared to any other way of watching television, much more likely to be mindfully and emotionally drawn into the story-telling conventions of programming and to sustain their involvement with them over the course of a given show or shows. It is in the story-telling conventions that the meaning of social life as it is depicted on television can receive its most elaborate treatment. In portraying a "content" to programs or parts of programs, the story-telling conventions represent the workings of mind and emotion in characters. In particular scenes, we can see characters think, feel, and act; we can also see them interact with others in varied situations, and, in this way, witness the ways that different thoughts and feelings, different needs and motivations, different desires, even, are acted out and reacted upon. The thoughts, feelings, and intentions of characters in scenes and segments of a show are situated by the broader movement and resolution of story-lines as they intersect, or run parallel to one another, or both, over the course of a show. The development of the story, including, of course, the selection of camera angles and the editing, gives a distinctive, meaningful perspective to the depiction of social action on television. And all of this unfolds *in time*. It has *duration*. Through story-telling conventions, depictions of social action can take on depth, complexity, and, above all, a developmental quality, which is what enables them to be understood as corresponding to "real-life."

In narrative-based viewing, people reconstruct the depth and complexity, but, especially, the developmental quality of social action as their own mindful and emotional involvement with the characters and stories and places depicted. The meaning elaborated in the story-telling conventions becomes the meaning that people elaborate in their own minds. In doing so, each person acts as a self. They place themselves in various situations; they judge and evaluate the motivations and actions of characters; they imagine the outcomes of actions, and they imagine what it would be like to lead the lives of the people they see on the screen. The fact that all of this took place in relation to televisual image worlds makes each person's action as a self different from what they are when other people are present in their lives. Nevertheless, their actions as a self were not any less real to them. Those I interviewed were indeed active participants in narrative-based viewing, as the following excerpts from the interviews demonstrate. For example, one viewer offered this account of how she actively reconstructed the meaning of what she watched:

I think that those shows . . . like *The People's Court* are probably best because I like to see what the outcome is . . . you know, like that one guy comes and says, "What do you think Judge Wapner will say?" So we try to guess before . . . you know . . . what we think. It's on an educational side too, as far as the law is concerned. You do pick up things from it. Like a lot of people . . . if it's an auto accident or something like that and they take you to court . . . he gets real upset if you don't have more than one estimate. So you know, hey, if this ever happens to you, you have to have more than one estimate, or you're going to get laughed at. We like things like that where you can try and figure them out before the judge does and see what he's going to say. On *Wheel of Fortune* we try to guess the clue before they do.

Similarly, another viewer, a regular viewer of *Our House* (a family-oriented, prime-time drama), offered this account of his active involvement in the story-lines presented in this show:

The show is not only stimulating from the standpoint of how families [*sic*] interact with one another to make it, but it's also got some educational value to it, because they take different problems and they deal with them. It teaches a real way to live.

I like the way the adults teach the children. They allow the children to make decisions for themselves, but they put input [*sic*] in how they would look at it. But they always leave room for the child to make the decision. They're never ordering them to do something, and I like that. It's hard to set that up in real life, but it's beneficial.

I'd like to be like the old man on *Our House*. He shows a human side where he does not always control his tongue, but 90% of the time he's controlled. Where he's thinking out what he's going to say. I admire him. When I'm watching, I can put myself in that situation of thinking that I would like to do things in this way [the way the old man does]. You can see where on certain issues he's stubborn, he's wrong, but he's never closed minded about it. I mean he might be for a period of a few days, but it ends up working on him and he always ends up doing what's right. I'd like to think I could be like that.

In either or both of these ways of watching, viewers must *continue* recreating *in their own minds* whatever developments in social action occur through the story-telling conventions. If not, they move – almost imperceptibly, in most cases – into other kinds of viewing relations, and the distinctiveness that comprises narrative-based viewing is lost, at least for that moment. To the extent that they do, the varied ways that they construct the meaning of programming are, at the same time, extending the discursive ordering and organizing of social life depicted in the story-telling conventions. In this way, what *they* generate as *their own* understandings of people, of their actions, of their social situations, or even of the broader contours of social life in the United States – indeed, in the world – is productive of television's power. And, because the meaning–making activity of people in narrative-based viewing is, as I said earlier, itself an extension of their capability to act as a self, this discursive power of television can be understood to produce this capability of self, too.

Critical viewing

It is obvious to even the most casual observer of the viewing culture that people who watch television do not simply accept as plausible everything they see and hear. This is true, even when they look for programming that is plausible and, because of that, become involved in narrative-based viewing. This was certainly the case in my research. The people that I interviewed and watched with were routinely critical of what passed before them on the screen. Even though much of the time they looked for things to be plausible, and wanted to become involved in characters' lives and the stories their lives were part of, most of them indicated that they found most programming to be implausible much of the time. They did, however, continue to watch, which is perhaps one of the reasons why criticisms of television programming occurred as frequently as they did.

Among these people, I found that three different kinds of critical viewing took place on a regular basis. The first was characterized by people questioning the plausibility of specific depictions of social action; the second by their moving beyond specific depictions and identifying broader patterns of implausibility; and the third by their recognizing the commercial basis of formulaic programming.

Questioning the plausibility of specific depictions

In its varied forms, critical viewing offers perhaps the clearest indication that watching television is a reflexive activity for people. Virtually everyone who watches television struggles to define the meaning of what they watch, even if they do not ordinarily articulate their criticisms as fully formed "oppositional" readings of the text that appears before them. Even those people in my study who said that they were less likely to become involved in narrative-based viewing regularly questioned the plausibility of what they watched. By questioning the plausibility of specific depictions, by generalizing from those criticisms, and by recognizing formula, people attempted to categorize the ways in which the commercial and institutional requirements of programming production and distribution shape story-telling conventions. Questioning the plausibility of specific depictions is the most elemental form of critical viewing. It is also the most limited. While they watched television, it was typical for people to take issue with one or another aspect of story-telling conventions. Whether it was the construction of situations or scenes, how a situation or scene "played out," how a story-line was constructed, or how it was resolved over the course of a given segment of a show or the show as a whole, people routinely questioned what they saw and heard.

For example, during the time of my research, a number of regular viewers of the daytime soap opera *General Hospital* voiced criticism of the way that a particular story-line, involving two regular characters, Bo and Hope, had become unbelievable in their eyes because the entanglement of these two characters with foreign intelligence agents and high-level Mafia figures seemed to "stray a bit too far" from the more personal, emotionally oriented issues of everyday life that were typical of the interactions that took place between these two characters. Similarly, a regular viewer of *All My Children* commented on the implausible way that the growth of one regular character's baby was portrayed:

I mean, they have a baby and within a year it's going to school, and not pre-school. They [the producers] move the story along, but there's no practicality . . . like I can't find a baby sitter, there's not enough money to buy clothes . . . we all wish we had that money available.

Another viewer of *All My Children* focused in our interview on the unreality of a particular story-line that had Jesse, a regular character, going undercover to assist the police in an investigation:

Some of the things, like Jesse for instance. If I wanted to go undercover to break a baby ring, just because I wanted to and I'm a city councilman, they wouldn't laugh you out of office, but they wouldn't give you a gun either . . . I'll just laugh and say that is not real.

And a regular viewer of *The Cosby Show* said that while she admired the "closeness and the loving feeling that goes throughout the show," there are occasions when what was presented was, in her eyes, simply not plausible:

When the kids come strolling through, I say, "Is this a typical family?" [Referring to a specific scene in a recent episode] . . . Do you know how much that sweater costs? I saw that sweater in the store and it costs $120.00 and it is on the little one – Rudy! She's going to outgrow it in three months.

In a similar fashion, another viewer commented on the implausible quality of a kidnapping previously depicted on *Knot's Landing* by saying that:

They do something that in real life, you wouldn't do. Like the guy who kidnapped Karen. It's ridiculous. The guy's obviously crazy. The way he did it – people who kidnap people don't do it like that. The guy in one scene is a clear thinking, normal human being and in another scene he's a total moron. It doesn't all fit together.

This questioning of plausibility is focused on specific depictions, primarily because people are following as it unfolds before them on the screen and they do not want to feel duped, or insulted, by what they recognize as patently false portrayals of social life. As a participant observer in different viewing situations, it was quite common to witness people verbalizing their criticisms. This was true when I watched with people who would otherwise be viewing alone, or when I participated in ongoing group viewing situations. This voicing of criticism was also evident in the interview accounts that people provided of their own viewing, both when others were present and when they were alone with television. This is particularly important, because it indicates that, even in situations that are, by definition, absent of the social interaction that we typically associate with critical viewing, people continue to question what they see and hear. The fact that they are alone with television does not stop them from monitoring, evaluating, and judging what is on. During these moments when they recognize depictions that fail to "ring true" for them, people are, in effect, having a conversation with themselves. They become mindful of implausibility much like they do when they or others voice criticisms in the conversations that take place when they view together. There is, after all, a sociality to critical viewing in solitary situations, too.

Generalizing from questions of plausibility

In another level of critical viewing, people *generalized* their criticisms of the presentation of social action in programming. In the interviews and in conversations that occurred while we watched together, many people said that in their day-to-day use of television, similar kinds of specific questions and criticisms occurred over and over again. This seemed to have had a cumulative impact on the mindfulness with which they watched television, enabling them to move beyond whatever attention they paid to specific depictions of social action and identify broader patterns of implausibility in programming. One viewer, in typifying the experience of many others, referred to this as a recognition of "the mind set" of a program: a patterning of subject-matter, settings, story-lines, characterizations, character interactions, and so on that, in this case, was understood to be *im*plausible. This generalizing from questions of plausibility was evident, for example, in one viewer's account of *All My Children*:

Sometimes, their [the producers'] story-lines are not believable, and your mind just tells you its not real, because he was just born and here he's 3 years old already, or here he's 10, or he's gone for three years and now he's 18. That's what I mean about unreality . . . And if there's a gun on one of these programs, a child always picks it up. Two or three times on *All My Children*, a child picks up a gun and you think the child is going to kill himself and he doesn't. I mean, even I know that you don't leave guns around and I'm not an actor. It turns your interest off because then you know . . . that's not real.

   Once you get the mind of a program down, sometimes you just really do not have to think about it. There's a sub-conscious format to the program and then they have all the little bits and pieces, but you know they're heading toward a certain end, and so it's really not hard when they have four different little sections, because, if you've watched for any length of time, you can follow it from that point on. Because when you notice them talking on the telephone, you notice, automatically, well Erica, she's going to be listening. That was her favorite thing about ten years ago. A phone call would come in while everybody [*sic*] . . . you know somebody else is listening. You don't talk on the phone and just pour out everything that you've done because someone else is going to hear it.

Other people expressed this generalized kind of criticism as well. Many regular viewers of the *Cosby Show* came to recognize the fact that Mr. and Mrs. Huxtable rarely seemed to feel the pressures of their day-to-day work in the medical and legal professions, and furthermore, that, even if they did, it never seemed to impinge in a negative way on their relations with each other or with their children. That, they thought, was simply not plausible. In this regard, one viewer said:

I think it is a little too pat, probably. Obviously they are both working in jobs –
whenever they work – that would leave them both stressed, and coming home and
acting as relaxed and easy going all the time . . . [it] doesn't appear that any of them
are ever terribly stressed where they would maybe take something out on the kids
that they hadn't meant to because maybe they were tired or somebody had done
something to them that day, you know?

Similarly, another regular viewer of *The Cosby Show*, thought that it presented "a nice little family, but it is also real phony, too. Their house is *never*
messed up, and no one ever yells at anyone else. I notice these things," she
said, "and it takes away a little bit from what I can get out of it." Still
another *Cosby* viewer remarked that "the *show* is so obviously contrived –
the *whole situation* that the show is about, I cannot believe that that would
happen in real life" (my emphasis).

At the time of my interviewing, the situation-comedy *Family Ties* followed immediately after *The Cosby Show* on NBC's Thursday night prime-
time schedule, and it, too, was a focal point for many viewers' generalized
criticisms. On the whole, the people I interviewed found it to be less plausible than *The Cosby Show*. One regular viewer commented that:

It seems that I'm seeing a truer portrayal of a family relationship and interaction
between husband and wife and parents and children [on *Cosby*] than I see on *Family
Ties*. The whole set up [on *Family Ties*] jars me. To me, it's like a star vehicle for
Michael J. Fox, who is amusing, he's very good in the role and stuff like that, but his
parents always come across as fools, or somehow inept, and he's somehow guiding
them through life, and it just rings false to me . . . I just find the situation very
obvious, trite, and contrived.

This more generalized kind of criticism was typical of the way that people
viewed other programs, too. For example, one woman said that she was a
regular viewer of *Dynasty*, but that, over the years, the growing implausibility of the characters, their interactions with one another, as well as the
unbelievability of the story-lines led eventually to her not watching the
show:

I quit watching it because they [the characters] went from being real people to being
. . . jerks, to being bitches. This person is going from a warm, sensitive, loving person
who also has a career and works, to being a bitch. "You are now in the bitch box.
You may not be human, you may not be warm and caring, you may not cry. You
must always be caustic and be a bitch. You may not have feelings. You [she refers to
a stereotypical man on the show] on the other hand must be strong and fatherly.
These are not real people.

Another viewer was a longtime fan of *Knot's Landing*, but he became
increasingly disillusioned by the implausibility of the show. "*Knot's*

Landing," he said, "has just carried all this garbage too far when you're talking about soap type shows. The characters are awfully implausible, and they do things that normal people wouldn't do." He went on to compare *Knot's Landing* to *Dynasty*. He said that he and his wife watched when it first came on, but, after a while, they grew tired of it:

> They [the creators] make it so that it [*Dynasty*] is exciting and interesting. Their argument . . . is that it's an escape. But I look at that and I say "Jeez, if I owned a big oil company, I wouldn't live like that, I wouldn't run my oil company that way." Real business people aren't like those people. [They] are morons, they're airheads. So when I see that I say "Sure, I want to be taken out of my element, I want to live in a fantasy world when I am watching TV just like everybody does. But I want to believe that it's a real world, not that it's some cartoon, and to me, *Dynasty* is a cartoon."

When they generalized from questions of plausibility, viewers' criticisms remained grounded in the story-telling conventions, but, unlike what occurred in the more elemental kind of critical viewing that I discussed, their meaning–making activity was now freed from the limitations that accompanied attention to any specific depiction in programming. People still found meaning in the discourse of story-telling conventions; but, because they identified broader patterns to the violations of what they thought that programming should, or could, mean, they became involved with discourse in a more mindfully and emotionally distanced way compared to when their attention was focused on specific depictions alone. Nevertheless, an important operative assumption of both of these critical viewing relations was that the intent of those who produce programming (meant here in the broadest sense) is to depict social life in a realistic way and thereby engage the viewer in meaningful communication *about* social life. From the viewers' standpoint, this can occur on the representational level, the "real" level, or both.

These two kinds of critical viewing usually occurred together and were intertwined with narrative-based viewing relations, too. This was true, as I said earlier, both when people viewed alone or with others, but it was more characteristic of viewing with others.

In the situations I observed, when people watch television together, their interactions with one another serve to draw out whatever questions or comments they may have regarding plausibility, something that is simply not possible when people watch by themselves. Typically, a comment or criticism by one viewer regarding a specific scene or action on screen would provoke further commentary by others who were present. This kind of interaction centering on the questioning of plausibility then serves as a jumping-off point for more extended discussions concerning developments within the show being watched, comparisons between that show and others, comparisons between the characters or story-lines of different shows, and so on. Talk of this kind inevitably involves the kind of generalizing that I documented earlier. In the process, the mindfulness exhibited in either or both of these critical viewing relations gives way to a more contextually oriented viewing practice in which people relate to one another various aspects of their previous participation in a range of narrative-based and critical viewing relations. In doing so, their viewing practice sometimes takes on a distinctly intertextual quality as they associate what they are presently watching with the multitude of televisual and filmic images stored away in their minds. Based on my observations, though, when people watch together, they wait until commercial breaks to engage fully in discussions of this kind because their primary intent is to *follow* what is on rather than discuss it.

Sometimes, in my research, what one viewer aptly characterized as "the game of television" emerged out of this sharing of criticisms and the associative connections that were made between them. In this game, viewers challenge one another to see who is the first to notice something implausible in what they are watching. This voicing of criticism becomes the basis for what people share while they watch. No doubt, this game, with its emphasis on recognizing what was implausible, was a source of much pleasure for those engaged in it. But, along with the pleasure they derived from playing it, the game also served as a means for them to continually recreate an awareness that they were not taken in, or duped, by the unreality of television programming.

Whether or not people make a game out of viewing television critically, the lack of plausibility that they find in programming can indeed replace their desire to find plausible programming as a basis for continuing to watch. This shift in the criteria for sustaining attention to television was evident in my interview with one woman when she said:

Every once in a while we watch something just God-awful like . . . was it *Lace* . . . no, no, it was *Mistral's Daughter*. We watched it because it was about an artist. It was so bad that we loved it.

Sentiments such as these were echoed by other people that I interviewed, too. Among them was a viewer who described why implausible programming could be so entertaining to watch:

I like watching stupid television programs . . . and stupid movies; anything that knows its stupid and has no pretensions of being anything else, as opposed to the prime-time soap operas which think they are real drama. That's one of the reasons I used to watch [daytime] soap operas – I used to make fun of them. They are great to watch because they are so stupid. I can't imagine people that actually think that this stuff actually happens. I can't think that the people who make it take that stuff seriously. But that is a different story. I'm talking about the people who make it – who are making you watch it. If they're honestly trying to tell me that this is a good program and it's a stupid program, I won't watch it; but if it looks like these people are laughing as they are writing this down, they're going, "This is the most idiotic thing I've written in my life," then I'll watch it. *Dynasty, Dallas, Falcon Crest*, and other night-time soaps . . . I enjoy laughing at that kind of stuff. As long as they know it's ridiculous. If they ever try to tell me that it is serious, well, that's insulting to sit and watch something that the people want you to believe.

By questioning the plausibility of programming and generalizing from questions of plausibility, people who watched television distance them-selves from the realities depicted via story-telling conventions. This, in turn, enables them to distance themselves from the preferred meanings – and the power – of the discourses that circulate in those story-telling conventions. In gaining this mindful and emotional distance from the social realities pre-sented to them, viewers I talked with often made use of their own real-life experiences and circumstances, or their own conceptions of real-life, as standards for judging the plausibility of programming. Yet, things did not remain so simple for people. As I pointed out earlier, I also documented a *shift* in the making of plausibility judgments – from such real-life reference points to televisual and filmic ones. And many of the people who exhibited such a shift in their reference points were, for the most part, unaware that their reference points had, in fact, shifted over the course of their making whatever judgments that they did regarding programming. Additionally, by looking for implausible programming to begin with, viewers moved as far as they could, it seemed, from the *realities* presented on television without abandoning the idea that developments of meaning in the story-telling con-ventions should form the basis of their continued attention.

Recognizing formula

The third and, in my opinion, most sophisticated, kind of critical viewing involves what I have termed the recognition of formula. It almost goes without saying that virtually everyone has constituted their own history of watching television. Integral to this history are, among other things, the seeking out of plausible programming and the involvement in narrative-based viewing. Also integral to this history is the making of critical judg-ments regarding what is seen or heard, including as I have said, questioning the plausibility of specific depictions as well as a critique of more general patterns of implausibility that people came to find there.

Some of the people that I interviewed and watched with, however, invoked yet another kind of criticism. They often employed terms such as "formula" and "predictable" in accounting for what they watched; they sometimes identified a "they" who were not necessarily the creators of a particular program, but whose interests they believed shaped programming more broadly; or they used the word "thing" rather than describing the particulars of what they saw and heard on television, and went on to say that they recognized the same *thing*, or *things*, occurring over and over again, not in a particular show, but across programming more generally. In these ways, people formulated a language that was at once more abstract and inclusive than that which they typically used in making the other kinds of criticisms that I discussed earlier. The use of this language, both within their own minds and in conversation with others, constitutes a distinctive way of seeing the implausibility of television programming. This was evident in the comments that surfaced in many of the interview accounts.

For example, one viewer said that he used to watch *60 Minutes* every Sunday night, but now, "it is so much alike – time after time it is the same *thing*" (emphasis added). Similarly, another viewer spoke in words that echoed those of many others viewers when he remarked that "most of the time, you can see *things* a mile off. Basically, you know what is going to happen because it is so predictable" (emphasis added). What follows is a sampling of still other viewers' comments regarding the recognition of formula in the viewing culture:

Most shows are built around formula, you know, and after a while you get familiar with that formula and after a while I get bored. That's why I prefer live performance type shows, because you do not know what's going to happen the next time around.

There is something manipulative about TV, and I do not mean this in an evil sense. Like laugh tracks. They'll tell you when something is funny, and they have to, because you wouldn't recognize it otherwise because it's not particularly funny. I don't like being insulted in that way. There is practically nothing that has any wit to it, or dramas that are in the least bit plausible, or have any human interest, really. The formulas are staring you in the face.

Most of the network stuff is so formula-ridden. I've watched the *St. Elsewhere* thing or *Hill Street Blues* a couple of times, and it is like, "oops," you can predict it, here it comes, and then they have four plots running at once and it's . . . it just becomes predictable.

I was drawn into *Simon and Simon* and *Magnum* . . . they are completely normal shows without those characters. If they put two other guys as *Simon and Simon* or if they took Tom Selleck away from *Magnum*, it would be just a formula show where the camera work is like . . . turn it on Harry and go get a sandwich.

If you look at a lot of the programs, they are all the same thing, especially these police programs. They just put another one on – *Houston Nights*. I just saw the ad on TV and in the *TV Guide*, and I thought, that's just another *Miami Vice*, which is another *Hill Street Blues*, you know? It's just a lot of noise and a lot of shooting . . . It's just the same stuff over and over again. The plots do not change, the noise level does not change. They are all predictable – you know what's going to happen.

The stuff on now is such garbage. I don't watch regular TV anymore – there's nothing on TV. They're stupid, they're predictable. With *Cheers*, I could tell you what the characters would say before they would say it. It's so banal. I lost interest in it.

We couldn't take our eyes off it [the mini-series *Lace*]. It was so predictable. I mean . . . it was so wrong. No one grew one iota. [laughter] . . . It was predictable, stereotyped, and a formula plot. You know the heroine is going to have some fatal flaw, like a bad temper; you know she's going to fall in love with a guy who treats her badly. It's a formula.

Generally speaking, in narrative-based viewing and in the two kinds of critical viewing that I already discussed, people operate with the assumption that the crafting of dialogue and stories, the presentation of visual imagery, or whatever else creative people do in making television shows, conveys meaning. Whether or not this meaning is consciously intended is less significant than the fact that it is, indeed, conveyed. From this particular standpoint, then, viewers understand programming as a representation *of* realities of one sort or another. When they recognize formula, viewers are, in effect, recognizing how the varied forms of this creative work carried out by writers, actors, directors, editors, and so on can be overshadowed by the more purely commercial concerns with generating popular, i.e., profitable, programming. In other words, they recognize the consequences that commercial concerns carry in constructing programming that, in their eyes, lacks plausibility. Some of the people who recognized formula connected this lack of plausibility with the production of programming as a commodity much more explicitly than others. At certain times, their language conveyed this awareness that commercial television often moves away from concerns with realism, authenticity, esthetics, or even politics, and moves instead toward a kind of predictability in the packaging of programming for increased market share. It was common for viewers to say that much of what was on television was "treadmill entertainment," with "no value in it" because "it is so predictable." For example, one viewer pointed out that she did not "have the patience for regular TV anymore," because "there's nothing on TV." The shows, she said, were "stupid, predictable," and aimed at "the lowest common denominator." Another viewer succinctly stated what he understood as the relationship between formulaic programming and the structure of commercial network television:

To a great extent, I find most of what is on TV mind-deadening . . . Its only real purpose is to sell products – it's a capital intensive medium through which business sells products. Shows are really not produced in and of themselves totally for their entertainment, but primarily as vehicles to sell, and certainly, they want them to look attractive so that people will tune in. Ultimately, they are less concerned about content, the value of the content or the program than they are about wooing the viewers to get the commercials.

I'll occasionally watch network programs . . . [but] I won't get involved in a two- or three-hour TV movie, just because they are junky – the low aim, the predictability, the lowest common denominator. The tendency is to play it safe; even if it's a TV drama about a social problem, they tend to want to avoid making statements.

Ideas such as these were on the minds of many other viewers as well. For example, one woman thought that "most TV plays it way too safe, because they are selling a product. They are not willing," she said, "to take the risk of going out on a limb. It would give me more stimulation, I would be far more interested if they did." And another viewer commented that he has seen a noticeable change in network television from the 70s to the mid 80s. "One of the reasons may be," he said, is that "TV series are not meant to last now – if you do not hit it right away, you're canceled, therefore not as much thought and care and attention is put into it. It's all a disposable commodity." Interestingly enough, this idea that the commercial requirements for television production and distribution have eroded the quality of programming over the last decade (at least) was a theme that ran throughout other interviews as well, and it was stated very clearly by one viewer:

In the last ten years, my TV watching of series has dropped off dramatically because of . . . it's just . . . I hate markets to be flooded. I can see that happening. All the sensationalism got to me. Shows like *Night Rider*, *Fall Guy* – these action movies that the kids like. There's so much sensationalism that these guys [his children] don't get to see a real good character actor. They may not see a story and a problem – it's dealt with, it's solved. You know, they see turning trucks, they see burning buildings. It's fun, but the market is glutted with it; the television industry is glutted with it . . . But people need it; apparently, people need it because the Nielson ratings wouldn't go up just because it costs a lot of money . . . I am so fed up with all the big money. Everyone can do anything they want without working for it.

In fact, some viewers found it virtually impossible to discuss the specifics of viewing – favorite shows, good shows versus bad shows, etc. – without first calling attention to what they believed was the formulaic nature of television programming in general.

When they questioned the plausibility of specific depictions, or when they formed more generalized criticisms of plausibility, viewers did indeed distance themselves, mindfully and emotionally speaking, from the preferred meanings that were conveyed through the story-telling conventions. When they recognized formula, however, they *thought through* the plausibility or implausibility with which social realities were represented there. They did this by symbolizing a commodity form to programming – what they named as formula, predictability, lowest common denominator, and so on. In this viewing relation, then, programming meant more than – or, better yet, something other than – what was conveyed through story-telling conventions, however plausible or implausible the realities they represented were taken to be. Viewers were no longer limited, as it were, to making meaning by accepting the realities depicted on a show, by criticizing them through conversation, by comparison with their own real-life circumstances, or by comparing them to the realities depicted in other television shows, films, newspapers, or magazines. When they recognized formula, viewers disengaged themselves from the social realities depicted in programming, including the varieties of creative work represented in them, and supplied instead a referent of another kind: commodification – a process that, in their eyes, interferes with programming being able to have or carry meaning in the first place.

The mindful qualities of recognizing formula, including this disengagement from the text, were reconstructed quite nicely by one woman, a self-described "lifetime TV viewer," when she said

Having watched TV as long as I have – since I was a little kid – there's a formula that works. It's one in which the hero does not get killed, because he has to be on TV the next week. Certain things have to be resolved within this format, and have to be resolved in 30 minutes time. So they set up their problem, people deal with that problem, and then the show is over. There's no depth to it. This cardboard character deals with this cardboard problem, and it's over. You can predict what's going to happen. You can recognize the formula, and you can see what's going to happen next, and you do dis-engage.

Interestingly enough, this recognition of formula does not appear to offer evidence of "resistant" or "oppositional" readings of the text, at least not as they are typically represented in cultural studies' accounts. To be sure, the viewers I talked with articulated more than mere opinions when they took issue with what they saw or heard on television. While it was more the exception rather than the rule, sometimes, something of these viewers' own more deeply held values and beliefs found its way into their criticisms of plausibility, either in specific or more general terms. When this occurs, critical viewing does indeed resemble the resistant or oppositional reading strategies that cultural studies' analysts associate with the workings of people's identities. For example, one woman voiced her own, feminist-based criticism of *Miami Vice*, a show that her husband and two teenage sons watched regularly:

Miami Vice really upsets me. Crockett and Tubbs just go from one sexy girl to another from show after show. And I can't believe that they, you know. That's part of why people watch it . . . the titillation of watching sex scenes. But I can't believe that they cared for the girl last week if they're that hot about the one this week. I resent that!

Similarly, another viewer used his working-class background to criticize the depiction of family life on *The Cosby Show* and *Family Ties* by pointing out that

Both *Cosby* and *Family Ties* are wealthy families. To me, you couldn't consider them middle class. You've got a doctor and a lawyer in one . . . and they got everything that they need. These are the unreal aspects of the show for me. I do not have any desire to be like that.

In a slightly different way, this kind of class-based critique was also articulated by one man when, in speaking about *All My Children*, one of his favorite soap operas, he said that "it is a life you'll never lead, you'll never have, but I think every American wants to have something like that. But, since you'll never have it, it is your fantasy watching something like that."

By contrast, when they recognized formula, viewers became involved in a significantly different form of cultural practice. As I said earlier, they no doubt disengaged themselves from the text, and, in this way, deflected the preferred meanings of the story-telling conventions. But, in doing so, they did not oppose, or resist dominant discourses by supplying alternative, identity-based discourses of their own, because they were no longer "reading" the text *as if* it were a representation of social realities. In this particular moment of mindful involvement with television, the way in which class, gender, race, or any other aspect of social life was depicted mattered less to people than at other times. They did not feel the need to draw upon their own class, gender, race (or other) identities, identities that were, in large part, still constructed outside the viewing culture, to comment upon or evaluate what they saw or heard. No, instead, they drew from their previous involvement with television itself to symbolize an altogether different referent for the discourses they encountered, namely, the commodity form.

The recognition of formula is a type of practical knowledge that emerges from the viewing culture. After all, it is in the viewing culture that people repeatedly encounter commercial programming and its standardized, commodity form. They encounter standardized representations in other arenas, too – going to the movies, reading magazines and newspapers, or listening to the radio, cassettes, and CDs – and this certainly contributes to the formation of their knowledge regarding the commodification of meaning. This is particularly true for younger viewers, who may be more likely than older viewers to participate in subcultures on high-school and college campuses. These subcultures sustain themselves, at least in part, through the shared activities of listening to and commenting upon music. The recognition of "top 40" music as something highly commodified is often a starting-point for listeners' disengagement from mainstream tastes and their turn to less commercially accessible alternatives. Still, television has often been the predominant mass medium in the lives of most people – including young people – and it stands to reason that a good deal of their insight regarding commodification stems from their repeated involvement with it.

As a form of practical knowledge, then, the recognition of formula is not based on identities that viewers *bring to* television from other social locations; that is, identities such as class, gender, race, ethnicity, sexuality, and so on. In fact, the knowledge and insight that comes with recognizing formula appears to cut across these locations. For this reason, I see this particular viewing relation as having the potential to provide a common cultural reference point among people whose lives consist, more and more, of repeated encounters with objects, ideas, and especially images that are marked by the commodification process.

The three kinds of critical viewing that I have discussed play a pivotal role in the viewing culture. They indicate that there are, in fact, multiple ways that people who watch television can and do distance themselves on a regular basis from its discursive power. This distancing is, for the most part, a momentary phenomenon: a specific depiction is criticized; if more generalized criticisms are put forth, they, too, occupy only one moment in the broader movement and flow of viewing relations; and, even if people go so far as to recognize what they watch as formulaic, this moment of disengagement is just that – a moment that must eventually be followed by other moments in which people again become mindfully involved with programming, begin to talk with others, or find something else to do. Yet, these moments are repeated over and over and over again, day-in and day-out, and, in time, the distinctive sociality that constitutes each type of critical viewing has become an ongoing feature, not only of the viewing culture, but of the capabilities that people have for acting reflexively in it. There is continuity in this momentary refusal to accept the ordering and organizing of social life that television proposes. This is especially true of the instances in which people generalized from questions of plausibility or recognized formulas, because these kinds of criticism are predicated on the identification of *patterns* of implausibility.

People I worked with did not sustain the mindfulness of critical viewing to the same degree that they did narrative-based viewing. This was due in large part to the fact that criticisms of programming were not supported, objectively, by developments in the story-telling conventions, as was the case with narrative-based viewing. But it was also due to the fact that, compared with narrative-based viewing, critical viewing does not generally require as consistent an identity-based reading strategy, since, as I said, criticisms were for the most part momentary, whereas following a story, for example, was not. As a result, people never really translate the continuity of critical viewing into the consistency and coherence that marks narrative-based viewing.

On the whole, I found that people typically move back and forth between the various narrative-based and critical viewing relations that I have discussed. In addition to whatever regularities television provides (in terms of the characters and stories depicted and the discourses inscribed there), it also presents people with a flow of different segments of social action; segments that are not necessarily consistent, normatively speaking, and that do not always add up to a discursively coherent whole. Commercial breaks and network promotional spots interrupt the development of story-telling conventions in any given show, they are juxtaposed to one another between shows, and the shows themselves often shift normative ground over the course of any given day or evening. Furthermore, the recombinant nature of television programming, in conjunction with the fact that most shows are designed to have a multiple-audience appeal, means that what is seen as plausible can shift, sometimes repeatedly and quite abruptly, from one moment to the next. Like the workings of flow and segmentation, these factors, too, may lead people to move from one or another kind of narrative-based viewing to one or another kind of critical viewing, and back again, over the course of their viewing activity. All of these characteristics apply, even when people seek out plausible programming to begin with, or when they eventually became highly involved with what they are watching. Even then, when people expect their viewing to be consistent or coherent, their minds are often in continual movement, back and forth between involvement and critical distance.

In the moments of critical viewing and in the longer periods of attentiveness that characterize narrative-based viewing, people interpret what they see and hear. Their minds are focused *in* the meanings they make. When they watch favorite shows or other "quality" programs, or when they expect to become more deeply involved with what they watch, or, when any of these factors come together, people sustain their involvement in narrative-based viewing. On such occasions, their meaning–making activity is more developed than at other times. It exhibits more consistency and coherence. It takes on a more elaborate form. All of this is to say, really, what I said earlier about narrative-based viewing: namely, that it centers the mindful involvement that people have with programming in the story-telling conventions, and, in a seemingly natural way, extends the workings of television's discursive power in their lives.

At the same time, however, the frequent movements that viewers make, back and forth between narrative-based and critical viewing, work to undermine this centering tendency. What might appear, from the outside, as mindfully consistent and coherent, is, from the vantage-point of those who must construct meaning from one moment to the next, a much more variegated and uncertain process. Their mindfulness can shift, say, from involvement in the realities depicted, to distance from them, to disengagement from the action altogether, and back again to involvement, this time at the representational level; or from involvement at the representational level of the realities depicted, to distance, and perhaps back again to involvement in the realities depicted; or, from involvement in the realities of a scene or interaction, to a critique of an interaction or what transpired in a scene, and then perhaps on to a more general critique of patterns within a show before settling back into a kind of involvement that takes notice of how lines are delivered or a scene written. I could go on in this way, perhaps mentioning as well the gaps and disjunctures that occur regularly when people attempt to follow and make sense of television's story-telling conventions. But, even if I did, I would be unable to capture *all* of the permutations and combinations of mindfulness that are possible when people who watch television – people, I might add, who want to stay mindfully involved in a consistent way with what they watch – employ their full repertoire of viewing relations. As I reconstruct it, and as people reconstructed it for me, this rather ordinary way of watching television is simply too complex, too unpredictable, to be understood only in terms that account for consistency and coherence in meaning–making activity, or by the even broader notion that one's mindful involvement is centered by television's story-telling conventions. Certainly, all of this takes place in the viewing culture. But that is not *all* that takes place there. Working simultaneously, and at cross-purposes with such centering tendencies are the decentering ones – the movements, gaps, and disjunctures, among other things, that do not always allow television viewing to "add up" and have a unified meaning for people.

Image-based viewing

Thus far, everything I have said pertaining to viewing relations has been predicated on the idea that, when people watch television, they want to follow the development of social action as it unfolds in the specific shows they have chosen to watch. Narrative-based viewing designates those occasions when people are mindfully engaged inside the discourses of story-telling conventions, and critical viewing designates those moments when they are distanced – and even disengaged – from them. Even though many things may vary when people orient themselves to television in this way – what they watch, whether they watch alone or with others, who they watch with, whether they are feeling relaxed or tired – it is generally the case that developments depicted through the story-telling conventions continue to provide the focal point of their mindful attention to programming. This is true, as I said, when narrative-based viewing predominates, when critical viewing becomes more frequent, even when, in the game of television, people look to watch *im*plausible programming, or when, in different ways, there is much movement back and forth between narrative-based and critical viewing.

But people do not always watch television with the idea in mind of consistently following the development of social action. Rather than grounding their mindful attention in the logic of story-telling conventions, quite often they base it instead in their understanding that programming is, after all, simply a series of images, and that it could be mindfully engaged on that level, too, either in conjunction with or in addition to their sustained attention to whatever depictions of social life it carries. I refer to this alternative way of watching television as "image-based viewing."

Image-based viewing is predicated on at least two factors: one is an objective structural feature of television itself, and the other, a disposition that has been cultivated by people who watch television regularly. Objectively, the commodity forms of television, notably the continual flow and segmented structure of programming, work in conjunction with one another and with the story-telling conventions, to generate for those who are watching a virtually endless succession of depictions of social action. This occurs both within and across channels. In considering all of the programming available to people, the succession of depictions found there is not always normatively consistent from one moment to the next; nor does it necessarily add up, on a broader level, to *only* coherent presentations of one sort of discourse or another. As I discussed in chapter 3, this is largely because programming is typically marketed to multiple audiences at the same time and, when it comes to any particular program, there is often uncertainty regarding what, in terms of settings, stories, or characters, will resonate best with different audiences. Keep in mind, too, that such strategizing is always changing, as cable and broadcast networks continually juggle their lineups in the pursuit of higher ratings. All of this is to say that normatively *unrelated* depictions of social action routinely succeed one another on any given channel, and are juxtaposed to one another at the same time across different channels. Add to this the fact that programming can be seen as movements of visual imagery that are distinct, really, from the meaning inscribed there by story-telling conventions. Objectively, then, television provides people who watch with the opportunity to move freely between multiple depictions of social action, between various movements of visual imagery, as well as back and forth from one level of programming to another – all of this across more than forty channels.

On the "subjective" side of things, people who watch television regularly are quite adept at critical viewing. After all, they have been doing it for years, really. They question the plausibility of what they see and hear, they formulate more general criticisms of story-telling conventions, and, perhaps most importantly, they recognize formulaic aspects of programming. In fact, the mindful disengagement that occurs when people recognize formula is, more than anything else that people do with television, indispensable to the emergence of image-based viewing. By repeatedly disengaging themselves from the story-telling conventions *altogether,* and doing so across a wide variety of different programs, people have come to cultivate a distinctive disposition toward television. It is a disposition that allows them to orient themselves to television knowing, in the back of their minds, that programming does not always require their full attention – at least not when it comes to following the story-telling conventions. Over time, then, people can approach their own television use with the idea in mind that any particular image (television is after all an image flow), any particular depiction of social action – whether it involves a setting, scene, story-line, character, character interaction, or whatever else – is *commercially equivalent* with any other. What follows from this is that any particular image, depiction, or even show, is *interchangeable* in their minds, with any other. This disposition parallels the recognition of formula in that it lends a taken-for-granted quality to the mindful movements that people make out of the story-telling conventions altogether.

As a result of these two factors – one objective, the other subjective – the possibility always exists in the viewing culture for people to become mindfully involved with programming, not as a representation of social realities, but, instead, as *manipulable images.* Certainly, experienced television viewers always carry with them the capabilities for finding plausible programming, for involvement in narrative-based viewing, and for the kinds of mindful and emotional distancing that can follow from their criticisms of implausible depictions. None of this ever leaves them, and all of it routinely surfaces in what I am calling image-based viewing. But the insights gained from recognizing formula, together with the disposition to treat programming as manipulable images, serve to put these other, narrative-based and critical viewing relations in a new context, and, in the process, alters the meaningful significance that they can have for people. This new context is, simply put, image-based viewing.

While recognizing formula provides an initial point of departure for involvement in image-based viewing, over time, this way of watching television itself becomes ritualized, and, consequently, takes on a life of its own in the viewing culture. Because a number of the viewers I talked to already had this knowledge of programming as manipulable images, they could become directly involved in image-based viewing, without having to first pass through narrative-based viewing periods and the particular kind of involvement in story-telling conventions that it implied. In image-based viewing, mindful movements between narrative-based and critical viewing relations could, and did, still constitute much of what was meaningful for this group. Such patterns of movement, however, did not constitute all that was meaningful for them in the viewing culture. What remained – the excess, if you will – worked in conjunction with these more engaged movements to constitute the distinctive sociality of image-based viewing.

In my research, I documented three different image-based viewing relations. The first is "simultaneous viewing," the second is "channel switching," and the third I refer to as "image-play."

Simultaneous viewing

As I discussed in chapter 4, this simultaneous viewing had become a routine practice in the viewing culture for many, if not most, of the people that I spoke with who used television. In that chapter I talked about the turn to simultaneous viewing as a distinctive way for people to make the daily transition from work to home life. Here, I want to extend this discussion and analyze simultaneous viewing as one viewing relation in the context of several others.

Obviously, when people watch television while simultaneously doing other things, programming is not the only thing that occupies their attention. One can see, too, that when people watch television in this way, and this is what I found, the disposition for mindful disengagement comes to the fore and remains an influential pattern. People know that television does not always require their full attention. They can opt out of involvement with what is showing at any time. This opting out was aided, certainly, by the fact that, from the outset, other activities were always available. As with television, these other activities can be taken up or put down at any time, as people see fit. This is exemplified in numerous extracts from the interview accounts:

Tv is pretty much what I do every night. If it is a show that I really enjoy, then I'll give it all of my attention; but if it is something that's less than compelling, then I might be doing a crossword puzzle, I may be reading the paper, or a magazine. Sometimes I'll have it on and use it as background noise, so I'll be listening but I won't be watching. Crossword puzzles are good because it is easy to listen and not have a continuous train of thought in trying to read something. It's almost like a crossword puzzle is competing with the TV for my attention, and if the TV is boring, I'll get more into the puzzle, and if I am frustrated with the puzzle, I'll end up paying more attention to the TV, and then it's just a back and forth thing all night.

I read a book and watch TV at the same time, and people go "how do you do that, that is nuts, you're wasting electricity," but I say that is a good show and I do not want to miss it and my book is too good to put down, so I do both at the same time. Once in a while I get a little engrossed in the book and lose what is on TV, but you just close the book for a minute and you pick up on it again. You basically get the gist of what is going on on the TV, and you don't have to watch everything that's going on all the time. A lot of the times I should because I end up going, "What happened, what happened?" and my boyfriend says, "Why don't you just watch the TV?"

It's easy to just drift away from *Wheel of Fortune* if there isn't a puzzle up there to be solved. If I am eating my dinner and watching *Wheel*, when it gets to the commercials or the picking of the prizes, I'll go back to reading the paper or doing a crossword puzzle, and sometimes I don't come back to TV, mentally or visually.

[When I watch TV and read] . . . it's like I think this show might be good but I'm not sure, but I'm really more interested in what I'm reading at the time, so I turn it on, you know, just to have it there, in case something interesting comes on . . . You're more interested in this [the book] and then they'll say something, and you'll say, "What's this?"

Sometimes, I have all three [reading a magazine, TV, and the radio on [*sic*] and it's really a question of what is more interesting at the time. I move back and forth, depending. If the news moves from an interesting story to one that isn't, then I just start reading this thing . . . I feel like I am more in control here in a sense, because I can turn the page, flip the TV, rather than having to sit there and wait for things to change.

During the week when we [his wife and their children] are watching TV I don't really pay attention to it any more. My relaxation nowadays is watching my fish in the tank next to my living-room chair. Something [on TV] might pull me in for a few minutes or so, but then I'll drift off again. My weekday viewing is really broken up into 10 minutes here, 20 minutes there. TV really doesn't hold my attention anymore.

If it is 9 or 10 o'clock and it's not *Cagney and Lacey*, or *Cagney and Lacey* is a repeat, and there's the *Monday Night Movie* or something like that . . . I come home from a meeting and I'm wired and I want to calm down and I turn on the TV and I get into that mindless kind of watching, where I get ice-cream, or I get undressed, or I wash my hair, and I come in and I've missed half an hour and it doesn't matter a damn.

In simultaneous viewing, those I interviewed continued to become mindfully involved in the developments of social action that are depicted through the story-telling conventions. That is, narrative-based viewing continues to occur. The degree and extent of it varies considerably, however. Sometimes, people continued to follow narrative developments, pretty much in their entirety, even if they were doing other things, like preparing dinner, housework, ironing, or sewing. They were able to keep up primarily by following the dialogue. They kept their ears tuned in to what went on, and, when the action became heightened, or their interests in other activities waned or was not needed, they were able to return to a more mindfully involved kind of viewing. On occasions such as these, simultaneous viewing exhibited a continuity and consistency, a developmental course even, that resembled the mindfulness of narrative-based viewing.

At other times, people were less consistently involved with what was on television. Their attention was for the most part elsewhere. Entire segments of a show – entire shows, for that matter – were ignored, or passed before them without their even noticing. People offered a rationale for this in the interviews. They told me that they were familiar enough with the format and formula of so much of what was on television that at those times they pretty much knew, they said, what was likely to occur. This kind of familiarity kept them at a distance, mindfully and emotionally speaking, from the discourses of programming; and it did not usually translate into a more mindfully involved way of watching television. There were, no doubt, short periods of time when people took up narrative-based viewing in the ways that I have described. That is, they positioned themselves inside the development of social action, far enough, that is, to mindfully and emotionally adopt the point of view of one or another character, to anticipate outcomes to interactions or stories, or to criticize the plausibility of what they saw and heard. But they did not do this all the time. More often than not, they were disengaged from the story-telling conventions, either ignoring things altogether or using their familiarity with what was on to refuse any deeper involvement. As a result, the consistency, coherence, and development characteristic of narrative-based viewing never really took root in this kind of simultaneous television use.

Compared to narrative-based viewing, or even to the intermingling of narrative-based and critical viewing, watching television while simultaneously doing other things was a much more disrupted mode of activity. The role that story-telling conventions play in the viewing culture is altered significantly in the sociality of simultaneous viewing. The degree of mindfulness, that people report having, shifts fairly frequently during this kind of viewing. They become involved in programming, they disengage from it, they become involved in it once again – and the process typically repeats over and over again. When viewing in this way people are much less likely to reconstruct the elaborations of social action that are developed, in time, through the story-telling conventions as the meaning they take away from programming. Instead, they tend to focus their mindful attention on shorter scenes or segments of a program and are less concerned, really, with supplying any overall consistency or coherence to what they watch, or with coming away from what they watch with such elaborated meanings intact. They are content, it seems, to "catch" the meaning of what is on in bits and pieces, perhaps using the aforementioned familiarity with programming to "fill in" the rest, or, alternatively, they move on to other things. As a result, the story-telling conventions can never achieve the same kind of centering presence in simultaneous viewing that they do in narrative-based viewing. Consequently, the discursive power of the story-telling conventions is contextualized differently, as well.

Channel switching

In another kind of image-based viewing, people watch more than one program at the "same time." Typically, in my research, they used a remote-control device to move back and forth between programs that aired simultaneously on different channels. Usually, they sustained this style of watching for a considerable period of time (for the duration of half-hour or hour-long programs, at least), sometimes for the entire time that the television remained on. As was the case with simultaneous viewing, people who watched television regularly by switching channels relied on their familiarity with the medium's commercial nature, in particular their knowledge of formula, to disengage from story-telling conventions at any point in time. In this style of viewing, too, programs were understood to be more or less interchangeable with one another. People used the continual flow and segmented structure of programming to move between different shows, segments of shows, or different depictions of social action and selected what, for a given moment at least, seemed plausible or entertaining enough to pull them in and hold their attention. Once this occurred, people resumed either narrative-based viewing, or the movements between narrative-based and critical viewing that typically occurred once they located themselves inside the story-telling conventions.

Sometimes, channel switching emerged from sustained periods of narrative-based viewing. As people became bored with implausible or slow-moving programming, they used the remote and switched to something else; something that, at least initially, seemed more plausible and could in fact hold their attention. If they decided to stay with this new program alone, then their viewing once again became narrative-based, and was centered in the developments of a single set of story-telling conventions. More often than not, however, people found this choice, too, to be boring or implausible, and they switched once again to something different, hoping that this might hold their attention. Here again, if this new program merited sustained involvement, they stayed with it, and narrative-based viewing ensued. But usually, however, people were unable to find a show that kept them involved, and their viewing took on a serial quality as they continued to switch between many channels in order to find the best of what was on. This way of watching television was exemplified in the interview account of one viewer when she said:

When I turn the set on, I just go right to channel 9. I see what's on, and if it is a little bit boring, I'll scan the dial and see what else is on. At that time of the evening, it's mostly sitcoms and things like that, so I keep scanning. If I find something that I'm really interested in, I'll try to keep it on, but then I have to deal with the kid's desires for something else.

At other times, people became directly involved in channel switching; they did not need to first pass through narrative-based viewing at all. This was an indication that channel switching had indeed become ritualized in the viewing culture. People would simply sit down to watch television with the expectation that they would continually switch between different programs in order to maintain their interest in what was on. This was evident in the interview accounts of two other viewers as well.

When I'm flipping around [looking for something to watch] it's like I have 14 different channels to choose from, so I go "click, click, click" and I narrow it down. Do I want to watch this or this, or flip back and forth sometimes, especially if neither one is enough . . . I flip around a lot, because there are very few things that will hold me . . . When I get bored, I just start flipping sometimes. A lot [of what I watch] is accidental: it's like "this is interesting."

Earlier [in the evening], we're not as discerning about what's on the tube. We just turn it on and say, "oh, that looks interesting, let's watch that for a while," or just flip around for a while.

Sometimes, some viewers deliberately selected implausible programming as they switched between channels because they wished to view television critically, almost as a parody of "normal," narrative-based viewing. This usually occurred in group viewing situations, and resembled very closely the "ironic" viewing that characterized the game of television, (described in my earlier discussion of generalizing from questions of plausibility). The major difference, of course, was that, when people were switching channels, the story-telling conventions continually shifted as particular scenes or stories were played out and people moved on to others that were more interesting or compelling.

Generally speaking, what typically happened in channel switching was that people eventually "settled" on two – or more – programs to watch. They used the remote to switch back and forth between them in order to follow, concurrently, what happened in each of them. As they "caught" the most interesting or exciting parts of each show, their viewing became, as I said, narrative-based. While people may have maintained a continuity and a developmental quality to their mindful involvement with any given program, their repetitive shifting between shows undercut the integrity of this kind of viewing and instead, lent a decidedly de-centered quality to their viewing. This was, after all, what made channel switching an image-based viewing relation.

Image-play

What I call "image-play" is a third kind of image-based viewing. It was described to me by viewers in the interviews and I also observed it occurring during my participant observation. Its occurrence was reported less frequently, though, than the other viewing relations.

Basically, image-play consisted of people using a particular image sequence, or a brief succession of image sequences, as a symbolic space in which they could engage in imaginative activity of various kinds. Viewers who I talked with sometimes spoke of "vegging out" or "spacing out" while they watched television. At first glance, terms such as these seem to imply a passive, relatively mindless way of watching television. But, as viewers discussed further what they meant by these terms, it became clear that they continued to think, feel, imagine, or fantasize about things when they "vegged' or "spaced" out; it is just that they were not explicitly looking for "meaning" as something that was discursively constructed in the text. I found, however, that viewers were hesitant to openly acknowledge that they "played" with images. This was partly due to the fact that such unorganized forms of adult play are often labeled as an unproductive use of time and, as a result, they tend to be devalued in the larger culture. For this reason alone, the frequency with which various kinds of image-play occur may be underestimated in my research.

For example, image-play often took the form of a free-floating kind of imaginative activity in which viewers simply played with the colors, contours, contrasts, and movements that appeared in visual imagery. They saw the bright colors or stark contrasts in an image or series of images and, in that brief moment, registered them in their minds as something esthetic. In some cases, they may even have associated these esthetic qualities with the creative work of those people who produced them – again, all of this occurring in a flash, because programming, and viewers, have moved on to other things. When they did this, people reported to feel things rather than think them. Those whom I interviewed mentioned commercials, music television, and sports programming as regularly providing them with the opportunity to engage in this kind of image-play.

Image-play also took the form of people placing themselves – again, for brief moments in time – inside the symbolic space of social settings or specific depictions of social action that were presented in an image or a series of images. In such cases, content mattered more than esthetics, although esthetics continued to play a role in drawing people into the imagery. People were drawn into the symbolism of imagery – a symbolism that was quite condensed, since it was designed to convey, almost instantaneously, widely recognizable and deeply held icons and values of the larger culture. So, for example, compelling images of glamor, masculinity, femininity, sexuality, poverty, wealth, individualism, technology or military strength – all of this, and much more, actually became what people imagined and felt, if only for the moment. They did not necessarily have to identify with the people or situations presented in the imagery; it was enough for them, really, to simply recognize and register the symbolism of this imagery in their own imaginative and emotional terms. In recognizing this imagery, people are drawn into the power that this presentational symbolism of programming has to structure their experience in accordance with recurring myths of the dominant culture. I adapt the term myth from the work of Roland Barthes. In *Mythologies* (1972), he was concerned, among other things, with understanding how the mere presence of images – including their repetition – can convey a meaning distinct from the kind that unfolds, discursively, in time. Here, I use this idea to account for the symbolically powerful role that images play in reproducing deeply rooted cultural values, or meanings, not discursively, but in a more *spatial* manner.

While these mythic moments represent definite patterns in programming, this does not necessarily mean that people reproduced these objective patterns as a part of their imaginative involvement with imagery. After all, viewers are active participants in the meaning–making process. Even though these myths may have been visually compelling and culturally attractive beyond words, viewers do not always, or only, locate themselves inside the symbolic space of imagery such that they automatically reproduce its power. As knowledgeable television viewers, they are able to disengage from the flow of programming at any time, or they can take up a more focused kind of narrative-based viewing, where a different set of power dynamics applies.

Furthermore, viewers reported that they also engaged in a kind of mindful maneuvering within the symbolic space of imagery. This enabled them to modify and deflect the power that these myths might otherwise have had in shaping their experience. People created brief but meaningful associations between the mythic content of the images in front of them and the content of similar images they had seen before on television or in films or magazines. For example, one viewer, watching a shooting scene in *Miami Vice,* recalled "it's like Rambo," referring to the film character, John Rambo, played by Sylvester Stallone, and to the sequel to *First Blood*, the film *Rambo.* Similarly, another viewer mentioned that, when he watched the Los Angeles Lakers' basketball team play on television, the skill or athleticism demonstrated by Magic Johnson or James Worthy, two of the Lakers' stars, when one or the other of them made a good pass or shot almost always provoked in his mind a recollection of similar moves made in the past by Johnson, Worthy, or other NBA players with comparable talents in previous games that he had watched. Some women viewers said much the same thing; only with them, it was more often than not images of glamor that would catch their eye and draw them in emotionally. Usually, they would notice in passing (rather than through any elaborate conversation they had with others, or with themselves) how a particular character "did" her hair and how it was different from a previous cut or style that she had worn; or how the clothes or jewelry worn by a character was similar, or different, from what she (or he) had worn before, or what other characters on the show typically wore. Again, all of this is momentary – they notice it, perhaps remark upon it with a few words, and then it passes.

People also, at times, associated recollections of their own and others' real-life experiences with the images that passed before them on the screen. Again, in a momentary fashion, resemblances between "the look" of a character, the movements they made, the things they said, or the ways that they acted – all of this was noted and then people passed on to other things. Sometimes, the associations that viewers made lent support to the mythic power of the images before them; at other times, the recollections that they associated with what they saw undercut this mythic power. The difference is significant. To the extent that such associations lend imaginative and emotional support to these myths, their power is magnified and people are drawn more deeply into meaning-structures provided by the dominant culture – without necessarily being aware that this had happened.

In another similar kind of image-play, viewers reported that they used the symbolic space of imagery as a starting-point for thinking about things in their own lives that were unrelated to what was on television. They might have started out engaged in narrative-based viewing, or they may have slipped into other kinds of image-based viewing, by playing with the colors, contours, or movements of images in, say, commercials, by being drawn into the mythic content of images, or by creating the kinds of associations that I just described. But at some point, quite spontaneously, they would "go off," as they put it, on short, imaginative excursions in which they brought forth thoughts and feelings about themselves, about people they knew, about past experiences or present circumstances, or anything else, really. None of this necessarily had anything to do with what was on television. Something in the image-flow may have prompted these little excursions, but that was pretty much the extent of television's role in shaping them. They – the viewers – might resume narrative-based viewing again, or engage in other kinds of image-play. These excursions were, however, distinctive. People had the opportunity to elaborate the meanings that they made, much the same as they did in narrative-based viewing; yet, they were not following the story-telling conventions. Rather, they moved in and out of the image flow. In this kind of image-play, there was a continual intermingling of mindful attentiveness to imagery with these imaginative excursions based upon one's own life. This way of watching television was exemplified in the account offered by one viewer:

At . . . about 8.0 P.M., we watch TV, and then that gets back to the "it depends if there's anything worth watching" or if there is something on my mind. If there's something on my mind, then I won't watch. I go into my "stare at the TV set" in order to take care of whatever I need to be thinking about. I just stare at the TV and think about it. I like to look at things that I feel comfortable with, but I don't care what goes on. If there's something that I haven't seen before, or if it's a new program, chances are that bits and pieces of it will catch me long enough to decide if it's stupid or not, and then I'll just go back to thinking about other stuff . . . For example, *Mike Hammer*. I've seen it once or twice, but it's one of those shows where there's nothing on [on TV that night]. It's one of those shows that I don't watch, but I feel comfortable staring at the TV when that's on, just because everything else is stupider than that show. So I can stare at *Mike Hammer* and every so often come back to see what's going on in the show, and then leave again.

In image-play, then, all sorts of imaginative activities took place. People make associations between visual images, between the visual qualities of images and the social settings or social action depicted in images. They make associations, too, between any and all of these qualities of visual imagery and other media images or real-life experiences recalled from memory. They associate one or another moment of social action that they see depicted in, say, a scene or character interaction with a similar, or different, moment in a succeeding scene or interaction. They draw connections between such moments and similar – or different – ones recalled from other television shows or films; or they see the relation between such moments and those recollected from depictions in newspapers or magazines, or between them and their own real-life experiences. Or, alternatively, they look right through television imagery and space out, taking off on imaginative excursions that are more wholly their own. As I said, some of these mindful associations and imaginings are more closely tied to what is on television than others are. In fact, the variations exhibited by viewers as they make these kinds of mindful associations are seemingly endless and impossible to predict. Nevertheless, what is common to all these forms of image-play is the knowledge that people carry with them regarding the *commercial equivalence* of television programming. When people engage in image-play, they know that any image, feature, or depiction in programming is, on one level at least, interchangeable with any other. In these viewers' eyes, programming is understood as a product. It is capable of being manipulated by programmers, hence it is something that is subject to manipulation by them, as well. They can disengage themselves from the meaning that unfolds through story-telling conventions, and play with images, associating them, instead, in whatever ways they choose.

Conclusion

When people watch television, they tend to look for programming that is plausible – programming that rings true with their own experience, or with what they take to be "real." What is "real" can vary widely – from one viewer to the next and even from one day to the next for a particular viewer. In some cases, the reference point shifts, often imperceptibly, from a person's own experiences to the image worlds of television, thus representing one important way that the medium's power works in the viewing culture.

With plausibility established, at least for the moment, people can enter into narrative-based viewing. Once they are involved with characters and stories, they generally try to stay involved to see how things turn out. Routinely, however, they question what they see, and, when they do, narrative-based viewing gives way to periods of critical viewing of different kinds. People move back and forth between narrative-based and critical viewing relations. In doing so, their meaning–making activity is premised on the idea that television's role, or purpose, is to represent social realities and, furthermore, that, as viewers, their role is to develop meanings about the social realities depicted. In this way, they imaginatively reconstruct the discourses of television's story-telling conventions as their very own understandings of the world. To the extent that they accept the depictions presented to them, and their meaning–making activity remains centered in the story-telling conventions, television exerts power by providing them with coherent ideas about social life.

But people who watch television do not always accept the premise that the medium's role, or purpose, is to represent social realities. When they recognize formula, they disengage themselves from the story-telling conventions, and from their representational premise as well. In doing so, people come to see programming as a commercial product – as a commodity – and they use that knowledge to then treat it, not as a representation of reality, but as manipulable images. This recognition of formula is a crucial factor in the formation of image-based viewing relations.

In image-based viewing, the situation is quite different than what typically occurs when people follow the story-telling conventions. Simply put, in image-based viewing, the elaboration of meaning encoded in the story-telling conventions is a much less significant factor than it is in narrative-based viewing. In simultaneous viewing, channel switching, and image-play, three forms of image-based viewing, people no doubt construct meaningful relationships of various kinds with programming. But such a relationship is simply less important for them at the times they are viewing in an image-based fashion. By watching television in these image-based ways, viewers do indeed deflect a considerable portion of the discursive meanings that are encoded in programming. In addition to whatever involvement they have with the story-telling conventions, then, people can use the commodity forms of programming, along with their knowledge of programming as movable images, to constitute a distinctive sociality of television viewing. I refer to this sociality as "disengaged," because, in image-based viewing, neither the story-telling conventions, nor the social identities that people bring to the viewing culture can provide the consistency, cohesiveness, indeed, the developmental course that characterizes narrative-based viewing. In the long run, watching television in image-based ways may accustom people to accept, if not expect, that their meaning–making activity need not exhibit a developmental quality or add up to a consistent and coherent practice.

In studying the viewing culture, analytical constructs such as plausibility, story-telling conventions, programming as a representation of social realities, narrative-based viewing, criticisms of plausibility, discourse and its power, and so on, are indispensable in any critical analysis of what people do with the medium. By themselves, however, they are inadequate. It seems to me that we must think of both the image worlds of television programming and the capabilities of people for mindful activity as making possible a wider range of sociality in the viewing culture than discursively based constructs presently allow us to envision.

8

A typology of television use

In this chapter, I construct a typology of television use. In formulating this typology, my intent is to bring together important aspects of the analysis I presented in the previous two chapters with additional documentation of viewing practices gleaned from the interview accounts and my participation in the viewing culture. I want to provide the reader with a way of understanding the relationship between the routines that people have established in turning to television on a daily basis and the specific, mindful ways in which they typically became involved with programming. In doing so, I want to make explicit how these viewing practices are situated amidst and shaped by the broader meaningful context that is people's everyday life. To a certain extent, I have already done this, especially in my discussion of the turn to television. In chapter 4, the very notion of a turn *to* television incorporated the idea that work, family life, household responsibilities, hobbies, and other free-time pursuits were significant factors that shaped in various ways the mindfulness with which people brought television into their lives on a day-to-day basis. In chapter 5, the sociality of viewing itself took center stage, but the lives people led outside of the viewing culture continued to play a role in shaping what they did with television. The judgments that people made regarding the plausibility of what they watched; their singling out certain shows as favorites; the ways in which they did, or did not, identify with the characters, situations, or stories; the kinds of criticisms they made regarding what they saw and heard – all of these, and more, were often very closely connected to what people understood and referred to as their own everyday experience of social life. So, even in my reconstruction of viewing relations, what people did besides watching television found its way into the analysis. Coming after analyses of the turn to television and viewing relations, then, this typology of use is designed to capture, in the broadest possible terms, the different meaningful ways that television worked in the everyday lives of the people who made use of it on a regular basis.

I employ a typology to identify the important interrelations that have developed in the day-to-day use of television and that have persisted over time to constitute distinct patterns of social organization in the viewing culture; what I refer to elsewhere as the sociality of the viewing culture. With this in mind, I will discuss, in turn, the sociality of "discrete," "undirected," and "continuous," television use.

Discrete use

What I call the "discrete" use of television is by far the most selective of the three patterns of use that I identified as occurring regularly in the viewing culture. The people who used television in this way were able to consistently separate their television viewing, as a distinct activity that occurred regularly, from other, equally distinct activities that also occurred regularly in the time that they spent away from work. Generally speaking, the people in my study who typically used television in this discrete way typically did so during the evenings that comprised their work week.

Approximately one-third of the people I interviewed used television in a discrete way. This pattern of use was typified by Jeanne, a white woman in her mid-fifties, who was an upper-level manager at the textbook publishing company. As she reconstructed it for me in the interview, Jeanne's typical day was as follows. It's five o'clock, she is just finishing up at work, and is beginning to make the daily transition to what she calls "my own time." She might stop at the store on her way home to pick up a few things or she might not. Either way, she then usually pulls up to the house, picks up the mail and, as she comes in the door, settles into her routine of unwinding after work. She checks the answering machine, changes into more relaxing clothes, perhaps waters the plants or tidies up a bit and, as she puts it, tries to "catch up on what is been going on."

For Jeanne, catching up means getting some sense of what has happened in her world while she has been busy at work. She can catch up in different ways. Sometimes this means sitting and reading the paper with the radio on as she contemplates what to make for dinner or, having made that decision, waits for it to cook. Catching up may mean turning on the television and watching both the local and national news. It may also mean reading through the paper while watching the news. Whether or not she watches the local news depends on her mood, but, more often than not, the national network news (and typically for her it is CBS) is an indispensable part of "catching up": whatever else may transpire, she tries not to miss *The CBS Evening News With Dan Rather*.

After work, Jeanne simply is not that attentive to what is on television. She is moving around the house a lot, coming in and out of the living room and working in the kitchen for extended periods of time, and it is difficult to stay focused and follow each and every story, especially with the local news. In addition to preparing dinner, the phone may ring, she may decide to return phone calls, clean up things in another room, or to unwind in ways that what is on television will pass unnoticed. She is, in this period after work, involved in simultaneous viewing. Typically, though, by seven o'clock, when *The CBS Evening News* comes on, Jeanne is seated in front of the TV and she is ready to devote more sustained attention to the screen. But, she admits, even at this point, her attention often drifts back and forth between following television news stories and reading the newspaper. At seven-thirty, however, Jeanne drops whatever else she is doing because her favorite show – *Jeopardy* – is on. She looks forward to her time with *Jeopardy* every day of the week (barring, of course, unexpected events that break her out of this routine). She is a fan of *Jeopardy* and she keeps her own scorecard to prove it.

When *Jeopardy* ends, it is decision time for Jeanne. She has had time to settle down from work, finish dinner, and catch up with what is going on in her world and, most importantly, she has had time to relax with her favorite show. So she asks herself, what do I want to do tonight? Watching television is one of numerous activities that Jeanne can turn to in her free time. She is not particularly attracted to television; in fact, reading mysteries, writing letters, visiting friends, or talking on the phone regularly provide Jeanne with more engaging alternatives to watching television. But, if she is going to watch, she checks the listings, sees what is on, and decides right then and there if the TV stays on; and, because she has selected a specific program, she knows in advance how long it will stay on. If she decides to watch a later show, the set goes off and she does something else in the meantime. Typically, she will select something from PBS – perhaps *Mystery*, *Nova*, or *Frontline* – or one of the "higher quality" network programs, which for her, at the time included *Cagney and Lacey*, *St. Elsewhere*, or *Hill Street Blues*. But Jeanne is not committed to watching these shows every week; they are simply not that compelling for her. The remainder of commercial television programming is simply too formulaic for her tastes and, as a result, she does not consider it a serious option.

Jeanne resists the temptation to lose herself in the image worlds of television. She is what I call a discrete user of television because she typically watches entire programs and regularly engages in other activities. Day in and day out, Jeanne maintains a continuity between her work life and her home life by integrating television into routines that she has already established in the rest of her life. Interestingly enough, it is viewers like Jeanne who, because they are so selective and attentive with regard to what they watch, are more likely than others viewers to center themselves in the discourses of television programming and to embrace them as their own.

Discrete users of television, such as Jeanne, exercised the most control, of all those I studied, over the conditions under which they allowed the medium to come into their homes. As I just described with Jeanne, these people made it very clear that other things besides watching television were important to them. Partly because of this, they were very purposive in the way that they went about watching television. They either knew, or selected ahead of time, the show or shows that they wanted to watch. Having made a conscious decision to finish up or turn away from whatever else they were doing, discrete users sat down to watch television and usually paid close or consistent attention to what was on.

Certainly, there were variations in discrete use. Some people did not watch television at all after work; they chose instead to do other things. In the evening, however, they did turn to television with some regularity, as they did to other separate activities, too. These people reserved only part of the evening for watching shows that were of particular interest to them. On a day-to-day, week-to-week basis, people who engaged in this particular pattern of discrete use typically approached their television viewing as mindfully as they did their involvement in other activities. In both cases, they were looking, they said, to stimulate their minds and become imaginatively engaged with things.

Others whose viewing I categorized as discrete use did, in fact, watch television after work, but they also said that at this time they were just as likely to become involved in other separate activities, besides watching television. Like those who waited until the evening to watch television, these people, too, deliberately chose particular programs to watch. They did much the same thing in the evening: sometimes choosing to watch a particular program that they already had in mind, and sometimes choosing, like Jeanne, to do any number of other things, such as read, visit with friends, sew, and so on. Furthermore, these discrete users approached television viewing as mindfully as they did other activities in the evening. They looked consistently to be stimulated and imaginatively engaged in things.

Still others who engaged regularly in discrete use did much the same thing as the people that I just described, except for the fact that their television viewing after work was not a discrete activity; rather, it occurred simultaneously with other activities. But its occurrence was rather limited and it did not preclude people from moving on to a more discrete and focused kind of viewing at other times. This was evident in Jeanne's case. Her simultaneous viewing typically came to an end by the early evening, at which time she made more deliberate choices in deciding whether or not to watch particular television shows or become involved in any number of other discrete activities. Others who became involved in simultaneous viewing early on did much the same thing. There were some people who chose to watch news or *Jeopardy* after work and in the early evening, and then later in the evening tuned in again to their favorite prime-time programs. In between, however, these people typically turned off the television and chose to read, sew, work on hobbies or household projects, undertake household chores, or simply spend some quiet time with their families. In these cases, I decided to categorize their viewing as discrete use. My rationale for doing so will become clearer, I think, once discrete use is contrasted to patterns of undirected and continuous television use.

In all of these variations of discrete use, a number of important things stand out. First, television viewing *as a separate activity* occurred regularly along with other discrete activities. People who use television in a discrete way simply have more – and more varied – options for mindful engagement available to them on a regular basis. Because of this, television viewing never really dominated the time that they spent away from work, as it did, for example, in continuous use (to be discussed below). Second, those people who used television in a discrete manner said that they turned to television and to other distinct activities with the idea in mind that they wanted either to stimulate their imagination and engage themselves playfully or to become thoughtfully and even reflectively involved with things, and they said this more often than any of the other people I interviewed. Furthermore, they also reported the most significant increases in these playful and reflective ways of doing things as they moved from the activities that occupied them in the transition time after work to their typical evening activities. In other words, people who used television in a discrete way were more self-directive in initiating activities of any kind, and they maintained this self-directive orientation to doing things clear through their evening leisure time.

When it came to television viewing itself, before people even began to watch, it was typical for them to have already narrowed down the possible programming choices to favorite shows or others that, in their eyes, were highly plausible. This meant that, in discrete use, people were much more likely to become involved consistently in narrative-based viewing. This meant, too, that they usually sustained such involvement throughout the time they spent with television. They watched with the idea in the back of their minds that their viewing did, in fact, have an end to it. Certainly, critical viewing occurred regularly in discrete use. In general, though, it tended to involve people questioning the plausibility of specific depictions in programming. People also generalized from questions concerning plausibility, and they recognized formula, too, but these two kinds of critical viewing played a less significant role in this type of television use. As a result, it was in discrete use, as opposed to undirected or continuous use, that viewers reconstructed in their own minds the elaboration of meanings found in the story-telling conventions of programming. Their meaning–making activity with television exhibited a developmental course, mirroring, in a way, developments in the character interactions and stories that unfolded before them. In this way, they actively and consistently reconstructed the dominant discourses of programming as their very own, common-sense understandings of the world. The power of television became their power to center meaning–making in themselves, which, in turn, led them to see the world "out there" with some consistency and coherence, and, because of that, place themselves in it in socially identifiable ways.

In discrete use, the involvement that people had in other activities was similar to that which I just described of their viewing practice. Because they tended to be selective in deciding what to do with their time, their approach to other activities was, as I said earlier, highly mindful to begin with. Their involvement in them, for the most part, exhibited a continuity, coherence, and, developmental course that was similar, really, to the way that they watched television.

All of this leads me to the conclusion that people who regularly used television in such a discrete way were aiming for a kind of meaningful integration of the various aspects, or segments, of their lives. They wanted to maintain a sense of continuity in the activities they pursued. They wanted what they did at one time – say, watching television – to connect with what they did at another time – reading, writing letters, completing a project – by feeling that they were in control of the conditions under which they decided to move in or out of these activities. In short, they wanted to think and feel that their actions, and their lives, developed over time; that they were "going somewhere" in their lives. The fact that these people were able to consistently work through workplace and household related stresses and strains and *direct* themselves into different discrete activities, including watching television, is testimony to the accomplishment of a kind of productive integration on their lives. So, too, is the fact that they regularly resisted the temptation to "lose themselves" in a more diffuse, open-ended, and "unproductive" involvement in television's image worlds.

Undirected use

"Undirected" use of television contained elements of the selectivity and focus that I just described, but, on the whole, it exhibited a more diffuse, fragmentary, and open-ended sociality compared to discrete use. In undirected use, people certainly monitored and controlled some of the conditions under which they allowed television to come into their homes; nevertheless, in contrast to discrete use, television was a more ever-present feature of the home environment.

People who used television in this way typically delayed their turn to television until the evening. Instead of watching television after work, they chose to become involved in what they understood as more mindful activities, such as reading the newspaper or a mystery book, hobbies of one sort or another, or ongoing household projects. In contrast to television viewing at this particular time, people said that they considered these activities, as opposed to watching television, as a "productive" use of their time. By the time that the evening had rolled around, these people reported that their energy for sustaining these more mindfully demanding activities had given out, and, at that point, they typically turned to television, seeing it as a relatively easy way to relax and enjoy themselves for a while. People said that then, for the remainder of the evening, they moved back and forth between periods of attention to these more mindful involving activities and television viewing. People did not just "give in" to television and keep it on all the time (as I found in continuous use), but they were no longer able so easily to maintain the distinction between television viewing and other discrete activities. It was in this sense that their use of television was undirected.

As was the case with discrete use, one-third of the people I interviewed used television in this undirected way. This pattern of use was typified by Steve, a single white man in his mid-twenties who worked as a production editor at the same book publishing company that employed Jeanne. Like Jeanne, Steve regularly uses television to ease his transition from work to home life. After work, Steve may go for a run, lift weights, or play a few games of pick-up basketball at the high school, but, once he has finished working out, he comes home and turns on the radio or the television for, as he describes it, "some company and a connection to what is happening out there in the world." Radio and television offer a comforting background as Steve settles in to enjoy his time at home. More often than not, it is television that wins out as his medium of choice. Oftentimes, Steve may begin to relax by listening to the radio or recorded music, but he ends up turning to television because, as he says, "it gives me more of what I want."

For Steve, news and sports programming best provide him with company and a sense of connection to the world. But at this time of day, he is simply not that committed to closely watching what is on, unless, of course, there is a noteworthy game or if one of his favorite teams, such as the San

Francisco Giants, is on. Usually he flips between channels, drifting in and out of news stories and sports action while at the same time alternating his attention to a variety of other things, including opening the mail, snacking, preparing dinner, cleaning up things around the house, or reading the local paper.

This is Steve's daily routine. If he is caught up in a game, or if a particularly interesting program is coming on, the television stays on. If not, like Jeanne, at about seven or seven-thirty, he will turn off the set to read, do crossword puzzles, make phone calls, or, if necessary, finish up work from the office. At this point, Steve wants to do something *other than* watch television. It's only later in the evening (and it varies from one night to the next), when one of his favorite shows comes on, that he sets aside time to sit down and watch television. When the particular show that he is watching is over, the set goes off and he returns to his plan of doing other things besides spending time with television. Like other viewers, Steve is adept at recognizing formulaic programming, and, once he has decided that a particular program is too formulaic for his tastes, he no longer even considers it as a possibility when it comes to his more mindful pattern of viewing.

By his own admission, however, Steve is not always successful in keeping to his plan. In fact, *not* watching television becomes an emotional tug of war for Steve. Television calls to him, enticing him, and promising relief from his having to sustain the more focused kind of mindful attention to other things that he would otherwise want to pursue. In contrast to Jeanne, Steve typically spends his evenings at home by reading, doing crossword puzzles, or even working sometimes, then taking a break by watching some television, moving back to reading, working, or doing puzzles, taking another television break, moving back to one or another of these other activities, and so on, repeating this routine on into the night. Sometimes, he simply leaves the television on, but with the sound off, and continues to intersperse his reading and working with glances at the television, sometimes turning up the sound and getting himself pulled in to more sustained viewing, and sometimes ignoring what is on for considerable stretches of time. It is for these reasons that I refer to Steve's television use as undirected.

Like I described in my account of discrete use, there were variations in people's undirected use of television. Since, in almost all cases, watching television after work was not an option for these people, it was in the evening that the significant variation in undirected use occurred. At that time, some people were initially more selective with regard to their television viewing. They turned to favorite shows, or consulted the listings to pick particular programs to watch. As a result, these people became involved in more focused, narrative-based viewing early in the evening. Typically, they sustained this kind of involvement throughout the time that the particular show, or shows, they had chosen to watch was, or were, on. To this point, the sociality of their television viewing was very similar, really, to that which occurred in discrete use. Sustained periods of narrative-based viewing may have been interrupted by questions that came up in people's minds regarding the plausibility of what they saw and heard, but, because their intent at this point in time was to follow closely what was on, they quickly left such criticisms behind in order not to miss what happened next. As with discrete use, other kinds of critical viewing, such as generalizing from questions of plausibility and recognizing formula, occurred less frequently in this phase of undirected use.

This particular variation of undirected use differed from discrete use, however, when, instead of turning off the television at the conclusion of a show, viewers continued to watch. Occasionally, they found another program that allowed them to sustain this same kind of narrative-based viewing, but, generally, people said that they ended up switching between different programs in order to find the best of what was on. They stayed mindfully involved with programming in this image-based way for a while, but eventually they became bored, turned the television off, and resumed other familiar activities, like reading, hobbies of various kinds, household projects, and so on. But they did not sustain their interest in these activities for very long either. Eventually, they tired of them, and turned back to television, switching around to find something that seemed interesting, or plausible enough for them to watch for a while, at least. This kind of mindful movement back and forth, from watching television (either in narrative- or image-based ways), to turning it off and taking up other discrete activities, to leaving these behind and turning to television once again, continued for a good portion of the evening.

In a similar evening pattern of undirected use, people were less selective at the outset of the evening when it came to what they were going to watch. In turning to television, they did not necessarily have favorite shows in mind, nor did they typically consult the listings to find particular programs to watch. They simply turned on the set and tried to find the best of what was on. They bypassed narrative-based viewing and instead began switching channels, which brought them directly into image-based viewing. If they found programming that appeared plausible enough to merit their sustained attention, then they settled into narrative-based viewing and stayed with it throughout the show. At the conclusion of such a show, they turned the television off and attempted to move back into doing other things.

Depending on their mood, energy level, whether or not there were other people at home – any number of things, really – they might or might not stay involved in other activities besides watching television. Generally, though, they either tired or lost interest in these other activities, and that, combined with their easy access to the more immediate pleasures of television, led them back once again to viewing. In turning back to television, people either again found a particular show to watch or they switched channels for a while, hoping to find something of interest. But again, at some point, their interest in television waned, they turned it off, and tried to resume doing other things. But, because none of this viewing was planned in advance, people could and did switch channels at any point; there was no need or interest that necessarily led them to become involved, and stay involved with programming in narrative-based ways.

Undirected television use is similar in many respects to discrete use. First, in turning to television and other activities, undirected users, like discrete users, were self-directive. They looked to stimulate their imagination and become playfully, or even reflectively involved in what they were doing. They just reported doing so less often than discrete users did – but more often, I might add, than continuous users. Second, viewing itself in undirected use was often narratively based, which was, after all, a defining feature of discrete use. And third, television viewing always took place in the context of other discrete activities. Such things as reading, hobbies, letter-writing, and household projects, for example, either preceded or followed viewing. Or, looked at in another way, television viewing could be understood to have preceded and/or followed people's involvement in any and all of these other activities. The point here is that, in undirected use, people moved back and forth between watching television and becoming involved in other activities. Taken together, all of this means that the sociality of undirected use contained elements of the continuity, coherence, and even the developmental course that typified discrete use of television.

But the movements back and forth between watching television and involvement in other, discrete activities and, when television was watched, the intermingling of narrative- and image-based viewing relations were, together, the principle factors that set undirected use apart from discrete use. Because people sometimes watched television without selecting a show, or shows, in advance, their commitment to programming often wavered; or, alternatively, was not that strong to begin with. This resulted in the periodic movements in and out of viewing and other activities that I described earlier. Furthermore, the uncertainty of their commitment to television viewing often led people to switch back and forth between channels in order to find something that they could watch in a more focused, narrative-based manner. While this sometimes occurred, it was just as likely that it did not. In that case, channel switching led people further along the path of image-based viewing. They became involved in simultaneous viewing or image-play for brief periods of time before turning away from television and returning to other discrete activities for a while. In undirected use, people still reconstructed in their own minds the discourses of story-telling conventions, but they did so in a somewhat more dissociated way compared to what typically occurred in discrete use. At times, their meaning–making activity with television and other activities still exhibited a developmental course, but, because of their image-based viewing and their frequent, mindful shifts between television and other activities which often interrupted such developments, they were much more dispersed in comparison to what happened in discrete use.

In my discussion of discrete use, I said that the power of television became the power that people had to center meaning–making activity in themselves. This was true, too, of undirected use. But, in the more open-ended kind of viewing that constituted undirected use, this discursive centering of meaning–making activity was not always sustained. People sometimes drifted in and out of the story-telling conventions, or they allowed themselves to space out with the visual imagery of programming. In either case, the discursive power of television was not experienced with quite the consistency or coherence that characterized its workings in discrete use. In its place, or set against it, was the power that television had to dissociate meaning–making and actually prevent consistent and coherent understandings of self, or the world "out there" from emerging in the first place.

Like people who tended to use television in a discrete way, undirected users certainly wanted to make productive use of their time away from work. Their commitment to remain productive, even in their free time, served as an important motivating factor in their ability to limit and control the place that television occupied in their lives. But the fact of the matter was, they struggled to remain productive, and this struggle was an ongoing part of what it meant to use television in an undirected way. This struggle took shape as a distinctive sociality. This was a sociality in which elements of consistency, coherence, development, and integration were continually juxtaposed with more open-ended, dispersed, and dissociated forms of involvement with television and other activities. People were split, in a sense, between what they felt as the demand that they remain productive, even in their "free" time, and the desire to let go of such control – to be unproductive.

Continuous use

What I have termed the "continuous" use of television involved a significantly less selective relationship to programming compared to what typically took place in discrete or undirected use. In this type of use, if the television was not already on when people came home from work, then they turned it on, and left it on pretty much throughout the time that they were home, turning it off just before they went to sleep for the night. While people were not always watching what was on, nevertheless, *the set* was on, and, because of that, television had a constant presence in their homes. Continuous users did not monitor as closely as other types of users did the conditions under which television imagery came into the home. One-third of the people that I interviewed routinely engaged in continuous use.

This pattern of continuous use was exemplified by Dennis and Brenda, who, you may recall, I introduced at the beginning of the book. I refer to my earlier account of their viewing practice because now, placed in the context of discrete and undirected use, it takes on a somewhat different significance. As I said earlier, Dennis and Brenda are white, recently married, and in their mid 20s. Dennis is a fork-lift operator at the Lipton plant, and Brenda a secretary at another company in town. After finishing work around five o'clock, arriving home has come to be synonymous, for both of them, with turning on the television and relaxing. As they unwind at the end of the work day and resume living their lives together, the television is on, but it is not the only focal point for their attention. With *Donahue, Oprah, Geraldo,* or the local news on, they talk about their respective days at work, shuffling in and out of the kitchen for snacks or to begin preparing dinner, or, on other occasions, they may just sit or lie down to relax and talk with one another, again, with the television on. If either of them remembered to tape *All My Children* – Brenda's favorite soap – they will rewind it and watch it, fast-forwarding through the commercials and the less interesting scenes. With either live or recorded programming, entire segments of a show may go unnoticed because their attention is elsewhere. Dennis, or Brenda, or both of them may be drawn into particularly exciting scenes, but only momentarily. At this time of the day, unwinding from work means that no single activity or program can sustain their interest for very long.

At about seven or seven-thirty, they have finished dinner, wound down from work, and, as evening comes upon them, the television typically stays on and they continue to live their home life in its presence. They may continue to watch television together, but, more commonly, Dennis will watch television in the living-room while Brenda moves to the bedroom and takes up reading or one of her sewing projects. Periodically, she will join Dennis to watch and talk together and then she will return to the bedroom to read or sew or do whatever else she does to occupy herself. It's impossible to predict how these patterns will unfold.

Dennis – more so than Brenda – is so thoroughly familiar with commercial television conventions that he knows the night and time of practically all the current prime-time shows. In fact, he credits himself with being able to recognize boring programming within seconds. As a result, he usually stays with a show just long enough *not* to be bored by it, using the remote to flip between stations to find, if only momentarily, the best of what is on. Without access to the remote, Brenda often tires of the abrupt changes in programming brought about by Dennis's seemingly constant selection process, and this is a recurring factor that precipitates her move to the bedroom to read, sew, or talk on the phone; but it is just as likely that she will continue to watch and talk – as long as Dennis agrees to stay with one program. Compromises must be made. As they watch together in this way, Dennis slips into what he describes as his "stare at the television mode," in which he finds comfortable images to "space out" with, often thinking of things completely unrelated to what is on the screen.

Throughout the evening, it is typical for Dennis and Brenda to move between talking with one another, watching TV, snacking, reading, sewing, talking on the phone, or whatever else may come up while they are at home. Of course they have favorite shows – *Dallas, Moonlighting,* and *Knot's Landing* topped the list at the time of my interview with them – that they try not to miss and that, when they are on, both Dennis and Brenda will watch attentively. Still, these patterns of movement between a variety of different activities, including periods of more focused viewing, continue until eleven o'clock or so, when they finally decide to turn off the TV and go to bed.

This is a typical evening for them, broken only by aerobics class, a night out to dinner or the movies, a visit with friends or family, or, during the spring and summer, by Dennis's softball games. Dennis and Brenda are far less selective in their television viewing than many other viewers. Simply having the television on is more important to them than closely following a particular program. And, ironically, while television imagery is a constant presence in their home, they are, compared to people like Jeanne, who watch more selectively, less likely to embrace the discourses of programming as their own common-sense understandings of the world.

With the flow of programming providing a constant backdrop of imagery and shows, many people, like Dennis and Brenda, went about doing the variety of things that were part of their everyday routine at home.

Depending upon what was on television, their mood, who else, if anybody, was present, and the mindful demands of other activities, people could pay more or less attention to programming, as they saw fit.

Narrative-based viewing occurred regularly in continuous use. People took the time to focus their attention on favorite shows, they rented movies, or they sometimes turned to pre-recorded programming of their own. As I found in discrete use, people actively reconstructed the developments of meaning found in the story-telling conventions as their own imaginative experience. As a result, they sometimes centered themselves in the dominant discourses of television programming and allowed those discourses to become their own common-sense understandings of the world – much like discrete and undirected users did. But much of the time in continuous use, people were far less attentive to what was on. Rather than mindfully grounding themselves in a single set of story-telling conventions, they were much more likely, really, to catch particular scenes or certain segments of shows, or other bits and pieces of programming, and find meaning there. When this occurred, the workings of discursive power were transformed. Instead of reconstructing the more elaborate meanings of social action that developed, in time, over the course of an entire show (as occurred in discrete use), in continuous use, people pieced together meaning out of the more abbreviated moments of mindful attention that characterized their image-based viewing. Consequently, the power of dominant discourses was now located in shorter, hyper-ritualized scenes and segments of social action which were not necessarily integrated with one another in people's minds.

There was, however, much more to the sociality of continuous use than the workings of discursive power, whether it was integrated or not. In continuous-use households, people often said that, in addition to its characters and stories, television provided them with "something to fall back on" if their interest in making conversation, reading, or carrying out household chores or projects dropped off. Simply having the set on allowed their attention to be drawn away easily from these other activities as exciting or compelling imagery or depictions were presented to them on the screen. As these passed, continuous users could then just as easily slip into other activities as a way to fill their time. But, because the set was always on, they invariably came across a good deal of programming that failed to exert enough of a "pull" on their attention to bring about the more consistently focused, narrative-based viewing that characterized discrete use. In fact, in continuous use, viewers drew upon the knowledge they had gained from repeatedly recognizing formula to routinely disengage themselves from any particular set of story-telling conventions and initiate image-based viewing. As was clear in the case of Dennis and Brenda, continuous users engaged much more frequently, and over longer periods of time, in simultaneous viewing, where they intermingled mindful attention to programming and other activities; in channel switching, where entire portions of parallel shows went unattended but the overall story-lines were somehow followed; and in image-play, where their involvement in the symbolic space of visual imagery outweighed the attention they paid to narrative developments.

Continuous use, then, is a complex and multi-layered practice that exhibited significant variation in the forms of mindful involvement that people had over the course of any given viewing period as well as in the long-term organization of the viewing culture. People chose to become involved with television in this way. Over time, this choice had itself become a ritual feature of continuous use; it provided people with a practical – though not necessarily conscious – point of departure for allowing television to be a part of their lives in this way. In continuous use, television was a constant presence in people's lives and its standardized image worlds served as a meaningful reference point for them. In the process, the coherence and developmental quality of a range of family oriented activities may have been compromised in ways that viewers were not fully aware of.

In contrast to what took place in discrete use, or even in undirected use, in continuous use people, in effect, chose to *not* make productive use of their time – at least not in the terms that the dominant culture defined as "productive." After all, they were not always selective about the programs they watched; if they watched particular programs, they were not always that attentive or focused in the way that they watched them. Much of the time, they said that they were "just watching television," something that many people – especially those whose opinions resonated with "official" perspectives concerning culture – had difficulty considering as an "activity" at all; or, if it was deemed legitimate to relax and enjoy oneself in this way, surely it could – should – only occur for a limited period of time before people moved on to more productive pursuits. Similarly, the fact that other activities typically took place around television certainly raises questions – again, among the arbiters of official culture and those who shared their view – regarding the commitment that people had to a productive use of time; or, at the very least, the commitment they had to a sustained and integrated kind of involvement that would enable them to *really* get something tangible and coherent out of what they were doing.

In continuous use, then, people altered, sometimes significantly, the conventional markers for what constituted meaningful social action. What they did was not always productive, or integrated, nor did it necessarily develop any broader coherence. Yes, they made judgments about what to pay attention to, and what not to pay attention to, in the flow of television imagery. They recognized what was plausible and implausible in depictions of social action. They reconstructed the meanings depicted in story-telling conventions, and, on occasion, they were critical of these depictions. But they also recognized formula and disengaged themselves from the story-telling conventions. They switched between channels. They played with images, interspersing thoughts and feelings about their own lives with those depicted on television. And, of course, they read, talked, worked on hobbies or household projects, sewed, wrote letters, or spent time together as a family. They did all of this with the television on.

Many working people actively sought out the lack of integration in continuous use precisely because they did not want to be productive; they did not want to focus their attention on any *one* thing; they did not want to make things develop – from one moment to the next or from one occasion to the next. All of this made sense to them, because they knew, in the back of their minds, that the tasks they worked on all day (or evening), despite whatever intrinsic rewards they may have carried, were not truly their own. The fact that people could disengage themselves from the story-telling conventions at any time, coupled with the fact of their not having, or wanting, to be focused in whatever they did – this is what enabled them to create a mindful space that was freed from ordered discourse. This, in turn, fostered the idea that they could, in fact, escape the mandate of official culture that they make productive use of their time.

Perhaps most significant in the sociality of continuous use were the "lateral" movements that emerged from the viewing culture. Rather than consistently moving *forward* through the narrative time of story-telling conventions, or through the developmental course of a variety of discrete activities, people moved *between* different contexts of social action; *between* depictions of social action and the image-flow; or *between* what they were watching and what they were reading or writing or fixing or saying to others. This was what occurred, repeatedly, throughout the time that they were home and the television was on. Of course, they sometimes moved forward in narrative time or in activities, too. That was an undeniable fact of continuous use, as I pointed out earlier. But, because people had already made a choice, practically speaking, *not* to integrate work and home life, and when they were home, *not* to focus on any *one* thing, they were freed from the constraints that these aspects of meaning–making placed on the sociality of their television use. Interestingly enough, in a somewhat paradoxical way, these lateral movements, the "unproductive" use of time, the lack of a sustained focus for activities, the lack of coherence in their meaning–making activity – in all of this, people seemed to establish a new kind of continuity for themselves. It was the continuity that came from using the image-worlds of television as a grounding for social life in the home. Rather than understanding this lack of productivity, integration, or developmental course in continuous use as a lack that must, in some way, at some point, add up to a more unified form of cultural practice, I choose instead to validate its multiple and non-integrated qualities and reject the premise that a higher ordering principle is needed to explain its discontinuities. Seen from this perspective, the sociality of continuous use is indicative of a post-developmental pattern of self-formation and cultural practice.

Conclusion: The politics of television reconsidered

I began this book with a scenario of continuous television use, something that I regularly encountered in the lives of television viewers. A guiding theme (or central argument) of the book has been that this way of using television, while quite common, is not well understood by cultural studies analysts, or, for that matter, by more conventional social scientists or social theorists. My initial presentation of continuous use served as a metaphor for the entire range of viewing practices – recognizing formula, simultaneous viewing, channel switching, and image-play – that I have analyzed, practices that largely escape the analytical frameworks that typically guide current accounts of television use. I conclude by returning to my initial claims regarding the limits of cultural studies.

One of my central arguments has been that the conceptual frameworks of cultural studies, (centered as they are on the construction of normative and resistant identifications with mass-media narratives) neither direct attention to nor explain these common and complex image-based viewing practices, and, because of that, fail to understand adequately the sociological significance of television use. My research demonstrates that there is more, much more, to the sociality of the viewing culture than discourses and identities, however multiple and complicated their workings.

The argument can be taken further. My earlier discussion of discrete use suggests that it is in this particular way of using television that the normalizing power of television, so central to cultural studies accounts, is prominently displayed. At the same time, this normalizing power works in ways that cultural studies does not anticipate and cannot capture, so that even here, at the very heart of its explanatory power, something is missing.

In discrete use, people constitute themselves as productive individuals, and, in so doing, simultaneously constitute themselves within the broader discursive frameworks of American individualism. In watching favorite shows, or in watching particular shows regularly, people connect, in their own minds, from week to week, what happens to characters as well as what happens in the social realities depicted in fictional programming. They do the same with the real people and events depicted in news and non-fictional programming of various sorts.

When they watch television, and when they become involved with other media, sometimes, people identify with the characters or people who populate these image worlds, or with the stories and events presented there; they are what I refer to as narrative-based in their involvement in media image worlds. Through these narrativized identifications, they locate themselves inside the meanings proffered though dominant discourses and place themselves in the broader context of American society. People are also critical of what they see and hear and read, and differentiate themselves from many of the characters and people, stories and events, that they are routinely exposed to. In this way, they could be said to "resist" or "oppose" what is presented to them. Such resistance is usually attributed to the "identities" they bring with them into the act of interpretation itself, identities based on class, race, gender, ethnicity, sexuality, and so on. My research suggests a different interpretation. There is more consistency exhibited in the identifications people make with what they see and hear than in the criticisms, or differentiations. This is because there is a consistency to the dominant discourses repeated on television (and in other media, such as newspapers, magazines, mysteries, or romance novels). While there are certainly multiple discourses at work in all of these media, it is safe to say that the same discourses are repeated with regularity, especially in commercial television, which, in my findings, is what most people, even discrete users, watch most of the time. This is not as true of the differentiations that make it possible for people to resist or oppose dominant discourses. I did not find the kind of consistency and coherence in identity-based identifications *or* differentiations that cultural studies accounts would lead us to believe occur when people watch television. Admittedly, I did not set out to examine this kind of interpretive activity alone. While I asked questions in the interviews pertaining to favorite shows and characters, likes and dislikes, and so on, I did not emphasize the exploration of dominant and resistant readings to the exclusion of other aspects of people's mindful involvement with television. My interest in moving beyond the interpretive dynamics of power and resistance led me to place less emphasis on this aspect of television use, relative to others. Still, I found that the interpretations that people routinely make when they are involved with the story-telling conventions of television or other media, but particularly with television, are too numerous, too varied, too momentary, and, in some sense, too superficial to exhibit a consistency in terms of people's identities – whether class, race, gender, sexuality, or any other identity.

What I found much more interesting was the simple fact that people establish continuities, not that they make identity-based contestations of normative power. When discrete users watch television, they can identify with or be critical of what is presented to them, but, either way, they enter into a process in which they are continually judging, monitoring, and evaluating things. Discrete users of television do much the same thing when they read mysteries, romance novels, biographies, non-fiction books, or, to a lesser extent perhaps, magazine articles. When they become involved in hobbies, household projects, family outings, or other activities, a similar kind of focused attention involving judging, monitoring, and evaluating also takes place. An elemental feature of this mindfulness, then, is its *continuity*, something that I also found in undirected and continuous use. Even though people's mindfulness often takes the form of textual interpretations that locate them inside, or in opposition to, dominant discourses, my argument is that the acts of monitoring, evaluating, or judging, and, especially, the expectation that these acts will continue to occur, become inscribed as capabilities that express the self's agency.

These continuities, and this capability of self, or agency, can certainly take the form of interpretive acts, either those that take place within power or oppose it; but these continuities and this capability are not synonymous with particular interpretive acts, or with the act of interpretation *per se*. This sociality of self is not discourse; it is not an identity; it is not a particular interpretation. In the developmental psychology literature it is such continuities that first define a sense of self, even before identities take shape and people learn to interpret their place in the larger scheme of things. This sociality is a capability for action, including interpretative and identificatory acts, something that I think cultural studies either assumes, skips over, or otherwise treats as too conventional and conformist a feature of cultural practice to take seriously.

In discrete use, this continuity of the self comes from watching shows, or reading books, or spending time with the family, day-in and day-out, week-in and week-out, month-in and month-out. It is a continuity that builds upon itself and, over time, creates a cohesiveness and stability that becomes an integral part of how people see themselves and their own actions in everyday life.

People who use television in a discrete manner see themselves as productive individuals. Their productivity at work – in terms of meeting its deadlines, fulfilling responsibilities, taking on new tasks, and so on – "pays off" in terms of salary increases, an addition to the house, perhaps a down-payment on a new house or condo, a trade-in on the car, family vacations, college tuition, or purchasing any number of new commodities. It can also pay off in terms of their meriting greater trust and responsibility at work, higher status among co-workers or colleagues, or a more lucrative retirement package. In short, productivity means more power. The productive individual is personally more powerful.

The desire to be productive – and, hence, powerful – carries over from the world of work and becomes an integral part of how people care for themselves in their free time. The developmental quality of the continuities exhibited in television use, the use of other media, and participation in other activities takes on added emphasis in discrete use because people are intent upon seeing themselves as productive individuals here, too. They order and organize practically all that they do so that they "get something" out of it. In this way, even when they are involved in these free-time activities, they are never very far from the world of work. Their productivity at work can, and needs to be, temporarily displaced. But discrete users know, in the back of their minds, that the world of work is a world that they will come back to, and, in a certain sense, by remaining vigilant in how they use their free time, it is a world that they never really leave.

For discrete users of television, discourses of productive individualism shape the very ways that they constitute who they are and how they place themselves in the larger society. As Foucault (1986, 1985) says about the crafting of the self in ancient Greece, constituting oneself as a productive individual is, for discrete users, inseparable from the discursive regularities of American culture that define what it means to be productive, to be an individual, in the first place. This *askesis*, as Foucault referred to it, is very personal and private and, at the same time, very much a part of the public domain. In the case of discrete users, the integrity they felt as selves was, simultaneously, a way of placing themselves, meaningfully, in the larger society. In this sense, far from carrying the debilitating consequences that, for example, the Frankfurt School, or liberal and conservative American intellectuals, attributed to mass culture, television use, at least among discrete users, actually contributes to the formation of the very directive self that these critics theorized as an alternative to mass culture. At the same time, I am suggesting that their figure of resistance – the productive individual – is fully implicated in normative, class-bound cultures of both work and leisure.

I turn now to a final discussion of those viewing practices that are not so easily identified or adequately explained in cultural studies: image-based viewing and the broader patterns of continuous and, to a lesser extent, undirected use. As I have said in different places and in different ways throughout this book, taken together, these practices are indicative of a distinctive sociality emergent from the viewing culture; a sociality that does not exhibit the kind of ordering and organizing of mindfulness that I found in narrative-based viewing or, more broadly, in discrete use. Certainly, even people who regularly use television in these ways also, at other times, become involved with television, other media, and other activities in more focused and normatively consistent ways. At times, they cultivate a directive sense of self; they experience the normalizing power of discourse that is exerted through story-telling conventions; and they even have moments, more so in undirected use, when they identify themselves within discourses of productive individualism.

But, despite and beyond all of this, there is a less clearly definable world of viewers' practical encounters with television, in which neither the discourses of programming, nor the identities that people have established in other areas of life, can provide them with the kind of consistency and coherence that has proven to be the hallmark of the productive individual who uses television in a more discrete way.

In contrast to what I found in discrete use, or what cultural studies analysts understand as the dynamics of power and resistance, in these viewing practices, people more often than not use their television-fostered capabilities of self, *not* their prior identities, to *disengage* themselves from the story-telling conventions of programming. Even though they do not "identify" with, or inside, various discourses, or with various socially constructed determinations of themselves, they continue to make *social* claims over the time and space of their cultural world. Yet, because these social claims emerge from repeated encounters with image worlds that are as fragmentary as they are discursively consistent, such claims do not always take a cohesive, coherent, or integrated form. In fact, in image-based viewing and in continuous use in particular, people do not necessarily strive for consistency or coherence in what they do, at least not in ways that have governed modernist understandings of what is most salient in television viewing or cultural practice, or, for that matter, of what is essential to personhood. While lacking cohesiveness, coherence, or direction in a conventional sense, the fleeting, constantly changing, and seemingly trivial relations that people have with programming, relations that shape, in a similar way, their involvement in other activities, are indicative of a kind of practical knowledge that many people come to have as they attempt to meet work, family, and household responsibilities as well as negotiate the transitions that must routinely be made between these different aspects of their everyday lives. Sometimes, as for example, when people recognize formula, this sociality actually represents avenues of insight that open up in the viewing culture regarding the ways that corporate power and the mass market work there, as well as in other domains of daily life. Furthermore, I found that the distinctiveness and importance of such knowledge and insights cannot be subsumed under the markers of discourse, text, identity, or the interpretive dynamics of power and resistance.

These disengaged forms of sociality – the recognition of formula, the variety of image-based viewing relations, and the broader patterns of continuous and undirected use – are indicative of emergent cultural forms that allow people *not* to be implicated in the workings of television's discursive power. They are also indicative of our entry, as a society, into a new historical era, one marked increasingly by the corporate production of goods, ideas, and imagery of all kinds – not just television imagery. Unlike what occurs in cultures that are more traditional, local, or clearly demarcated in terms of class, race, gender, or other social distinctions, in a corporately controlled culture, the mass market becomes perhaps the most powerful and sometimes, final, arbiter of tastes. Among other things, this means that, in the corporate production, distribution, circulation, and exchange of goods, ideas, and images, there is a kind of indifference shown toward the norms or values of any particular culture. And, to the extent that the mass media predominates as the communicative form of a corporately controlled culture, the circulation of ideas, and even goods themselves, is increasingly image-based.

From the sellers' perspective, a market is not defined by the norms or values of those who compose it, but by the sales, revenues, and, ultimately, the profits that result from consumer behavior. Of course, the images of things that can circulate in the market are bound differently at different times by political struggles and cultural pressures, and, in some cases, they are even regulated by the state. Powerful corporations are powerful, in part, because they must regularly contend with hegemonic interests and satisfy their discursive requirements. Even so, the mass market constitutes a relatively open field in which a plethora of depictions, images *of* things, whether personalities, characters, stories, settings, events, or goods, circulates continually. And, since these images or depictions typically reference one or another recognizable social reality, or one or another aspect of a recognizable social reality, their mass circulation ends up multiplying the normative precepts, or principles, that are part of those realities.

All of this can be tremendously exciting – liberating, even – for the people who live amidst these image worlds, representing a democratic tendency of the mass media that I identified in the Introduction. These media image worlds provide people with the opportunity to see and hear and read about and purchase new things; things that are not necessarily part of the other kinds of cultural worlds that they inhabit, and, because of that, not so deeply embedded in the normative precepts found in those other worlds. At the same time, all of this can be understood as problematic, too. In John Hewitt's (1989) eyes, for example, this mass circulation of imagery, with its indifference to any particular norms or values, is constitutive of the increasingly fragmented and differentiated conditions that characterize modern society. It contributes, he says, to an inability to form stable and lasting community-based relationships in which readily identifiable and socially relevant norms and values play an important part. I argue that this proliferation of corporately produced and distributed image worlds is not only responsible for increasing fragmentation and the declining significance of community, but that, perhaps more importantly, it actually creates the conditions in which time-honored assumptions about the intersubjective formation of meaning, self, and identity no longer apply, and people accept the fact that they live in a culture that is not always, or only, normatively based.

Yet, this is not simply another cycle of modern dilemmas about individual identity and community formation. It is, instead, a distinctively postmodern condition. The proliferation of image worlds generates disjunctures, a time and space of split-off experiences, in which, as I have said numerous times before, continuity does not occur, meanings do not add up to anything, people no longer construct a developmental sequence to events and unified experience is no longer a given. It also generates flows, eruptions, and interruptions of desire on a *social* level that are analogous to what, in psychoanalysis, is theorized as the individual experience of unconscious processes. As a result, establishing the boundaries of self becomes increasingly problematic, as does the very formation of a stable and coherent self – with its various identities – as a normatively based reference point for social action. And, because this social field of unconscious processes is corporately produced, the formation of self and culture – whether we think of them as integrated or not – becomes a political concern.

None of this is cause for celebration. Some writers, theorists, and critics have attempted to explore this postmodern condition in ways that identify patterns of identity-formation and cultural practice that are distinctive to it. In *The History of Sexuality, Volume III*, for example, Foucault (1986) discusses the ability that people have to make judgments regarding the images of themselves that they confront in daily life. This reflexivity provides a line of escape from the discursive construction of subjectivity. Deleuze and Guattari (1983) theorize the "deterritorializations" and the "lines of flight" from ordered discourse – again, as a way of highlighting what is emergent in cultural practice. Rosaldo (1989) uses the construct of "borders" to illuminate how subjects move, create, or play with the disjunctures of discourses. In this way, he proposes, they disrupt the normalizing power of discourse, and emphasize its processual, and, hence, changeable qualities. Anzaldua (1987) uses the construct of the mestiza to articulate how movements and shifts across and between discursive determinations make for a more fluid process of identity formation, one that recognizes and validates simultaneity and cultural difference. Butler (1990, 1995) proceeds with the idea in mind that the repetitions of discourse generate instabilities, gaps, and disjunctures in the workings of power, providing a space for transgressions of power to emerge. And Wellman (1993) speaks of Blacks and Latinos in Los Angeles beginning to forge new, hybrid identities out of the disjunctures provided by their neighborhood borders.

Like these writers, theorists, and critics, I want to explore the kinds of social maneuvering and practical knowledge that emerge from the image worlds of corporate culture. My documentation of the viewing culture is a first step in this direction. In recognizing formula, image-based viewing, and continuous use, people cultivated an *indifference* to much of what was held out in the story-telling conventions as normatively appropriate for them. They routinely distanced themselves from the normative reference points inscribed in the discourses of programming, and from their own identity positions as well. As I have emphasized, theirs is a *disengaged* sociality. I documented it in the viewing culture, but it is increasingly characteristic of how people live in an image-based culture. To be disengaged is to be situated outside the logic of social action depicted *in* images, but not outside the logic of images themselves. That is, mindfully, people can place themselves outside the perspective of an "other" who requires a reflexive response from them. In doing so, they can continue to *look at* the people or characters who are located in the social action depicted in images, and observe from a distance what it is that they do. By suspending the more conventional dynamics of role-taking in this way, they can then see others, not as intersubjectively based social actors, but *as images*. This image-based sociality can then be extended beyond involvement in the image worlds *per se*, to any variety of settings in which people routinely encounter one another. Only now, their relations are constructed through the projection of an image rather than by taking on more conventional interactionally based identities. People see others as the images they project, and, in turn, they expect to be seen by others as an image of themselves. They become image-objects to each other and, consequently, image-objects to themselves. They are, as T. J. Clark (1984) has said in discussing spectacle, "a separate something to be looked at."

As a result, people do not need to construct an internal "Me" as a way for social interaction to proceed. A knowledge of intersubjectively based role expectations regarding what they do or how they think is no longer needed, because, now, people are drawn to each other in terms of the images that they project. Consequently, their sociality emerges as something more spatial than temporal, since intersubjectivity need not unfold for relations to be meaningful.

This is not to say that the more conventional avenues of reading, listening, watching, buying, and interacting are not still present and important in the postmodern condition; they are, as my earlier discussion of discrete use demonstrates. Nor is this to say that there are not problems, serious problems, that people face in trying to use conventional markers of self, meaning, and culture to craft themselves, and their lives, in normatively consistent ways; undoubtedly such problems persist. Nevertheless, disengaged forms of sociality exist, too. Not only that, but they are probably on the rise, given the prevalence of corporately controlled image worlds and their growing presence in people's everyday lives.

All of this takes me a bit far from the sociality of image-based viewing and continuous use. I want to return to them now, and make some connections. When people adopt a critical perspective toward their own and others' viewing practices, they are quite capable of recognizing that television does indeed have the power to dissociate their meaning–making activity and disrupt whatever integration they do try to establish. They can see, too, how it blocks them from consistently making meaningful connections to the larger society, and how it sometimes prevents more cohesive and coherent forms of self-understanding from emerging. Furthermore, people who use television in image-based ways indicate that they want more out of life than just watching television. While such sentiments are not stated with any more heightened emotion or any greater sense of urgency than many of the other statements, critical or otherwise, that they make about television, they *are* stated, and stated regularly. People want more than television in their lives, but they do not really do anything to change things, and they acknowledged this as an ongoing problem. They readily admit that they waste too much time watching television. And yet, even if it is on practically all the time, television does not completely take over their lives. They continue to participate in various activities, including significant rituals of family and home life. And, when they watch television, people continue to have thoughts – sometimes, critical thoughts – about both the televisual and the non-televisual worlds around them, even as the boundary between them may be increasingly hard to draw. The fact of the matter is, people are well aware that they occupy a relatively powerless position in corporate culture. But they also recognize that the exigencies of daily life require them, practically speaking, to continue living life *in* corporate culture, not outside of it.

A final word regarding power and politics. As I have said throughout the book, the power of television, the mass media, and mass culture more broadly conceived has been a long-standing concern of scholars working in a wide range of different fields of study, but especially in cultural studies. One framing of the power issue has led to an interrogation of how mass culture shapes political participation, especially the influence it carries in enhancing or thwarting the democratic workings of public life. This conceptualization of cultural politics is found in the work that emerged from and was subsequently inspired by the Frankfurt School, as well as the perspectives advanced by conservative and liberal critics of American mass culture. A second framing of power was based on Gramscian-inspired perspectives on cultural politics. This is largely the perspective of cultural studies, and it is used as a basis for theorizing and documenting both the acceptance and contestation of discourse that occurs in the reading of cultural texts. In this perspective, it is not so much a question of what, or how "culture" contributes to "politics" (although this contribution remains a concern), but, rather, to what extent contestations of elite power take place *within* the cultural domain itself. It presupposes that power has infiltrated even the most profane realms of everyday life, and, in contrast to the Frankfurt School as well as the conservative and liberal critics, proponents of this perspective emphasize how the interpretive dynamics that take place in the image worlds of corporate culture can preserve an oppositional politics without necessarily advancing beyond the cultural domain to an explicit contestation of policies through collective, public action.

In my research, there was little evidence that people attempted to bridge their everyday involvement with media imagery and any ongoing participation on their part in politics, conventionally understood. Similarly, identity-based contestations of power within the cultural domain itself – oppositional interpretations – were not displayed very consistently, either. This is not to say that the issues of power and politics raised by these perspectives are unimportant. They *are* important; very important. But, in the absence of such overtly political, or politicized forms of cultural participation or involvement, the disengaged sociality that I documented – particularly the recognition of formula, image-based viewing, and continuous use – merits further consideration, as political. After all, it is clear from my account that these viewing practices are not merely reproductive of power. They have to do with somewhat subtle processes of self-formation that emerge between discourses and identities, and remain beyond their reach as persistent social forms of the viewing culture. I think this sociality is significant because it forces critical analysts of television or other media to take seriously the mindfulness that people exhibit and maintain regarding the socially constructed nature of their own participation in corporately controlled image worlds, including, perhaps, the corporately controlled televisual world of contemporary politics. If it is taken seriously, then political questions and concerns can be posed in a new, different, and, hopefully, more illuminating way.

I conclude the writing of this book with the television continuously on, channel-surfing between the spectacles of the impeachment hearings and the bombing of Baghdad. Are the ability to recognize formulas and the capacity to disengage from and look at the competing narrative interpellations of "the American people" perhaps critical–political resources in this moment? Are they resources with which to confront and contest this strange and dangerous disjunctive and disordered time and space of postmodern politics?

References

Adorno, Theodor. 1974. "The Stars Down to Earth." *Telos* 19.

    1957. "How To Look At Television." In *Mass Culture: The Popular Arts in America*, edited by B. Rosenberg and D. White. New York: The Free Press.

    1945. "A Social Critique of Radio Music." *Kenyon Review* 7:2.

Adorno, Theodor, and Max Horkheimer. 1972. *Dialectic of Enlightenment.* New York: Seabury.

Allen, Robert., ed. 1987. *Channels of Discourse.* Chapel-Hill: University of North Carolina.

Ang, Ien. 1985. *Watching Dallas: Soap Opera and the Melodramadic Imagination.* London: Methuen.

Anzaldua, Gloria. 1987. *Borderlands.* San Francisco: Spinsters/Aunt Lute.

Bandura, Albert. 1965. "Influence of Models' Reinforcement Contingencies on the Acquisition of Imitative Responses." *Journal of Personality and Social Psychology.* 2, 1–55.

Barthes, Roland. 1972. *Mythologies.* New York: Hill and Wang.

Benjamin, Walter. 1968. *Illuminations.* New York: Harcourt.

Berelson, Bernard. 1971. *Content Analysis in Communication Research.* New York: Hafner.

    Psychology. Vol. 2, 359–69.

Blumer, Herbert. 1969. *Symbolic Interactionism.* New York: University of California.

    1933. *Movies and Conduct.* New York: MacMillan and Co.

Bourdieu, Pierre. 1977. *Outline of a Theory of Practice.* Cambridge University Press.

Brunsdon, Charlotte. 1991 "Text and Audience." In *Remote Control: Television, Audiences, and Cultural Power*, edited by Ellen Seiter, Hans Borchers, Gabriele Kreutzner, and Eva-Maria Warth. New York: Routledge.

Butler, Judith. 1995. *Bodies That Matter.* New York: Routledge.

    1990. *Gender Trouble: Feminism and the Subversion of Identity.* New York: Routledge.

Cantril, Hadley. 1935. *The Psychology of Radio.* New York: Harper.

Clark. T. J. 1984. *The Painting of Modern Life.* Princeton University Press.

DeFleur, Melvin and Sandra Ball-Rockeach. 1982. *Theories of Mass Communication.* New York: Longman.

Deleuze, Gilles. 1983. *Nietzsche and Philosophy.* New York: Columbia.

Delueze, Gilles and Claire Parnet. 1987. *Dialogues.* New York: Columbia.

Deleuze, Gilles, and Felix Guattari. 1983. *Anti-Oedipus: Capitalism and Schizophrenia.* Minneapolis: University of Minnesota.

Dunn, Robert. 1991. "Postmodernism: Populism, Mass Culture and the Avant-Garde." *Theory Culture and Society* 8, 111–135.

Durkheim, Emile. 1967. *The Elementary Forms of the Religious Life.* London: G. Allen and Unwin.

1938. *The Rules of Sociological Method.* New York: The Free Press.

Ellis, John. 1982. *Visible Fictions: Cinema, Television, Video.* Boston: Routledge and Kegan Paul.

Fiske, John. 1987. *Television Culture.* London: Methuen.

Foucault, Michel. 1986. *The Care of the Self: History of Sexuality, Volume III.* New York: Vintage.

1985. *The Use of Pleasure: The History of Sexuality, Volume II.* New York: Vintage.

1980. *The History of Sexuality, Volume I.* New York: Vintage.

1970. *The Order of Things.* New York: Pantheon.

Gerbner, George, Larry Gross, Michael Morgan, and Nancy Signorielli. 1986. "Living With Television: The Dynamics of the Cultivation Process," in Bryant, Jennings., and Zillman, Dolf., eds. *Perspectives on Media Effects.* Hillsdale, N.J: Lawrence Erlbaum.

1982. "Charting the Mainstream: Television's Contribution to Political Orientations." *Journal of Communication*, 30:2.

1980. "The Demonstration of Power: Violence Profile No. 11." *Journal of Communication* Summer. 1980.

Gerbner, George, Larry Gross, Nancy Signorielli, Michael Morgan, and Marilyn Jackson-Beets. 1977. "The Demonstration of Power: Violence Profile No. 10." *Journal of Communications* 29:3, 177–196.

Gitlin, Todd. 1983. *Inside Prime Time.* New York: Pantheon.

1980. *The Whole World is Watching: The Media in the Making and the Unmaking of the New Left.* Berkeley, CA: University of California Press.

1979. "Prime-Time Ideology: The Hegemonic Process in Television Entertainment." *Social Problems* 26:3, 251–266.

1978. "Media Sociology." *Theory and Society* 6:2, 205–254.

Goffman, Erving. 1979. *Gender Advertisements.* New York: Harper.

1959. *The Presentation of Self in Everyday Life.* Garden City, NJ: Doubleday.

Goodwin, Andrew. 1992. *Dancing in the Distraction Factory: Music Television and Popular Culture.* Minneapolis: University of Minnesota Press.

Grossberg, Lawrence. 1988. "'It's a Sin': Postmodernity–Popular Empowerment and Hegemonic Popular." Paper presented at Rice University Conference on the Sociology of Television, Houston, TX.

——— 1987. "The In-Difference of Television." *Screen* 28, 28–45.

Grossberg, Lawrence, Cary Nelson, and Paula Treichler (eds.). 1992. *Cultural Studies*. New York: Routledge.

Hall, Stuart. 1980. "Cultural Studies: Two Paradigms." *Media, Culture, and Society* 2, 57–72.

——— 1975. "Television as a Medium and Its Relation to Culture." Stencilled Occasional Paper, Centre for Contemporary Cultural Studies. Birmingham, England.

Hall, Stuart, Dorothy Hobson, Andrew Lowe, and Paul Willis, (eds.). 1980. *Culture, Media, Language*. London: Hutchinson.

Hewitt, John. 1989. *Dilemmas of the American Self.* Philadelphia: Temple University Press.

Hoggart, Richard. 1966. *The Uses of Literacy*. Boston: Beacon.

Iyengar, Shanto. 1991. *Is Anyone Responsible?* University of Chicago Press.

Iyengar, Shanto and Donald Kinder. 1987. *News That Matters*. University of Chicago Press.

Jameson, Fredric. 1991. *Postmodernism Or, The Cultural Logic of Late Capitalism*. Durham: Duke University.

——— 1983. "Postmodernism and Consumer Society." In *The Anti-Aesthetic: Essays on Postmodern Culture*, edited by Hal Foster. Port Townsend, WA: Bay Press.

Katz, Elihu and P. Lazarsfeld. 1955. *Personal Influence*. New York: The Free Press.

Kellner, Douglas. 1990. *Television and the Crisis of Democracy*. Westview Press: Boulder, CO.

Klapper, Joseph. 1960. *The Effects of Mass Communication*. Glencoe, IL: The Free Press.

Kubey, Robert William, and Mihaly Csikszentmihalyi. 1990. *Television and the Quality of Life*. Hillsdale, NJ: L. Erlbaum.

Lacan, Jacques. 1977. *Ecrits: A Selection*. New York: Norton.

——— 1968. *The Language of the Self: The Function of Language in Psychoanalysis*. New York: Dell.

Langer, Suzanne. 1957. *Philosophy in a New Key*. Cambridge: Harvard University Press.

Lasswell, Harold. 1938. *Propaganda Techniques in the World War*. New York: P. Smith.

Lazarsfeld, Paul, Bernard Berelson, and Hazel Gaudet. 1948. *The People's Choice*. New York: Columbia University Press.

Lazarsfeld, P. and R. Merton. 1977. "Mass Communication, Popular Taste, and Organized Social Action." In *The Process and Effects of Mass Communication*, edited by W. Schramm and D. Roberts. Chicago: University of Illinois Press.

Lembo, Ron. 1994. "Situating Television in Everyday Life: Reformulating a Cultural Studies Approach to the Study of Television Use." In *From Sociology to Cultural Studies*, edited by Elizabeth Long. Boston: Blackwell Publishers, pp. 203–233.

Lembo, Ron, and Ken Tucker. 1990. "Culture, Television, and Opposition: Rethinking Cultural Studies." *Critical Studies in Mass Communication* 7, 97–116.

Macdonald, Dwight. 1983. *Against the American Grain.* New York: Da Capo Press.

Mahler, Margaret. 1975. *The Psychological Birth of the Human Infant: Symbiosis and Individuation.* New York: Basic Books.

Malamuth, Neil, and Victoria Billings. 1986. "The Functions and Effects of Pornography: Sexual Communication versus Feminist Models in Light of Research Findings." In *Perspectives on Media Effects,* edited by Dolf Zillmann and Jennings Bryant, Hillsdale, NJ: Ablex.

Marcuse, Herbert. 1964. *One Dimensional Man: Studies in the Ideology of Advanced Industrial Society.* Boston: Beacon Press.

McRobbie, Angela. 1991. *Feminism and Youth Culture.* Boston: Unwin Hyman.

Mead, G. H. 1934. *Mind Self and Society.* University of Chicago Press.

   1932. *The Philosophy of the Present.* University of Chicago Press.

Merton, Robert. 1968. *Social Theory and Social Structure.* New York: The Free Press.

   1946. *Mass Persuasion: The Social Psychology of a War Bond Drive.* New York: Harper & Bros.

Meyrowitz, Joshua. 1985. *No Sense of Place: The Impact of Electronic Media on Social Behaviour.* Oxford University Press: New York.

Miller, Mark Crispin. 1988. *Boxed In: The Culture of TV.* Evanston, Ill: Northwestern University Press.

Morley, David. 1994. *Television, Audiences, and Cultural Studies.* New York: Routledge.

   1986. *Family Television and Domestic Leisure.* London: Comedia.

   1980. *The Nationwide Audience.* London: British Film Institute.

Nietzsche, Friedrich. 1968. *The Will To Power.* New York: Random House.

Postman, Neil. 1985. *Amusing Ourselves to Death.* New York: Viking.

Press, Andrea. 1992. *Women Watching Television.* Philadelphia: University of Pennsylvania.

Rabinow, Paul and Hubert Dreyfuss. 1983. *Michel Foucault: Beyond Structuralism and Hermeneutics.* University of Chicago Press.

Radway, Janice. 1984. *Reading the Romance.* Chapel Hill: University of North Carolina.

Rosaldo, Renato. 1989. *Culture and Truth.* Boston: Beacon Press.

Seldes, Gilbert. 1957. *The 7 Lively Arts.* New York: Sagamore Press.

Shils, Edward. 1969. *Literary Taste, Culture, and Mass Communication.* Englewood Cliffs, NJ: Prentice-Hall.

Silverstone, Roger. 1995. *Television and Everyday Life.* New York: Routledge.

Spigel, Lynn. 1992. *Make Room for TV: Television and the Family Ideal in Postwar America.* University of Chicago Press.

Thompson, E. P. 1966. *The Making of the English Working Class*. New York: Vintage.

Tichi, Cecilia. 1991. *Electronic Hearth: Creating an American Television Culture*. New York: Oxford University Press.

Wellman, David. 1993. "Honorary Homeys, Class Brothers, and White Negroes: Mixing Cultural Codes and Constructing Multicultural Identities on America's Social Borderlands," Paper Presented at the American Sociological Association Annual Meetings, Miami Beach, Florida.

Williams, Raymond. 1983. *Culture and Society*. New York: Columbia University.

1982. *The Sociology of Culture*. New York: Schocken.

1974. *Television, Technology, and Cultural Form*. London: Fontana.

Willis, Paul. 1978. *Profane Culture*. London: Routledge, Kegan, Paul.

1977a. *Learning to Labor*. London: Saxon House.

Winnicott, D. W. 1971. *Playing and Reality*. New York: Tavistock.

1965. *The Maturation Processes and the Facilitating Environment*. Madison, Wisconsin: International Universities Press.

Wright, Charles. 1975. *Mass Communication: A Sociological Perspective*. New York: Random House.

Zillmann, Dolf and Jennings Bryant. 1982. "Pornography, Sexual Callousness and the Trivialization of Rape." *Journal of Communication* 32:9.

Index

LYNN RAPAPORT, *Jews in Germany after the Holocaust*
0 521 58219 9 hardback 0 521 58809 X paperback

CHANDRA MUKERJI, *Territorial Ambitions and the Gardens of Versailles*
0 521 49675 6 hardback 0 521 59959 8 paperback

LEON H. MAYHEW, *The New Public* 0 521 48146 5 hardback
0 521 48493 6 paperback

VERA L. ZOLBERG AND JONI M. CHERBO (eds.), *Outsider Art*
0 521 58111 7 hardback 0 521 58921 5 paperback

SCOTT BRAVMANN, *Queer Fictions of the Past* 0 521 59101 5 hardback
0 521 59907 5 paperback

STEVEN SEIDMAN, *Difference Troubles* 0 521 59043 4 hardback
0 521 59970 9 paperback

RON EYERMAN AND ANDREW JAMISON, *Music and Social Movements*
0 521 62045 7 hardback 0 521 62966 7 paperback

MEYDA YEGENOGLU, *Colonial Fantasies* 0 521 48233 X hardback
0 521 62658 7 paperback

LAURA DESFOR EDLES, *Symbol and Ritual in the New Spain*
0 521 62140 2 hardback 0 521 62885 7 paperback

NINA ELIASOPH, *Avoiding Politics* 0 521 58293 8 hardback
0 521 58759 X paperback

BERNHARD GIESEN, *Intellectuals and the German Nation*
0 521 62161 5 hardback 0 521 63996 4 paperback

PHILIP SMITH (ed.), *The New American Cultural Sociology*
0 521 58415 9 hardback 0 521 58634 8 paperback

S. N. EISENSTADT, *Fundamentalism, Sectarianism and Revolution*
0 521 64184 5 hardback 0 521 64586 7 paperback

MARIAM FRASER, *Identity without Selfhood* 0 521 62357 X hardback
0 521 62579 3 paperback

LUC BOLTANSKI, *Distant Suffering* 0 521 57389 0 hardback
0 521 65953 1 paperback

PYOTR SZTOMPKA, *Trust* 0 521 59144 9 hardback
0 521 59850 8 paperback

SIMON J. CHARLESWORTH, *A Phenomenology of Working Class Culture*
0 521 65066 6 hardback 0 521 65915 9 paperback

ROBIN WAGNER-PACIFICI, *Theorizing the Standoff* (2)
0 521 65244 8 hardback 0 521 65479 3 paperback

RONALD R. JACOBS, *Race, Media and the Crisis of Civil Society* (2)
0 521 62360 X hardback 0 521 62578 5 paperback

ALI MIRSEPASSI, *Intellectual Discourse and the Politics of Modernization* (2)
0 521 65000 3 hardback 0 521 65997 3 paperback